D1300539

I am rousing everyone here to love, and I will try to show the superheated and supernatural feeling of love to everyone. —RICHARD ROLLE

This Image Book Original contains a pair of treatises written by Richard Rolle, a fourteenth-century English mystic. His appeal in the twentieth century lies as much in his manner of addressing his intended audience as in the experience he wishes to share and the message he wants to convey. Taken together, these two works provide a coherent pattern of living.

The Christian, summoned by the touch of God's grace to seek "the mending of life," needs practical, orderly guidance so that this impulse to conversion may bear fruit in the love of God. Having followed these graces faithfully and been set ablaze by "the fire of love," he needs instruction in order to recognize this new action of God without fear and to follow it faithfully in freedom, responding with joy to the ever-deepening union God offers. In both these areas, Rolle is a sane, experienced, and thoroughly reliable guide as well as a comforting friend.

This edition is the only modern English rendering of *both* these classics in one volume. As such, it takes its rightful place beside *The Stairway of Perfection* by Walter Hilton and *Revelations of Divine Love* by Juliana of Norwich.

Now the works of the three greatest fourteenth-century English mystics are available in Image Books.

THE FIRE
OF LOVE

and

THE MENDING
OF LIFE

by Richard Rolle

Translated with an Introduction by
M. L. del Mastro

IMAGE BOOKS
A Division of Doubleday & Company, Inc.
Garden City, New York
1981

Library of Congress Cataloging in Publication Data

Rolle, Richard, of Hampole, 1290?–1349.
The fire of love and The mending of life.

Translation of Incendium amoris and Emendatio vitae.
Bibliography: p.
1. Spiritual life—Catholic authors—Early works to
1800. 2. God—Worship and love—Early works to 1800.
3. Love (Theology)—Early works to 1800. I. Del Mastro,
M. L. II. Rolle, Richard, of Hampole, 1290?–1349. De
emendacione vitæ. English. 1981. III. Title: Fire of
love.
BX2349.R67413 1981   248.4′82

ISBN: 0-385-15839-4   AACR2
Library of Congress Catalog Card Number: 81-65660
Copyright © 1981 by M. L. del Mastro
Printed in the United States of America
First Edition

CONTENTS

INTRODUCTION

I. The Author

Little is known of the man Richard Rolle beyond what he tells us himself in various of his works[1] and what appears in the lessons of the *Office* prepared for his feast and its octave,[2] probably by or for the community of Cistercian nuns at Hampole Priory,[3] against the day of his canonization—which, for various reasons,[4] never occurred.

Many manuscripts provide us with the year of his death, 1349, and several indicate the day as the feast of St. Michael, which falls yearly on September 29,[5] but none states the date of his birth. Scholars in general agree that he must have been born around the year 1300, perhaps a few years earlier.[6]

In order to give a chronological account of what is known about Rolle, then, it is necessary to follow the account given in the *Legenda* of the *Office*—the nine lessons composed for the hoped-for feast itself. (The *Miracula*, twenty-one lessons to be used in the *Office* during the octave of the feast, are accounts of apparitions of the saint and of miracles worked after his intercession had been asked at his tomb.[7] These are less important in establishing the facts of Rolle's life than in indicating the extent of his cult and in offering proofs of his intercessory power with God, which derived, in the view of medieval Christendom, from the sanctity of his earthly life.)

In spite of the fact that the lessons found in the *Legenda* share with traditional hagiography the tendency to glorify their subject by showing him as a quasi-legendary figure[8] somewhat larger than life, practicing heroic virtue from unimpeachable motives and to the general admiration of all, scholars agree that there is no reason to doubt the general authenticity of the work[9] nor its accuracy in its strictly biographical aspects,[10] particularly as many of these are taken from Richard's own autobiographical asides in other works.[11]

The first lesson in the *Legenda* declares that Richard Rolle was born "in the village of Thornton, near Pickering, in the diocese of York."[12] This Thornton has been identified as Thornton-le-Dale,[13] and genealogical research indicates that the Rolle family had been living in the neighborhood since around 1160.[14]

Young Rolle was sent to school by his parents—we do not know where[15]—and apparently proved to be a promising pupil, for, as Lesson One reports, "When he was of adult age Master Thomas Neville, at one time Archdeacon of Durham, honourably maintained him in the University of Oxford, where he made great progress in study."[16] Of his career at Oxford we learn only that, again according to Lesson One, "He desired rather to be more fully and perfectly instructed in the theological doctrine of Holy Scripture than in physics or the study of secular knowledge."[17]

This preference did not precisely match the prevailing emphasis at the Oxford of Richard's time,[18] and the discrepancy fueled the suggestion,[19] based on three appearances of his name in a seventeenth-century compilation of the history of the Sorbonne which included lists of its fellows and guests (perhaps copied from an authentic medieval source now lost)[20] that Rolle had spent a period or periods of time[21] between 1320 and 1326[22] in theological study at the Sorbonne. Since the Sorbonne then specialized in the study of theology "as much as possible divorced from dialectic,"[23] a direction matched by Rolle's instincts,[24] this hypothesis made good sense. It was further supported by the evident learning revealed in Rolle's writings, particularly in his commentaries on Scripture,[25] a discipline that was rather a specialty of the Sorbonne.

However, the absence of the hypothetical "lost" medieval source, the difficulty of fitting the sojourn(s) at the Sorbonne into the unequivocal chronology of the *Office* without accusing the *Legenda*'s composer of having left "a (wilful) gap in the Legend,"[26] the absence of a known patron to underwrite the costs of one or two journeys abroad, the absence of records of the awarding of a doctoral degree by the University,[27] and the possibility of Rolle's having attained his learning through private reading[28] led even supporters of the Sorbonne theory to hesitate and qualify their acceptance of it.[29]

The Sorbonne theory, though it "was conclusively shown to be a mare's nest"[30] has not been replaced with any other explanation of the "gap of more than twenty years of his later life"[31] nor of the sources of Rolle's "training or the materials for the elaborate commentaries which seem to be a dominating interest in his years twenty-five to thirty-five (or thereabouts)."[32]

In any event, the *Office* is quite clear as to Richard's flat rejection of an academic career. In his nineteenth year, according to Lesson One, after probably three or four years spent at Oxford,[33] "considering that the time of mortal life is uncertain and its end greatly to be dreaded . . . by God's inspiration he took thought betimes for himself, being mindful of his latter end, lest he should be caught in the snares of sinners,"[34] he left the University for good and returned to his father's house in Yorkshire. His return, most likely without the Master's degree his studies were intended to obtain,[35] was probably made at the end of the term, during the University's summer vacation, which, before 1350, began about July 5 or 6.[36]

Shortly after his return, he embarked upon his life as a hermit, as Lesson One records. His methods were direct, if somewhat flamboyant. Says the Lesson,

> Hence, after he had returned from Oxford to his father's house, he said one day to his sister, who loved him with tender affection: "My beloved sister, thou hast two tunics which I greatly covet, one white and the other grey. Therefore I ask thee if thou wilt kindly give them to me, and bring them me to-morrow to the wood near by, together with my father's rain-hood." She agreed willingly and the next day, according to her promise,

carried them to the said wood, being quite ignorant of what was in her brother's mind. And when he had received them he straightway cut off the sleeves from the grey tunic and the buttons from the white, and as best he could he fitted the sleeves to the white tunic, so that they might in some manner be suited to his purpose. Then he took off his own clothes with which he was clad and put on his sister's white tunic next his skin, but the grey, with the sleeves cut out, he put on over it, and put his arms through the holes which had been cut; and he covered his head with the rain-hood aforesaid so that thus in some measure, as far as was then in his power, he might present a certain likeness to a hermit. But when his sister saw this she was astounded and cried: "My brother is mad! My brother is mad!" Whereupon he drove her from him with threats, and fled himself at once without delay, lest he should be seized by his friends and acquaintances.[37]

That, as far as anyone knows, was Rolle's last contact with the members of his family, though not with Yorkshire.

Having fled from his family, he had made his way by August 14, the vigil of the Feast of the Assumption of the Blessed Virgin, to a church that happened to be frequented by an old friend of his father, John de Dalton, Constable of Pickering Castle.[38] Richard was still dressed in his makeshift hermit's "habit" and had apparently not thought to consult local church authorities as to his formal entrance to the vocation of hermit.

The hermit, like the anchorite, after proving to his bishop that he had means to sustain himself,[39] had to be licensed by the bishop in a ceremony of dedication[40] in order formally to enter upon and follow the solitary way of life. The hermit, unlike the anchorite or recluse, was not confined to a single geographical location or cell.[41]

There is, however, no record that Rolle ever obtained either license or blessing.[42] He seems simply to have begun, and having begun, to have persevered in this calling virtually without challenge, until his death.[43]

Once at the church, Rolle settled himself to pray. He

chose, unwittingly it seems, the seat where the squire's wife was accustomed to pray. Lesson Two describes the scene. "And when she entered the church to hear vespers, the servants of the squire's house wished to remove him from their lady's place. But she from humility would not permit them, lest he should be disturbed in his devotions."[44]

After the service, Rolle was recognized by the squire's sons "who were scholars and had studied at Oxford."[45] They told their mother "that he was the son of William Rolle, whom they had known at Oxford."[46] None of the family approached Rolle at this point, nor, apparently, was he aware that he had been identified, for he returned to the same church on the following day for the celebration of the Feast. Lesson Two reports,

> Then on the day of the aforesaid feast of the Assumption he again entered the same church; and without bidding from anyone, he put on a surplice and sang matins and the office of mass with the others. And when the gospel had been read in the mass, having first besought the blessing of the priest, he went into the preacher's pulpit and gave the people a sermon of wonderful edification, insomuch that the multitude which heard it was so moved by his preaching that they could not refrain from tears; and they all said that they had never before heard a sermon of such virtue and power.[47]

Even allowing for the hyperbole of the hagiographer, this must have been a remarkable performance. Certainly Rolle was not licensed to preach, and at eighteen, even after extended exposure to Oxford, a sermon like the one described is not usual. It impressed the squire, who promptly invited Rolle to dinner at the manor.

Rolle seems to have had some difficulty in resolving the conflict he saw between his newly embraced vocation to the solitary life, living on alms alone, and the hospitality the squire offered. He went along to the manor, but instead of following the rest of the family to the table, Richard, according to Lesson Three,

. . . betook himself to a certain mean and old room; for

he would not enter the hall but sought rather to fulfil the teaching of the gospel, which says, "When thou are invited to a wedding, sit down in the lowest room; that when he that bade thee cometh, he may say unto thee, 'Friend, go up higher,'" and this too was fulfilled in him. For when the squire had sought for him diligently, and at last found him in the aforesaid room, he set him above his own sons at the table.[48]

Once at the table, Richard's behavior reflected the continuing conflict between the asceticism to which he aspired and the demands of common politeness. The compromise at which he arrived is indicative both of his character and of his inexperience. "But he kept such perfect silence at dinner that not a word proceeded from his mouth. And when he had eaten enough he rose, before the table was removed, and prepared to depart. But the squire who had invited him said that this was not customary, and so prevailed upon him to sit down again."[49]

The squire, in spite of his reputation for ruthless self-seeking,[50] substantiated by the methods by which he dealt with the vicissitudes of his career,[51] seems not to have been unduly concerned in this instance with offenses to his own dignity. He seems instead to have been curious about the young man whose brusque, boorish manners stood in such marked contrast to the eloquence of his preaching. His sons may have already identified Rolle to their father as a fellow student from Oxford (we are not told), but the squire chose not to use this information in dealing with the aspiring hermit. Instead, he proposed to let Richard tell his own story in his own way, and to that end, relates Lesson Three, he held Rolle back after everyone else had left the hall. Then, "he asked him if he were the son of William Rolle. Then he rather unwillingly and with reluctance answered: 'Perchance I am,' since he feared that if he were recognized the plan on which his mind was set would be hindered. For this squire loved his father as a friend with warm affection."[52]

As it turned out, Richard need not have been concerned about Dalton's connection with his father, whose house he

had fled (presumably because the latter would not have allowed him to abandon his career in the world for the hermit's life). For reasons best known to himself, Dalton decided to assist Rolle in the pursuit of his chosen vocation. It
may be that he "hoped to attach himself to an eloquent
young preacher—for who knows what half-political purpose."53 Again, it may simply be that Dalton, sharing the
same direct approach to the gaining of his own ends as the
young would-be hermit, and seeing his own headstrong
ruthlessness in Richard, rather admired his wholehearted, if
imprudent, determination and decided to help him in his
defiance of the world. Neither the *Office* nor Rolle himself
supplies a motive. Lesson Four simply reports,

> And when the aforesaid squire had examined him in pri-
> vate, and convinced himself by perfect evidence of the
> sanctity of his purpose, he, at his own expense, clad him
> according to his wish, with clothing suitable for a her-
> mit; and kept him for a long time in his own house, giv-
> ing him a place for his solitary abode and providing him
> with food and all the necessaries of life. Then he began
> with all diligence, by day and night, to seek how to per-
> fect his life, and to take every opportunity he could to
> advance in contemplative life and to be fervent in divine
> love.54

Though Richard was intent upon learning the ways of God
in this new calling, and though Dalton had carried out his
decision to help the young man with not inconsiderable material assistance, Richard's way was not smooth. Difficulties
seem to have risen from the distinct differences which, in
spite of similarities of temperament, divided the young hermit from his first patron at the outset. These differences were
inherent in the responsibilities that fell to each in his own
chosen sphere of action. Rolle sought solitude for prayer, but
the cell Dalton provided was accessible to all the members of
his household55 and, in addition, from June through Novem-
ber was subject to the noise and distractions related to storing
the harvest and preserving other products of the manor to

feed the Dalton dependents (including Richard) for the winter.[56]

The situation became unbearable for Rolle, and apparently he decided to move on. From this point in the narrative the *Office* becomes vague as to the chronology of events, their geography, and the persons involved, and we must consult other sources—those autobiographical references made by Rolle in various of his works—in order to fill in the gaps.

The *Office* itself concentrates on Richard's progress in holiness and on those quasi-miraculous events which demonstrate that sanctity. Lesson Five repeats the first section of the Prologue of the *Incendium amoris* and remarks in general terms upon the penitential austerities Richard practiced in response to this gift.[57]

In Lesson Six we read of an instance of automatic writing which confirms the sense that, in Dalton's household, Rolle was considered a dependent of the family and so had to be accessible to family members and guests at their pleasure. One day after dinner, the lady of the house (not named as Squire Dalton's wife, though scholars conclude that it was probably she)[58] came to Richard's cell with her guests, interrupting him as he was writing some spiritual work or other, and asked him

> . . . to leave off writing and speak a word of edification to them, which he immediately did, exhorting them most eloquently to virtue and to renounce worldly vanities and stablish the love of God in their hearts. Yet in no way on account of this did he cease from writing for two hours without interruption, but continued to write as quickly as before, which could in no wise have been possible unless the Holy Spirit had at that time directed both his hand and tongue; especially as the occupations were discrepant one from another, and the spoken words differed utterly in meaning from those which he wrote.[59]

Apparently Rolle left the Dalton household some time after the second full summer spent there, for another patron and another abode.[60] Lesson Seven, recording his temptation by the Devil in the form of "a very beautiful young woman, whom I had seen before and who loved me—in honorable love—not a little"[61] may supply another reason for Rolle's willingness to quit the Daltons if, as has been suggested, his cell there was the scene of this crisis.[62]

The *Office* does not specify where or to whom Rolle went when he left Squire Dalton. Lesson Eight, having described his effective dispersal of troops of demons for various friends and for himself, simply remarks, "After this the saint of God, Richard, betook himself to other parts," adding, "doubtless through the providence of God so that dwelling in many places he might benefit many unto salvation, and sometimes also that he might escape impediment to contemplation."[63]

The passage that follows offers a vigorous defense of Rolle's changing of abode, citing the example of the Desert Fathers; it by no means defends the kind of vagabondage which Rolle himself denies in the *Incendium*,[64] but it does suggest the kind of vilification and persecution to which Rolle seems to have been (or to have felt himself) subject for the early part, at least, of his life as a hermit. Lesson Eight remarks,

> For frequent change of place does not always come from inconstancy; as is the accusation of certain who are given to quick and perverse judgment of their neigh-bours, but whose crooked interpretations and habits of detraction ought not to make a sensible person neglect those things which he has found by experience to be good and conducive to virtue. For in the canon and decrees of the Church many causes sometimes are as-signed for which change of place may be made; of which the first is when pressure of persecution makes a place dangerous; secondly, when some local difficulties exist; and thirdly, when the saints are harassed by the society of evil men.[65]

A great deal of the hostility Rolle engendered seems to have been his own fault. As a young man, at least, his tem-perament seems to have been difficult,[66] his temper short, his manners lacking and his condemnation of locally observed vice, whether clerical or lay, blunt in the extreme.[67] When he preached to reform, his condemnations were probably merited, but his youth[68] and his manner seem to have combined to render these home truths more than usually unpalatable.[69] In addition, these condemnations ring with the shrillness of self-defense in some cases.[70] This quality seems further to have irritated those he condemned, urging them to counterattack[71]—even to the point, he claims, of turning various of his patrons against him.[72]

The *Office* passes over all this warring in silence, and Rolle himself buries the specific details in the Latin alliterative intricacies of the *Melos Amoris* and the earlier *Judica Me*.[73] Apparently the situation eased after a time—probably as Rolle grew up! No one seems to have taken formal action against the young hermit[74] and in his later writings he concentrates on sharing with his audience his marvelous experiences of the love of God.

The *Office* picks up the chronological narrative in Lesson Eight, near the end of Richard's life, recording his removal to Richmondshire (place unspecified), and his friendship with the recluse Margaret Kirkeby, whom he cured of what seems to have been an epileptic seizure, and to whom he promised, on a second occasion, freedom from the disease "as long as I shall remain in this mortal life."[75]

The recluse in question was originally a member of the Cistercian community at Hampole. She was enclosed not at Anderby, as the *Office* suggests, but at East Layton on December 12, 1348, ten months before Rolle's death.[76] On January 16, 1356–7, the Bishop allowed her to be transferred to Anderby because she could not "see the sacrament of the altar or hear"[77] the services. It was not, in all probability, until 1381–83, the period when miracles began to occur at Richard's tomb, his cult to flourish, and the *Office* to be composed,[78] that Margaret moved to Hampole to occupy Richard's cell,[79] experiencing the completion of her cure described in Lesson Eight.[80] She lived there until her death, probably twenty years later.[81]

The *Office* records only one seizure that Margaret suffered between Richard's promise to her of health while he lived and her removal to Hampole. That attack, according to Lesson Eight, coincided with the day and time of Rolle's death. Having suffered the seizure, Margaret sent a man to Hampole to inquire after Rolle's health, for "she doubted not that he had passed from this world, because she knew that he was faithful to his promise, and he had promised her that as long as he lived in the flesh she should never again suffer such torment."[82]

The returning messenger confirmed her belief: ". . . after diligently inquiring the hour of his passing, he found that the aforesaid illness had returned to the recluse shortly after the hour of Richard's departure."[83] Margaret's subsequent removal to Hampole (which the *Office* suggests is immediate, though it cannot have been)[84] seems to have completed her cure.

Neither the *Office* nor the manuscripts provide information about Rolle's death beyond the date—September 29, 1349, the feast of Saint Michael. It was a time when the Black Death was raging in Yorkshire[85] and most probably the hermit succumbed to this plague.[86]

The process of canonization—the formal declaration by the Church that the subject has led a life of heroic sanctity and is now enjoying the reward of Heaven—if begun, was never completed. The plague, with its consequent depletion of Church and monastic personnel,[87] difficulties between England and the papacy,[88] the Lollards' (or Wycliffites') adoption and heretical adaptation of some of Rolle's positions,[89] and Rolle's own determination not to be formally affiliated with either the monastic or the ecclesiastical established social organizations[90] have been suggested as reasons for the failure to formalize Richard's cult, and for its eventual decline and disappearance. As is true of most circumstances surrounding Rolle, there is no way of resolving the question beyond these probabilities.

In spite of their failure to have Rolle canonized, the work of the writer or group responsible for the *Office* has not been wasted. Though the *Office* focuses on the deeds of the hermit to show that he was a saint, the primary effect of this information, at least for a modern audience, is to show us the man as a human being, and an engaging one, in spite of his emphatic faults. Rolle himself provides autobiographical incidents only for their spiritual applications in teaching his readers. His lack of self-consciousness and his candor enhance his charm, though that was not what he had in mind. The portrait of Rolle that emerges from a consideration of these sources is limited, necessarily, by the fact that all this biography and autobiography centers on the beginning of Rolle's career as a hermit, covering in some detail his adventures from the age of eighteen to (at the outside) twenty-six. The mature Rolle must be inferred from the matter and manner of his religious teaching and sharing.

The picture which finally emerges is that of a man governed by his heart and his generous instincts, rather than of the calculator governed by cold, undeviating reason. Rolle's warmth shows itself in his youth in indignation against, and vigorous condemnation of, abuses, whatever the rank or power of the offender; he also resents criticism of his own conduct, and by his reaction seems to aggravate the attacks made upon him.[91] He is single-minded, often ruthless, in pursuit of what he sees as his God-given way of life and all of its duties, as we have seen in his precipitous adoption of the hermit's life. Prudence seems to have had little part in shaping these responses, and were they the only, or even the dominant manifestations of his temperament, we should be faced with a very unpleasant man indeed.

But Rolle was chiefly a lover—of God and of his fellows—not a warrior, and as he grew into his vocation, love began to dominate him. The *Office* makes this point by implication. Lesson Nine, the last of the readings prepared for the feast itself, quotes in its entirety Richard's summary description of the process by which he entered into mystical union with God: Chapter Fifteen of the *Incendium amoris*. This, it seems, was the point of his life, and the essence of his sanctity.

In Rolle, this love found two chief means of expression—in

his dealings with people and in his writings about God, for their sakes.

For the first, we have seen him dealing with Margaret Kirkeby in her illness, and the *Office* notes his rescues of various persons from diabolical possession. His evident affection for his friends is also shown in the treatises he wrote for them, at their request. For Margaret Kirkeby he wrote the English Psalter,[92] and for William Stopes, a younger friend (who seems to have become his literary executor),[93] he composed, near the end of his life, the *Emendatio vitae*. He sometimes made several copies of a work, a time-consuming job, and sent them, apparently at their request, to various of his friends and disciples (of whom we know nothing else).

In the *Incendium amoris*, the more general dedication found in the Prologue suggests that Rolle not only considered himself responsible for sharing his experiences in prayer with those who had no other instructor, but that he felt a protective affection for these simple seekers.

It is, however, in the subject matter of his works, all of them, even those most marked by astringency and impatience, that Rolle's central preoccupation declares itself. Rolle is a scholar, as his Scriptural commentaries and treatises attest, but for him the God of Whom the Scriptures speak is the point. Always he turns the attention of the reader back to God, to Love. As love came to dominate his personal relationships eventually, with grace smoothing out the "prickles" of his youth,[94] so the Love Who is God dominates his writings.

This love expresses itself in his prayer as tangibly experienced sweetness, heat and song, but for Rolle the importance of these manifestations lies not in the sensations themselves but in the God, Love, Whose presence and abiding love they make physically and psychically so real for him. Sharing this experience, warmly encouraging his brothers and sisters to allow God to love them and to recognize and trust Him when He does so, provides Rolle with his central, and finally his only real, lasting motive, for writing as for living.

II. *The Works*

As is the case with many popular and hence widely copied medieval texts, there is no holograph extant for either the *Emendatio vitae* or the *Incendium amoris,* and no certain way to date the composition of either. There seems to be no conclusive disagreement with Allen's conclusion that the *Emendatio* was written near the end of Rolle's life[1] and that the *Incendium* was written earlier, probably after the *Contra amatores mundi,*[2] though when Rolle was well advanced in spiritual growth; Allen suggests 1343 as a probable date for the *Incendium.*[3]

A. AUDIENCE

In both works, Rolle speaks as a teacher instructing those who are eager to learn. Though in the *Emendatio* Rolle does not specify his proposed audience, in his prologue to the *Incendium* he describes those he writes for in some detail. What he asks as a prerequisite is not learning, but the desire to love.

> Therefore I offer this book for consideration not by philosophers, not by the worldly-wise, not by great theologians ensnarled in infinite questionings, but by the unsophisticated and the untaught, who are trying to love God rather than to know many things. (IA Prologue, p. 3)

Rolle's reason for this limitation is simple. God, he says, "is known in doing and in loving, not in arguing." (IA Prologue, p. 3)

The exclusion of the learned from the audience is more apparent than real, however. In the first place, it must be remembered that Rolle was writing his work, rather than teaching it orally. Thus, for the truly *rudibus et indoctis,* the work would be inaccessible, unless they could find someone lettered to read it to them.

Further, Rolle was writing—by choice, not by necessity—in Latin. Indeed, Rolle was a capable prose stylist and a passable lyric poet in English, as his three English Epistles and his English Psalter attest. By his deliberate choice of Latin, then, Rolle limited his direct reading audience not only to the literate but to those who counted a fair ease in Latin comprehension among their accomplishments—not a great number of people, if the professional academics—the philosophers and theologians—were to be excluded. In fact, some ninety years later, Richard Misyn, the Carmelite Prior at Lincoln, was preparing his English versions of the *Emendatio* (1434) and the *Incendium* (1435) at the request of a recluse, the Lady Margarete Heslyngton. In his prologue he declares to her that he is making this English version "for you and others who do not understand the intricacies of Latin." His translation exists in at least fifteen extant manuscripts, which argues that the Lady Margarete's was not an isolated case. In Richard's own time the Latin reading audience among non-theologians and non-philosophers must have been considerably smaller.

That Rolle did not intend to exclude learned men simply because of their academic training, however, is made plain in the next paragraph of the prologue. It is not the learning, but the attitude accompanying and fosters its pursuit that Rolle finds unacceptable. The attitude, suggested by the description of the usual activities of the theologians and philosophers, and by the coupling of them with the "worldly-wise" in the paragraph previously cited, is one which values words *about* realities in preference to the Reality Itself. Such men, making learning an end in itself, seek preeminence in knowledge *about* God for the sake of the fame it brings, or for the sheer fascination of the intellectual exercise—the unending game of scholastic reasoning. Rolle excludes such men from his audience not because he does not wish to speak to them, but because, given their priorities and preoccupations, they would simply be unable to hear him or to take in what he was saying in a fruitful way. For Rolle, all learning, like every other created good, is only a means to union with God, the Uncreated Good.

Hence, if the learned are to join Rolle's audience, it will not be until they have changed that attitude and refocused their energies, when "having put aside and forgotten all things which have to do with the world, they burn to be enslaved by single-minded desires for the Creator." (IA Prologue, p. 3)

Conditions for such a transformation of attitude aim first at external change, and then at spiritual training. Richard continues,

> First, however, in order that they may flee all earthly rank, they must hate all the ostentation and empty glory of learning; then, conforming themselves most strictly to poverty, they must continually place themselves in the love of God by praying and meditating. (IA Prologue, p. 3)

The conditions Rolle sets down here for the learned to join his *Incendium* audience are, in distilled form, the subject matter of the first eight chapters of the *Emendatio*, a treatise whose audience is not specified either by inclusion or by exclusion. The *Emendatio* speaks, in fact, to any Christian who wants to advance in union with God, particularly in the union of contemplation. It moves through the same steps Richard outlines above, from the Christian's initial conversion or conscious turning to God, to purity of spirit (Chapter Ten), the condition he demands of his prospective *Incendium* audience.

In chapters Eleven and Twelve, the *Emendatio* deals with the love of God and contemplation. These realities are described by Rolle in the *Incendium* prologue in the paragraph immediately following the one just cited. As a result of their change of attitude, says Richard of the learned who have met the conditions for joining his audience,

> without a doubt, a certain small interior flame of uncreated love will appear to them and, centering their hearts on the seizing of this fire (by which all darkness is

consumed), it will raise them up in lovable and most pleasant burning ardor. Thus they will transcend temporal things and cling to the throne of tranquillity forever. (*IA* Prologue, pp. 3–4)

So it would seem that the learned are not to be excluded after all! If by changing their attitudes, by being converted or completely turned toward God, the learned can arrive at the same contemplative union offered as a goal to readers of the *Emendatio*, then the *Incendium*, which describes that union in its processes of development and in its effects, is very much meant for them.

Further, the very learning which, in their unconverted condition, barred the learned from that union and from Rolle's audience, when freed from this encumbrance by the process of conversion, becomes for them an inestimable enrichment of the contemplative union, and thus makes them preeminently candidates for the *Incendium* audience. Rolle explains,

Indeed, because these men are more learned, they may, by that fact, be better adapted for loving, if they truly despise themselves and rejoice to be rejected by others. (*IA* Prologue, p. 4)

It would seem, then, that the audience intended for the *Incendium*, like that for the *Emendatio*, was to be marked only by the desire to love God and to enter into as close a union with Him as it pleased Him to grant. The "exclusion" of the learned from the group seems to have been Rolle's shock tactic, a way of getting the attention and redirecting the (currently wasted) energies of this group so eminently suited to union with God.

The supposition of a universal audience is confirmed in the very next sentence, the last of the *Incendium* prologue. Appropriately enough (given Rolle's radical declaration of exclusion tempered by the *if*'s we have just examined), the confirmation appears in a subordinate clause:

Accordingly, because I am rousing everyone here to love, and because I will try to show the superheated and supernatural feeling of love to everyone, the title *The Fire of Love* is selected for this book.

B. Arrangement of This Text

As we have seen, the *Emendatio* and the *Incendium* share a common end: to show their audience the way to contemplative union with God. Their chief difference lies in their emphasis. Where the *Emendatio* focuses principally on the preliminary ground-clearing of attitude-conversion, and on the processes of disposing the converted Christian for union, the *Incendium* deals chiefly with the union itself, in its physical, psychic, and spiritual manifestations. Although the *Incendium* seems to have been composed first, the work of the *Emendatio*, in the experience of the reader—as indeed, of Richard himself, as he attests in autobiographical passages in the *Incendium* and elsewhere—actually occurs first. For that reason, the *Emendatio* appears before the *Incendium* in this translation. This arrangement seems psychologically more useful than the reverse, based on chronology of composition, and it seems (from colophon dates) to repeat Richard Misyn's process of making the first English translation of the paired texts. (It does not reflect the chronological arrangement found in the manuscript from which Harvey made the Early English Text Society's printed edition, however.)

C. Style

In writing the *Emendatio* and the *Incendium*, Rolle faced the same problem—that of reducing to words experiences not naturally congenial to this medium.

Words, by their nature, are linear and sequential. They are the tools and the mode of expression of the ordering intellect, and are most effective in expressing the processes and conclusions of reason. They work fairly well in describing concrete realities, provided these can be considered piece by piece. Where simultaneities occur, or wholistic impressions must be conveyed, or complexities of thought and feeling exist in conflict, words become labored and prove more cumbersome than valuable. In these instances, a picture is indeed worth a thousand words.

Consequently, where Richard speaks of reasons for taking specific actions, describes the sequence of steps in a process designed to achieve a particular end, or explains the causes of a condition or the results of a course of action, words serve him well. He is clear, concrete, and logically ordered. This is the case through most of the *Emendatio*, which spends the greater part of its time urging conversion and showing means for the accomplishment of this end. In this treatise Rolle's language is fairly sober and prosaic, enlivened by occasional images and some use of alliteration, with a modest use of rhetorical flourishes.

However, when Rolle comes to describe the experience of union itself, drawing his material not from "the authorities" beloved of his contemporaries, but from his own perceptions of it as an overwhelming reality, words are less effective and logic gives way to another kind of order. Then his language leaps to lyric flight. Alliterations abound, apostrophe dominates, images proliferate, rhetorical flourishes elaborate idea after idea, the whole sings in bright colors, and language is pushed to its limits.

This occurs in the last two chapters of the *Emendatio* and in most of the *Incendium*. The reason for both the difficulty and the change is plain enough. The experience of contemplative union—of love of any kind, for that matter—is centered in and apprehended not by the rational powers of the intellect, but by the affective powers of the will and by the power of intuition, neither of which takes kindly to verbal expression. Indeed, in an experience where the affective and intuitive powers are dominant, words, at best, approximate or suggest the reality—and then only by being pushed to (or past) their limits. Hyperbole, metaphor, paradox, lyric flight—all these are exhausted by the man who, for one reason or another, must find words to express the essentially inexpressible.

Such is the case of the lyric poet and the teaching mystic. Dissatisfied with each attempt, driven to try to communicate what he has perceived in heart and vision, each returns again and again, in ways that change even as they remain constant, to the experience at its source.

In the case of the mystic, the Source is God, and the experience is perceived union with Him. The cyclic returns to the Source for a means of expression of the experience of union, intensify the experience and deepen the union, so the mystic prays as he writes and writes as he prays.

The result can seem chaotic, unless the reader, too, turns and returns to the Source as he reads, joining the writer in prayer (or at least in the realization that that is what is happening) and, the mystic hopes, in union with the God they both love. To read this way, the reader, like the writer, must be shaped, prepared to receive the gift of perceived union with God. And this is why the mystic writes in the first place.

In these two texts of Richard Rolle, the problems of comprehension and communication outlined above are somewhat simplified, because wherever he can Rolle uses concrete images drawn from daily life—homely, vivid pictures sketched to reveal analogous spiritual truths. Further, he never loses sight of his human audience, even when he is most absorbed in addressing God, his Beloved. He suggests appropriate practical actions for them to take in arriving at the same union, and offers them the mirrors of concrete examples of proper and improper attitudes and behavior as checks for their own practice.

Finally, with charming candor, he takes down the protective barriers the authority and dignity of his role as teacher, learned man, and experienced mystic allow him, and in autobiographical passages he reveals himself "warts and all." He speaks to his audience as a loving, concerned elder brother, open and responsive. He teaches by virtue, not of academic sanction, but of having traveled the road he would share with his readers.

Because he has erred and learned from his mistakes, he can warn those who follow of dangers and delusions of the world, of the specific, unceasing hostilities of the unsleeping enemy, the devil, and of the particular pitfalls the flesh itself offers in its war against the spirit.

Because he has also succeeded in receiving and returning Love, he can share the joy of this communion to encourage his following brothers and sisters.

Thus, by revealing himself and his experiences, good and bad, unguarded, Rolle allows his readers to unmask themselves before themselves and before God—the essential precondition for initial conversion and eventual union with Love Unguarded.

D. *Emendatio vitae*

In the *Emendatio vitae*, Rolle is chiefly concerned with the means by which the Christian may first be turned toward Christ, then cleansed, and finally prepared to receive the gift of contemplation, a direct experience of the love of God.

In this treatise, which is more an outline with examples than an intensive analysis of a state of soul, or an exhaustive examination of all the ins and outs of the process of human sanctification, Rolle arranges the chapters in what may be called psycho-chronological order: the order in which the seeker becomes aware of the progressive stages of development in his own spiritual growth. Each chapter is so ordered that it leads inexorably to the next.

The tone, for the most part, is mild and matter-of-fact, whether Richard is exhorting his audience to seek God, warning them against the snares of the world, the flesh, and the devil, or describing the distance delusion can put between the appearances of external practice and the reality of the inward state of soul. Clarity, common sense, and cheerful, steady encouragement mark the whole.

The only extensive exception to this rational approach occurs in Chapter Eleven, where Rolle waxes passionate and lyrical on the love of God. In long passages directly addressed to God, his own soul, love, and again, God, Rolle rises to a level of excitement rare in this work, though characteristic of the *Incendium amoris*. The reason seems plain. For Rolle, who is (as he demands his *Incendium* audience shall be) "enslaved by single-minded desires for the Creator," the experience of the love of God generates its own intensity. For him this is the only reality worth spending the self on—and spend he does, with abandon! This is the goal toward which all the spiritual labors he has described tend, and the only real reason for doing them. And so, having carefully worked his way, in chapters One through Ten, through the processes leading up to this point, when at last he arrives there, he soars!

There is nothing particularly radical in Rolle's ascetical advice offered in the first ten chapters, though he misses the pedestrian by a fairly wide margin.

Rolle tends to expand the meaning of the virtues he treats by insisting that they must transform the spirit as well as change physical behavior. Poverty (Chapter Three), for instance, is to be a rejection, not only of the world's goods and gold, but also of the things that belong to it—like its standards of judgment, which lead to detraction and arrogance. The injunction of Christ to the rich young man, "Go, sell what you have," demands of a Christian, according to Rolle, a transformation of his thoughts and affections. On the other hand, poverty is to mean accepting the necessities for life—food, clothing, and shelter—but doing so without greed, without wishing for anything in particular (Chapter Twelve), and without complaining, should any of these be lacking at any time (Chapter Three).

Mere external deprivation, Rolle remarks, "is not of itself a virtue but a great misery" (Chapter Three). Without humility and mercy, a man can be damned, even if he practices willing poverty, but with these virtues, however great his riches, he "will be established at the right hand of Christ" at the Judgment. Finally, when things must be possessed, their possessors can still rise to contemplative union if they possess the things without attaching their hearts to them.

Similar expansions, qualifications, and applications are

made for each of the other steps in Rolle's progress from conversion to contemplative union. The steps themselves are clear enough, as are the connections between them and their individual and collective relationship to the goal, and much of what Rolle says is squarely in the ascetical tradition. Where he departs from that tradition, or contributes to it, he draws on personal experience. It might be useful to take a look at some of these differences to get an idea of this experience, which comes to fuller expression in the *Incendium*.

Of abstinence (Chapter Four), Rolle remarks that it must be practiced with discretion, lest it weaken the body so much that a man be unable to pray—the reason for which abstinence is practiced in the first place! Again, as in the "exclusion" of the learned from the *Incendium* audience, a distinction is made between using a thing as an end in itself or as a means to another end. Abstinence, says Richard, is not sanctity, but, practiced with balance, can be a means to it. Charity far surpasses it in value, despite the judgment of men who value only what they can see. (The same subject-cluster is treated in Chapter Eleven of the *Incendium*, analyzed below. Reading the two side by side illustrates clearly the differences in language and approach produced by subject matter and context.)

Speaking of patience (Chapter Six), Rolle notes wryly that people think they have patience until they are attacked—then they discover how little they actually have.

It is when Rolle arrives at Chapter Seven and defines true prayer as occurring "when we do not think *about* [italics mine] anything, but our whole will is directed toward the highest things, and our soul is set ablaze with the fire of the Holy Spirit" that the heart of his mystical experience (detailed more fully in the *Incendium*) is suggested. The description of the effects of this enkindled prayer suggests the rich invention characteristic of the earlier treatise.

Says Richard, "And our whole prayer will be made with affection and effectiveness, so that now we do not hasten past the words in our prayer, but we even offer almost every syllable to our God with a powerful cry and an intense desire. For the very intention in our heart, by means of burning love, also sets our very prayer ablaze, and from our mouth it is consumed by fire in the sight of God, in an odor of sweetness, so that to pray is a great delight. For when ineffable sweetness is found in prayer, the prayer itself is transformed into a song of rejoicing."

Meditation (Chapter Eight), "recalling" events in the life of Christ, being "mindful" of them, is more a function of the intellect than of the will, but it is to be used to move the will to love along one path or another. Here Rolle stresses that the path a man takes to God, while he is directed to it by his own "disposition, meditation and affection" is not his choice but God's choice for him. If he wants to arrive at God and enter union with Him, he must accept that choice and pursue it faithfully. And because the path, like God's will for the individual, cannot be seen, the meditations proper for a particular man cannot be taught him directly by another person. "I might be able, therefore," Rolle says to the reader, "to describe my meditations for you, but I do not know how to explain which kinds will be more fully effective for you, for I have not seen your interior affections." God must provide the seeker with His gifts, in His time, and He will give each the gifts most suited to him.

Nevertheless, human teachers, Doctors of the Church, experienced men of prayer (even Rolle himself, by implication, though he does not say so) have a use for the seeker. God uses their experiences and their writings to teach His lessons and, presumably, as a means by which to grant His individually selected gifts to each man in turn. Again, humility is stressed—in this case as openness to God and acceptance of His love from any source He may choose to use as a channel of communication.

In his final remarks in this chapter, Rolle declares that his reader should practice most diligently those meditations in which he finds most sweetness, "For to meditate without sweetness produces little, except in that condition on account of which the sweetness is not felt." This somewhat cryptic remark is not explicated, either in this treatise or in the *In-*

cendium. It may refer to the state of aridity or darkness described by St. John of the Cross, among others, which, it would seem probable from the rest of his works, Rolle never experienced. If this is the case, his lack of explication would be characteristic: Rolle was writing here, as elsewhere, of what he knew from experience.

Rolle's remarks on reading (Chapter Nine) echo the "exclusion" of the learned from the *Incendium* audience, discussed above. Here he assumes that his reader is *not* one of the professional philosophers. He recommends the reading of Scripture as a means to goodness, love, and penitence, not vainglory, and urges that the knotty texts be left to the experts trained in handling them. Again, knowledge is to be a means to an end—the knowledge and glory of God and the good of the neighbor, to whom one's insights are to be transmitted—not a means for self-aggrandizement.

The "heavenly melody" of which the *Incendium* makes so much appears in Chapter Ten as a result of purity of spirit, which also brings with it the destruction of sin, especially unavoidable venial sin, in Christ's love, "as a drop of water is dispatched in a burning furnace," and the transformation of fear from fear of hell to the fear "lest he should offend his most dearly Beloved."

This purity of spirit, acquired by steady progress through chapters One through Nine, leads to a single goal, the love of God, ecstatically hymned in Chapter Eleven. Chapter Twelve deals with contemplation itself, in a much calmer tone. It serves as a kind of reprise, in which the major points made in the treatise, most of them those that Rolle has added to or developed within the ascetical tradition, are repeated and fitted into this new context of contemplative union.

Though the *Emendatio* seems to have been composed four or five years after the *Incendium amoris*, it can serve the modern reader as a suitable introduction to the earlier treatise. The *Emendatio*, as we have seen, deals with the ascetical ground-clearing and the proper laying of foundations of virtue, prayer, meditation, and reading which must precede the mystical union of contemplation described in the *Incendium*. The *Emendatio* ends with the following paragraph.

> Therefore, nothing is more useful, nothing more delightful, than the grace of contemplation which raises us from the depths. For what is grace except the beginning of glory? And what is the perfection of glory except perfection consummated? In it there is preserved for us a delightful happiness and a happy delight, a glorious eternity and an eternal glory, to live with companions, to stay with angels, and (what is above all), to know God truly, to love Him perfectly, and to see Him in the splendor of His Majesty, and, with ineffable jubilation and melody, to praise Him eternally. To him be honor and glory and the giving of thanks, forever and ever. Amen.

This is the point at which the *Incendium* begins.

E. *Incendium amoris*

In the *Incendium amoris* Rolle thinks and writes in a way quite different from the orderly, sequential mode of the *Emendatio*. The differences in subject matter, it seems to me, more account for this than the explanation of "greater youth." Six years, at most, is not much time, when there are no major internal or external upheavals. Rolle had received his gifts of "heat, sweetness, and song" in divine contemplation some twenty-four years earlier, and had grown quietly in them in the interim.

Further, he was quite capable, at this point, of using the strict formality of language and the order that characterized scholastic argumentation. Chapter Six and the beginning of Chapter Seven, which together present an exposition of the orthodox doctrine of the Trinity, offer a model of this kind of writing and thought. When Chapter Seven moves on to the love of Christ as a logical response to the doctrine, however, style, tone, and language change to those characteristic of the treatise as a whole. Here Rolle begins in reason and ends in prayer.

The subject matter of the *Incendium*, the love of God and the direct contemplative perception of Him experienced in transformed prayer, does not, as we have seen, lend itself to being rendered in words. Nor does it yield gracefully to the logical organization that shapes scholastic disquisition.

Wisely, Richard does not attempt to force-fit his material into the *Emendatio* form, in either the organization or the arrangement of his chapters. Instead, he calls upon the associative powers of the mind, those responsible for the creation of metaphor and paradox, and for the best expression of emotional and intuitive complex experiences possible in words.

The result, while irritating to the essentially linear mind (which tends to judge it "rambling," "circular," "messy," and "disorganized") is probably the most accurate verbal reflection possible of one man's essentially incommunicable experience of love.

The associative principle underlies not only the arrangement of the elements of the experience, and the images, metaphors, and paradoxes in which it is to be expressed, but the preliminary selection of these details and, indeed, in some measure the very perception of these details as bearing upon or central to the experience.

A close look at Chapter Eleven may make Rolle's perception and procedure clearer. Here, as in every part of this work, all elements come to their proper focus in love. Every detail springs from and/or leads back to love—the power, the experience, the Person as sought and as joined. Here, as elsewhere, no matter what the starting point, what the route, Rolle and his reader end in Heaven in the joy of experienced contemplative union.

The chapter begins with a proposition: "Nothing less than God can fill the human soul which has a capacity for God alone." The first conclusion, immediately following, is that, for the lovers of God, rest is found only in union with Him.

The description that follows, of the nature of this union,

repeats the images of fire, song, and sweetness worked out in earlier chapters, with a wealth of loving detail. It is followed by the introduction of two themes which will alternate in shaping the rest of the chapter—the opposition between appearances and reality, and the choosing of the man for the work by God, not by anyone else, including the man himself.

The distance between appearances and reality, a favorite theme of Rolle's in the work as a whole, is focused in this chapter upon the problem of abstinence, which seems in the judgment of men to be a virtue. So it is, Richard affirms, but only when practiced in moderation.

Further, it is inferior to the gift of love, the union described above, in its ability to prepare the spirit for prayer; indeed, if excessive, fasting weakens the body too much, it may even prevent the union it is designed to facilitate.

Rolle then delivers a brisk response, based on this superiority of love over fasting, to those who have been accusing him of gluttony and of choosing his friends for the delights of their tables! In doing so, he brings in a second application of the appearances/reality conflict. It is better to conform to the lawful outward habits of those around one, than to "feign sanctity" by a greater abstemiousness, and thus be praised for virtue one does not possess.

Rolle returns to the larger topic of the relative worth of union with God and fasting, and notes that love also purifies one of desires for "fleshly pleasures" and enables one "to command the unruly petulance of the spirit" better than fasting (which is intended to do both jobs), because the "ardent fire" of divine love extinguishes carnal concupiscence.

The mention of contemplative union leads Rolle to rhapsodize on a line from the Canticle of Canticles (5:8): "Say to my Beloved, I languish for love," in characteristic lyric and exclamatory flight. He returns to prose in a development of the nature of contemplative union as a gift of God to the chosen one, who is consequently inspired by the Holy Spirit in the arrangement of his own life. Other people's advice, based on what they can see of his life (appearances again), is likely to be less helpful than his own sense of his life, based on the indwelling Reality of God, with Whom he is in union.

On the other hand, Rolle warns, no man must be too quick to assume that he is one of these chosen souls (appearances!) for, "The grace of contemplation is not, in truth, granted to everyone, but rarely and to the extremely few, who, taking on the deepest quiet of mind and body, are chosen exclusively for the work of divine love."

That *caveat* offered, Rolle sounds another note that serves as a minor theme for the work. Such rare men as there are who have this gift "are therefore held as dear, and they are desirable and beloved before God and men." The usual corollary—that therefore they will be despised by the worldly, who judge by appearances—is absent here, but the dangers of passing such judgments serve as the subject of the next chapter.

Rolle ends Chapter Eleven where he began it, with those who are in union with God. These are they who are satisfied because He fills their souls; they are those who "frequently offer their prayers to God in great devotion and delight, and who are able to taste the sweetness of contemplation by praying or meditating, who do not run back and forth, but remain in quiet."

Throughout the *Incendium*, Richard is plagued by the inadequacy of language to reflect accurately the complexity of his experience of union with God. His principal metaphors for the experience—heat, sweetness, and song (*fervor, dulcor, canor*)—operate thematically in the work as a whole, and one or another of them usually serves as starting or ending point for any associative train of thought.

Nevertheless, there is still a problem. Richard must make clear that these three are metaphors, that they are real experiences (neither imaginary nor hallucinatory) *and* that their reality is spiritual (not physical), without reducing them to simple (and for his audience, unreal), images, words without substance. He solves, or attempts to solve the problem, by leaning on the image and developing its ramifications, without stressing the fact that it is metaphor. With the image of fire, for instance, only once does he break off and state, flatly,

"I have called this love 'fire' as a metaphor, because it burns and illumines." (Prologue). For the rest of the work, he treats love *as* fire and describes its actions in those terms without qualification.

"Sweetness" and "song" are similarly handled. Each is identified as metaphor once, and then used in its own terms to describe the spiritual reality it images.

The reason for this solution of the problem lies, I believe, in Rolle's sense that the dominance of intellect in studies about God had led men to a great deal of knowledge but not into union with Him in love. Stress on the metaphoric function of the image would have supported that dominance; stress on the image itself, the picture as spiritual reality, would assist the affective and intuitive powers of the soul through which love was expressed and union made. Since Rolle aimed to feed the "poor," the non-professional Christians, "starving" for the love of God, his choice here seems inevitable.

A second means of dealing with the complex, apparently contradictory realities of an experience is paradox. Richard uses paradox as he does metaphor, stressing the separate realities, in discord and as resolved, while dealing only sparingly with the intellectual process by which the resolution is effected. Perhaps the clearest instance of this use of paradox lies in Richard's attitude toward women. He sees them as at once dangerous and attractive (chapters Twelve and Twenty-nine), as able to instruct (Chapter Twelve), and in need of instruction (Chapter Thirty-nine), as the seducers of men (Chapter Twenty-nine), and their victims (Chapter Thirty-nine). Men, consequently, must avoid them (chapters Twelve and Twenty-nine) and may not avoid them (Chapter Thirty-nine)!

The resolution of the paradox is made silently. Having established these discordant realities, and having previously established that women can serve as friends of men (though this is dangerous), Rolle ends Chapter Thirty-nine with a paen to friendship, unspecified as to sex; it is the complement of his plea to God for a friend of his own (chapters Thirty-four and Thirty-five), and the completion of the definition and description of friendship with which he began the chapter.

Rolle, in attempting to force language past its natural limits in order to convey the reality of his experience of ecstatic union with God, Love, often explodes in the verbal equivalent of a shower of sparks, not unlike a Roman candle. He soars in lyric flights of prayer—agony or ecstasy—and takes the willing reader with him.

He is also capable of a crisp analysis of human frailty, particularly when vice masks itself as virtue. Chapter Nine offers examples of both, in the prayer for misery in this world instead of in the next, and in the description of the behavior of proud, stubborn men. (The depiction of the simulators, Chapter Ten, brings Molière's Tartuffe to life some three centuries before his time, but Rolle is not amused.)

In short, in the *Incendium* Rolle lives in Love, and brings the reader to see the Love toward which the *Emendatio* is designed to lead him.

THE MENDING OF LIFE
(Emendatio Vitae)

CHAPTER ONE – *Concerning the Conversion to God*

Do not be slow to be completely turned to God, converted to Him, and do not put it off from day to day, for the rigor of death seizes wretched men suddenly, and now bitterness unexpectedly devours with punishments those who were reluctant to be converted. Nor can there be numbered how many dissolute worldly men there are from among us, whom presumption has pulled down. For it is a great sin to trust in the mercy of God and not cease from sin, judging the mercy of God to be so great that He will not inflict just punishment on sinners.

Therefore He says, "While it is daytime, work; night is truly coming in which no man will be able to work" (John 9:4). He calls this present life "light" or "day." In it we ought never cease from good works, knowing that while death is a certainty for us, the hour of death is uncertain. He calls death "night." In it our limbs are tied up, our senses are laid aside and we can now do nothing for our salvation, but we shall have to receive joy or torment as a result of our deeds.

We live within a point—rather, in less than a point, for all of our time, compared to eternity, is nothing. Thus it is not without the most serious damnation that we consume our life in the love of vanities and stand idle all day long, negligent and impenitent.

> Therefore, O Lord, convert us, negligent and impenitent, and we shall be completely turned toward You. Save us, and we shall be healed.

For many shall not be healed; they are corrupted and their wounds putrefy. For today they are turned toward God, and tomorrow they are turned away from Him; today they are penitent, and tomorrow they go back to their original evils. Of such people has been said, "We have cured Babylon and it has not been healed," for they are not truly turned to Christ.

For what is conversion, complete turning to God, except turning away from the world, turning away from sin, turning away from the devil, and turning away from the flesh? What is turning away from God except turning from Unchangeable Good and turning toward mutable good, turning toward delight in the beauty of a creature, turning toward the works of the devil, turning toward the pleasures of the flesh and of the world? For it is not by the walking of our feet that we are completely turned to God, but by a change of our affections and of our customary behavior.

A conversion or complete turning to God is made when we direct the sharpness of the mind toward Him and incessantly meditate on His counsels and commands, so that they may be fulfilled by us and, wherever we are, whether we stand up or sit down, that the fear of God may not depart from our heart.

I'm not speaking about the fear which has pain, but about that fear which is in love, by which we offer reverence to the presence of such great Majesty and always fear lest we should offend Him in the smallest thing. Indeed, when we are thus disposed, we are truly converted to God, and we are turned away from the world. Moreover, to be turned away from the world is nothing else but to place behind us all its delectations, to endure all its bitterness willingly, for the sake of Christ, and to consign all useless occupations and worldly business to oblivion.

To the extent that our soul has been converted entirely to God, it dies in its very marrow to all those things that must be loved and sought in the world. Stretched out toward heavenly desires and delighted by them, such a soul always holds God before his eyes, and gazes at Him almost unweariedly, as the most holy Psalmist declares. He testifies that he has done this when he says, *"Providebam Dominum in conspectu meo semper"* ["I keep Yahweh before me always"] (Ps. 15:8). He says "always"—not for an hour, as those men do who keep before the eyes of their hearts any beautiful and lovable earthly thing which they contemplate, in which they are delighted and which they desire to enjoy.

And again the Psalmist says, *"Oculi mei semper ad Dominum, quoniam ipse evellet de laqueo pedes meos"* ["My eyes are always on Yahweh, for He releases my feet from the net"] (Ps. 24:15). It is perfectly evident from these words that unless we train our interior eyes indefatigably on Christ, we shall not avoid the "nets" of temptations.

And indeed, lest the eye of the heart should be fixed on God and it should be perfectly converted to Him, there are many obstacles, of which we shall list several. These are the abundance of riches, the flatteries of women and the physical appearance or beauty of youth.

These make up a three-strand cord which can be snapped only with difficulty. Nevertheless, it must be snapped and held for nothing, so that Christ may be loved. For whoever desires to love Christ truly, not only without sadness but even with immense joy, must go away from all the things which have the power to impede him; in this cause he spares neither father nor mother nor his very self.

He does not look for the approval of anyone else; he bears violence from everyone; he breaks all obstacles to pieces; whatever he is able to do so that he may love God seems small to him. He flies from vices as a drunken man flies toward those things which belong to the world. He does not look back at their solaces; on the contrary, directing himself wholly into God, he almost lets go of his exterior senses and, entirely collected within himself, he is entirely raised up into Christ, so that when those seeing him think him sunk in sadness, he rejoices intensely.

But there are many who say they are willing to be completely turned toward God, but they claim they are not yet able to fulfill this desire, because these or those occupations hold them back. With sorrow we censure the frigid spirit of such people, for without a doubt, if they were touched by the smallest spark of the love of Christ, they would at once, in solitude, seek in every way to find by what road they might come to the service of God. Nor would they cease from searching until they had found it.

They frequently offer excuses that accuse them even more, for riches drag many men back, and the flatteries of women deceive them. And those who have done well for a long time sometimes, through these things, plunge into the deepest pit. For beauty is quickly loved, and when it senses itself to be loved it is easily attracted, and when it has been attracted, it is thrown down headlong—and on account of his conversion, the man may be in a worse state than he was before. Then his reputation is blackened and he who was praiseworthy before is despised by everyone; he is judged abhorrent.

For I have seen a man of whom it has been said that, after fifteen years in which, by marvelous rigor, he thoroughly tamed his body, he next fell into sin with his own servant's wife, from whom he would not be separated even up to the moment of his death. But at his death his servants said that he cursed the priests who came to him and refused to receive the sacraments.

Therefore, neophytes, that is, those who are newly converted, ought to flee from the occasion of sinning, and to avoid with their whole will the words and deeds and sights stirring them up to evil. For where a thing is the more unlawful, there it will be several times the more fully desired! For the devil rises more vehemently against those who, he sees, have been turned away from themselves and fully turned toward God, and he does not cease to enkindle the desires of the world and of the flesh. He pours into the soul the delectations previously enacted, he proposes the abandonment of penance, and he rouses the innumerable phantasms of vain thoughts and useless affections which had previously been put to sleep.

Against these things, the penitent man must exercise himself. In manly fashion, he must take up spiritual arms; he must constantly resist the devil and all his suggestions; he must extinguish fleshly desires; he must ever sigh for the love of God, and contempt of the world (about which we shall speak next) must never withdraw from him.

CHAPTER TWO – *Concerning Contempt of the World*

To have "contempt of the world" is to hold in contempt all temporal and transitory things, to pass through this life without love of those things, to seek on this pilgrimage nothing outside of God, barely to accept, ungreedily, the necessities from all vain joys and comforts—and, should the necessities be absent at any time, to bear it cheerfully. This is "contempt of the world"; have it, if you do not wish to be utterly destroyed.

And thus it is a shame for a man to honor excrement—which is to love earthly things. Hence it is that greedy rich men make themselves slaves to the vilest foulness. And they rejoice to have themselves called the lords of men, though they are slaves to vices. That a man rules another man is the property not of nature but of chance; that a man is overcome by vices is the property of his own perverse will. Therefore, lay aside your evil will and you will be free both from sin and from the devil; you will be made a servant of justice which teaches you not to love worldly things.

For greed for the world and the love of God are opposites, nor can they rest in the same man at the same time, for the place is so strait that one of the two must fall out. Therefore, the more thoroughly you cast out greed, the more intensely you will savor divine love. The greater the greed, the less the love.

> O wretched soul, what do you seek in the world, where you see all things are transitory and deceptive? These things deceive you the more quickly which flatter you the more. Why are you satisfied by mortal things? Why do you desire with such intense emotion the things that will perish? You do see, don't you, that they perish more quickly than they are acquired? But I know that where you dwell is where Satan's seat is! He has blinded your

eyes, and through his illusions he makes a fool of you, so that you desire fleeting things, you love hateful things, you hold permanent realities in contempt, and you cling to vanishing things. And thus you base yourself upon a fallible foundation. When you think you stand, you fall down into the fire!

Those who dwell in temporal abundance are deceived by five things which they love: by riches, by dignity, by pleasure, by power, and by honors. These things chain them in sins, tie them up in faults; they are fettered in these delectations, nor are they released except by death. But then the unchaining is too late; for them nothing remains except eternal damnation.

These things keep them back from contempt of the world, from the love of God, from self-knowledge, and from an appetite for the kingdom of Heaven. In fact, no one can be saved unless he ceases to love the world and all things that are in it. Therefore cease, while the warmth is still in your body, and the beautiful age of youth still remains!

For what shall delight him who has disposed himself for loving Christ? He has trod youth underfoot. He shall preserve his fortitude for God. He shall assess riches as valueless. He shall learn that favor is false, and shall perceive that beauty is vain. But shall I discourse at length on everything, item by item? He shall hold completely in contempt all things which pass by like shadows in this world.

O carnal lover, what do you find in the flesh, that you delight in it so? Does its beauty please you? Or, by chance, do you glory in its skin? Why do you not attend to what lies hidden under the skin? But do you not know that the beauty of the flesh is the garment of ugliness, the kindling-wood of corruption and often the cause of perdition? Therefore, let it be sufficient for you that you despise other things to love God, to praise God, to be with God, to rejoice in God, not to draw back from God, but to cling to Him with inextinguishable desire.

The world itself compels us to contempt of the world, which is filled with so many miseries! In it malice perseveres, persecution shatters, jealousy consumes, and detraction corrodes. In it there is the false naming of crimes and the bitterness of scandals. There all things are confused; there all things are out of order. There justice is not loved, nor is truth approved. There fidelity is unfaithful and friendship is cruel, for it stands firm in prosperity but in adversity it fails.

And here are other things that can move us to contempt of the world: the mutability of time, the brevity of the present life, certain death and the uncertain result of death, the stability of eternity, the vanity of present things, and the truth of future joys.

Choose what you will! If you love the world, you will perish with the world. If you have loved Christ, you will reign with Him.

CHAPTER THREE – *Concerning Poverty*

"Si vis perfectus esse vade et vende omnia quae habes et da pauperibus et veni sequere me." ["If you wish to be perfect, go and sell all that you have and give it to the poor and come, follow me" (Luke 18:23).] This injunction indicates that perfection lies in abandoning the things that belong to the world and in exchanging them for the things that belong to Christ. For not all those who have left their goods behind come to Christ. For some are worse after abandoning their goods than they were before!

For then they zealously serve detraction. They do not fear greatly to take away the good reputation of their neighbors. Then they corrode with jealousy; they gnash their teeth in malice. They place themselves before others. They praise their own state; all others they either censure or hold in contempt.

Whatever you may think, it is by such things that the devil deceives those who have neither the world nor God. Through diverse nonsense he leads them to eternal torment.

But you, knowing these things which have been said, must accept poverty in another way. When it says "Go and sell" it means a transformation of the affections and of the thoughts, so that the man who previously was proud now must become humble, the wrathful man must become meek, the jealous man must become loving, the greedy man must become generous (with discretion)—and if a man was impure he must struggle to abstain not only from every evil but from every evil appearance. If, moreover, in another case a man has gone to excess through food or through drink, then he must amend through fasting. But he who loved the world too much now must bind himself entirely to the love of Christ. He must fix all the dispersions of his heart in a single desire for eternal things.

Thus, certainly, that poverty, freely chosen, will be most

fruitful, and the straits which he suffers for the sake of God will be a most glorious crown. For *"Beati pauperes spiritu quoniam ipsorum est regnum caelorum."* ["How happy are the poor in spirit; theirs is the kingdom of heaven" (Matt. 5:3).]

For what is "poverty of spirit" but the humility of spirit by which a man recognizes his own infirmity? Seeing himself unable to attain to perfect stability, except by the grace of God, he forsakes all those things which are able to block him from that grace which ought to be seized, and he places his desire in the joy of the Creator alone. And just as from one root many branches spring, so from voluntary poverty, taken up in this way, virtues and inestimably good habits come forth.

This is not like the behavior of certain men who change their tunic and not their soul. On the contrary, these men seem to abandon riches and do not cease from gathering innumerable vices. For what is worse than a proud pauper? And what is more execrable than an envious beggar?

But you, if you abandon all things for the sake of God, look rather at what you hold in contempt than at what you are relinquishing. Examine diligently in what manner you may imitate Christ in your habits.

He says, *"Discite a me quia mitis sum et humilis corde."* ["Learn from me for I am gentle and humble in heart" (Matt. 11:29).] He does not, indeed, say, "Learn from Me because I am poor." For poverty is not, of itself, a virtue, but a great misery, nor is it praiseworthy for its own sake, but only because it is the means to obtain virtue.

Poverty both helps one to acquire beatitude and makes one avoid the many occasions of sinning. Therefore it is praiseworthy and desirable. Indeed, it causes a man not to be honored, however virtuous he may be, but rather to be despised and confounded, and to be degraded among the lovers of the world! And to endure all these things for the sake of Christ is the highest merit.

On this account Christ, as an example for man, led a poor man's life while He was on His pilgrimage, because He knew that those people who abound in riches and delights would enter the kingdom of Heaven with difficulty. Whence, so that men would embrace poverty greedily and fervently as the greatest honor, to those who, for the sake of God, abandoned all things and wished to follow Him, He promised judiciary power, saying, "*Vos qui reliquistis omnia et secuti estis me sedebitis super sedes duodecim iudicantes duodecim tribus Israel.*" ["You who have left all things and have followed me shall sit upon twelve seats judging the twelve tribes of Israel" (Matt. 19:28).]

But those who hold to poverty, even willingly, and lack the humility and mercy which He teaches are more miserable than all those who abound in riches. Nor will they receive in the Judgment a seat of apostolic dignity. But they will be clothed with a double cloak of confusion, which is the damnation of body and soul.

Moreover, those who are strong in humility and mercy, however great the riches they possess, nevertheless will be established at the right hand of Christ when He judges them.

Indeed, certain men say, "We are not able to relinquish all things! We are infirm! It is necessary for us to retain the necessities, so that we may live!"—and this is lawful. But these men are of less worth, because they do not dare to endure narrow poverty and penury for God. Nevertheless, they are able to attain to the summit of virtues through the grace of God, and to raise themselves to the contemplation of heavenly things, if they abandon occupations and secular business and rise up unceasingly to prayer and meditation, and if they do not possess those things which they have by loving them, but relinquish them in possessing them.

Moreover such men must continually consider that to seek for what is superfluous belongs to vile cupidity, that to retain the necessities belongs to infirmity, but to relinquish all things belongs to perfection. Therefore, when they consider that the higher things are what they do not attain, let them not boast nor presume concerning the lesser things which they have, so that they may deserve to ascend to the instruction of an ordered life. The points concerning that topic, consequently, will follow next.

Chapter Four – *Concerning the Establishment of Life*

So that a man, for the honor of God and his own advantage, and for the profit of his neighbor, may rightly be directed, four things which ought to be said present themselves.

First, what are those things that defile a man? These are your sins. There are three kinds of sins: those of thought, of word and of action.

A man sins in thought when he thinks anything against anyone. He does this if he does not occupy his heart with the praise and love of God, and if he allows it to be dragged away by diverse meditations and to wander about in the world.

A man sins in word when he tells lies, when he perjures himself, when he curses, when he backbites, and when he brings forth foolish talk, foul language and vain or idle conversation.

A man sins in deed in many ways. By lust he sins in lascivious touching and kissing, in voluntarily defiling himself either by procuring or by sustaining, without great necessity, occasions by which he believes he can be defiled. He sins also by stealing, by deceit, by striking blows and by other different kinds of deeds.

The second thing that must be discussed is, what are the things which make a man clean? These also are three, opposed to the three mentioned above, namely:

—Contrition: This requires the expulsion of the thought, and the exclusion of every affection which does not pertain to the praise, honor and love of God.
—Confession of mouth: This ought to be seasonable, unadorned and complete.
—Satisfaction of deed: This has three parts, namely, fasting (because the man has sinned against his very self),

prayer (because he has sinned against God), and alms-giving (because he has sinned against his neighbor). Nevertheless, I'm not saying that he ought to give alms from someone else's goods, but he must make restitution of these, because he will not be absolved of his sin unless that which has been stolen is returned.

The third thing that must be discussed is, what are the things that preserve cleanness of heart? There are also three of these, namely,

–Wakeful meditation on God, so that there is no time in which you do not meditate on God, except in sleep, which is common to all.
–Solicitude for custody of the exterior senses, so that taste and smell, hearing, sight and touch are wisely restrained under the bridle of discipline.
–Honest occupation, whatever it might be: reading, or saying anything about God, or writing, or doing anything useful.

Similarly, there are three things that preserve cleanness of word, namely, thinking before you speak, avoiding a multitude of words, and detesting lies.

Again, there are three things that preserve cleanness of deed, namely, moderation in foods, avoidance of vicious society, and continual meditation on death.

The fourth thing that must be discussed is, what are the things which draw us into conformity with the will of God? There are three, namely,

–The exemplarity of creatures, which is attained through considering it.
–The familiarity of God, which is acquired through prayer and meditation.
–The rejoicing in the kingdom of heaven, which is experienced, in a way, through contemplation.

And thus in this pattern of living is a man of God established. He will be like a tree that has been planted beside running waters (Ps. 1), that is, flowing graces, so that he always grows green in virtue and never grows dry with the aridity of vice, a tree that will give fruit in good season—that is, good works in example and good gifts—and he will give assistance for the honor of God; he will not sell it for the sake of vainglory.

"In good season" it is said against those singular people who give an example of fasting when it is time for feasting, and against the greedy people who give away fruits when they are rotten, or put off giving to the point of their death.

Consequently, therefore, he has prayed wisely who has said, "*Bonitatem et disciplinam et scientiam doce me.*" ["Teach me goodness and discipline and wisdom" (Ps. 118:66).] For what is "discipline" but the establishment or correction of habits? First, therefore, we are made ready in uprightness, through discipline, so that we may be reformed of our evil habits, and then we recognize and know what we ought to do and what we ought to avoid. At length, we savor not fleshly and earthly things, but heavenly and divine things.

Who is there who can direct himself totally to the will of the Creator and grow in virtues through discipline in uprightness? And the man who, by his desire for Christ, has, by chance, surpassed in the constancy of his living, other men who have gone before him, ought not boast, on that account, of what has been given to him, nor even to judge himself superior to other men who seem depraved. On the contrary, he ought to reckon himself to be the most wretched and the most vile.

Let him judge no one man except himself; let him set all men ahead of himself; let him desire to be judged by all men not as holy but as despicable. When he comes among men, let him arrange that he may be the last in their number, and let him be judged least in the opinion of all men. For when you are greater in humility among men, then in the sight of God you will find grace, namely, that of exaltation.

For great is the power of God, and He is honored by the humble. Therefore, He is held in contempt by the proud, who seek their own glory, and not the glory of God. Moreover, if you should glory in the goodwill of the people (which is opposed to humility), and should, with joy, assume honor for yourself for the sake of fame offered in your lifetime by the masses, know that you have received your reward here, however marvelous you may seem for penitence or continence. For when you rejoice more in the glory of men than that of the angels, nothing will remain to you in the future except torment.

Therefore, you ought perfectly to despise your very self, and to refuse every glory of the world, neither to think nor to act except in consideration of divine love, so that your entire life, inward and external, may cry out the praise of God.

In food and in drink, be spare and discreet, and, as the occasion demands, nothing ought to be rejected which is laid hold of with the action of grace. When you eat or drink, let the memory of God, Who feeds you, not fade from your mind. On the contrary, praise and bless and glorify Him in every morsel, so that your heart may attend rather to the praise of God than to your food, and so that there may be no hour when your spirit is separated from God.

For acting in this way in the sight of Jesus, you will earn, through service, an ineffable crown, and you shall flee the temptations of demons, which most particularly lie in ambush for people in food and drink, and deceive them. For the demons either cast down the incautions from the stronghold of virtue through their immoderate intake of food, or through too much abstinence they shatter them in their very virtue.

For there are many who in eating always fluctuate, so that they continually take in either less food or more; they never perfectly hold on to one form of living, when they first judge this one and then that one the better. For the unwise and the uninstructed, who have never experienced the sweetness of the love of Christ, judge that indiscreet abstinence as sanctity, nor do they imagine that they can become great in merit before God except through rare and almost excessive abstinence, and unless they become known to men as outstanding in this regard.

But in truth, abstinence is not sanctity, in itself, but if it is discreet it may be a help, so that a man may become holy. If abstinence is indiscreet, it keeps him from being holy, because it thus destroys discipline, without which virtues are transformed into vices.

If a man wishes to take on singular abstinence, he ought to avoid the sight of men and their praise, lest he should grow proud, as if for nothing, and lose everything. For men often judge those people as more holy in truth, whom they see to be the more abstinent, when in reality they are inferior.

But indeed, the man who has truly tasted the sweetness of love will never judge that he overcomes anyone in abstinence; on the contrary, the more he is judged inferior, in his own judgment, so much the more does he seem marvelous in abstinence in the judgment of men. It is best to be pleasing to God, I judge, so that a man should conform himself in food and drink according to the place and the time, and, with honesty, to those with whom he converses, so that he may not appear either to be superstitious or to be a simulator of religion. For let him know without doubt that if one or two think well of him, the rest will call him hypocrite or simulator!

But there are certain men greedy for foolish glory, who in no way acquiesce to be held among common men. Wherefore, either they eat so little that they attract all the words of men, or they arrange for food of another kind to be brought for them, so that they seem different from the rest in something. May their insanity and obstinacy be far from me!

Nevertheless, the advice that those who are less abstinent prefer themselves to those who abstain more is health-giving; since they are not able to abstain in this way, they are stung in spirit!

Moreover, those who are marvelous for abstinence should judge as superior to themselves those others, whose virtue (in which they excel other men) lies hidden to men. For while their virtue (namely, abstinence) is praised by many people, unless it is supported by great humility and charity, in the sight of Christ it is held as nothing. Truly, the virtue of the other people is the greater in that it is not seen by men.

For who can recognize with how much love a man burns toward God? Who can recognize with how much compassion he shines toward his neighbor? Without a doubt, the virtue of charity incomparably exceeds every abstinence or fasting, or any other deeds that can be seen exteriorly. For the most part it may be that the man who seems less abstaining in the sight of men may, meek in the sight of Christ, be more burning in his love.

For it is necessary that a man be strong who will exercise himself in divine love in manly fashion. His flesh debilitated and made infirm by too much affliction, a man often is not strong enough to pray; however much greater his desire for burning in love may be, he will not lift himself up to the heights.

Therefore, I would prefer that a man fail on account of the magnitude of his love rather than on account of too much fasting. As the spouse testifies concerning herself, *"Nunciate dilecto meo quia amore langueo."* ["Tell my Beloved that I am sick with love" (Cant. 5:8).]

You, therefore, be constant in all your ways. Direct your life according to the rule taught to you, and even though in the beginning you will not be able to obtain what you desire, do not desist, but persevere because, through a long time and exercise, you will arrive at perfection. Whether you are a pilgrim or a man refraining from action, or one sitting down, or whatever you may do in this life, always direct the eyes of your spirit to God. Do not permit your meditation to withdraw from Him. Consider that time in which you do not meditate on God as time that you have lost. Praise God in the night and desire His love, that sleep may not discover you occupied in any other way than either praying or meditating on God.

Watch lest you melt away in vain thoughts, or subdue yourself to superfluous cares. But desire to seek and retain this constancy of spirit, so that you neither fear the evils of the world nor in any other way immoderately desire its goods.

The man who fears to endure adversities does not yet know how it behooves him to hold the world in contempt, and he who rejoices in earthly goods is far distant from eternal goods. But it belongs to the virtue of fortitude to hold in contempt all adversities and prosperities—and even death itself—for the sake of eternal life. And love is to desire only heavenly joys. For perfect love rejoices to die, and it endures life patiently. If, Christ granting, you have ascended to that perfection, nevertheless you will not be without temptation or tribulation. This discourse is now turned to a discussion of that topic.

When the devil sees one man from a thousand to be perfectly converted to God, to follow in the footsteps of Christ, to despise present things, to seek only invisible things and to love to take on perfect penance, and to purge himself from every contagion of spirit and body, he prepares a thousand frauds to harm him and a thousand arts to attack him, so that the man may turn away from the love of God to the love of the world, so that he may pollute himself again with the filth of crimes, so that, at the least, he may, by libidinous thoughts, render himself hateful to God alone.

The devil stirs up against him persecutions, tribulations, calumnies, impositions of false judgments, and all kinds of hatreds, so that these things may almost terrify him and thus break the man whom prosperities have been unable to deceive. Now the devil places before him prosperities, now flattering things. He brings into the man's mind the images of physical things. He composes phantasms of vices. He recalls in a terrifying way the delectation of ancient charm and love; he inflames the heart and flesh with hazardous fires.

He begins from the smallest persuasions, but he arrives, in this way, at the greatest flame of wickedness, and the more he desires with greater anxiety to blow up against all kinds of torments and tribulations, the more he grieves that we have already been rescued from his jaws through the mercy of God. For the devil seeks nothing except that he may separate us from the spiritual, the most chaste and the most agreeable embraces of eternal love, and that he may disfigure us again in the cistern of misery and in the filth of the dregs—which would, indeed, be more miserable for us than I have the power to explain.

For who can imagine the insanity of the man who would descend from the delights of kings to the food of pigs? And, by this token, he is more insane who rejects the most delicate feasts of uncreated Wisdom and submits himself to the uncleanness of the flesh. Are not lust and gluttony swinish filthiness? And demons eat them—and those who practice them!

Therefore, how we ought to act against tribulations and the temptations of our enemies, and how we ought to resist them, patience will teach us—and of that we shall speak now.

CHAPTER SIX – *Concerning Patience*

The sons of the king do not deign to be tumbled down to be the fodder of irrational animals. On the contrary, they spurn all illicit pleasures and the comforts of the world for the love of Christ.

For the man who fills himself with that Bread Who came down from Heaven does not bend his affection to those things that might be suggested by the devil. When temptations or tribulations surge up, he ought to put on spiritual arms and march forward to the warfare. For temptations are vanquished by the constancy of faith—that is, of love—but tribulations are overcome by patience.

For what is patience except the free and willing bearing of hostile things? Therefore, the man who is patient murmurs against no adversities, but rather, at all times he praises God with the prophet. For the greater a man's patience is in adversities, the more glorious he will be in heavenly things.

Therefore, tribulations, anxieties, bitternesses—and, I may say, infirmities and penury—ought willingly to be endured because through these and other such things many sins are purged and merits are increased. For it behooves us either to be burned in this life by the fire of divine love and by tribulation, and thus to be purged from the filths of the world, or to be crucified most sharply after this life by the fire of purgatory or of hell. We choose what we will; we cannot evade one or the other!

Here, moreover, by an easy penitence—on the contrary, with joy—we are able to wash away every future punishment, if we truly cling to God. Therefore, tribulations are allowed to come in so that they may call us back from the love of the world and so that we may not be punished more seriously for our sins in the other life. For it behooves us to be purged by sorrows of what we have perpetrated in pleasure.

If sinners build upon our backs, they will not harm us (if we bear it patiently), but themselves. Although they bring us a little pain, nevertheless they bring us a crown and prepare torment for themselves. But evil men are permitted here to get through this present life without many tribulations, where no glory is reserved for them in the future.

It is on this account that holy men love tribulations, because they know how to arrive at eternity through these things. On the other hand, reprobates always complain in adversities and avoid them as much as they can, because while they have been given over immoderately to visible things, they are deprived in the hope of eternal things. In exterior goods alone, they have found solace, because at their foundation they have lost the savor of celestial things.

But there is no rational soul living in this world who does not cling either to the Creator or to the creature. If he loves the creature, he loses God, and with his love he goes forth to ruin. For such love in the beginning is labor and foolishness, in the middle is sickness and misery, and in the end is hatred and suffering.

If a man loves his Creator, he resists all things that are in the world. To speak about Him and with Him he considers sweet; to meditate on Christ seems a refreshment to him. He closes off his exterior senses, lest death go up through these "windows," and lest he be occupied in some useless vanity.

And sometimes contempt, shames, mockeries and scandals are raised against him. Therefore it is necessary that he at once snatch up the shield of patience, and that he rather be prepared to suffer injury than to be ignorant of it. Let him pray for the conversion of those who hate him and oppress him. Nor should he be anxious to be pleasing to men, but let him fear to offend God.

Again, if he is tempted in the flesh, let him subdue it, lest the spirit succumb. For a temptation, when it is not consented to, is material for the exercising of virtue.

Certainly, no one comes to know for himself by experience whether he is strong or weak, unless he is tempted. For thus he who is in peace ought not be called patient, but when he has been aroused by an injury, then he will see whether he possesses patience!

Many men seem patient when they are not attacked, but immediately when a light breath (I do not say of injury, but of correction), touches them, in the face of it their spirit at once turns itself into bitterness and wrath. And if they should hear a single word against their will, they try to return twice as many from a harsh mouth. May my soul not come into their ways of judging!

The darts of the enemy must be extinguished by humility and by the sweetness of the love of Christ. Nor should temptation be yielded to, be it as extremely severe as you will, because where the battle is the greater, the victory is the more glorious and the crown the more sublime. *"Beatus vir qui suffert temptationem quoniam cum probatus fuerit accipiet coronam vitae."* ["Blessed is the man who endures temptation, for when he has been tested, he will receive the crown of life which God has promised to His lovers" (James 1:12).]

Moreover, you will not doubt then that you are on the road to perfection if contempt is like praise to you, poverty like wealth, scarcity like a feast, so that you may endure either with the same spirit and fall from the height of the spirit in neither case.

Flee and abominate, as much as you can, the praise of men because in this life it is most greatly worthy of praise, if you are praiseworthy and are not praised by men. The tongues of praisers deceive many, and the lips of detractors confound more. But you, despise favor and honor and every vainglory. Freely endure hostilities, hatreds and detractions, and thus, through infamy and good reputation, through tribulations and flatteries, you will not cease to hasten to the heavenly kingdom.

We fall often, so that, instructed through many failures, we may afterward stand the more steadfastly. The strong man does not fear. Patient in adversity, he does not grow sad, as it is written, "The just man will not grow sad, whatever befalls him."

Thus disposed, you will, without a doubt, overcome every temptation, you will extinguish all malice, you will judge those who trouble you inferior to you, and you will cling to Christ with your whole mind.

CHAPTER SEVEN – *Concerning Prayer*

If you should be placed in temptation or in tribulation, you should run immediately to prayer. For if you pray purely, you will have help.

Whenever there come distractions and wanderings of the heart, they snatch the thoughts away to different things, nor do they allow the heart to stand still in the praise of God. Then, perhaps, it would be good to meditate for a change on divine things, until the spirit is better stabilized, and thus to fill out one's prayers.

But if men have put aside all occupations of the world for the love of God, and have entirely bound themselves to heavenly meditation and holy prayer, I judge that, through the grace of God, within a short time they will find their heart made stable for loving and adoring, so that they do not flit past, now into this thing and now into that, but rather, they rest again in tranquillity and in eternal peace.

It greatly contributes to obtaining stability of heart to persist in numerous prayers and to sing the psalms devoutly. For by continual prayer we conquer the demons and we unman their wiles and disturbances. For they are rendered weak and as if without strength when we are strong and persevere, unmoved, in prayer.

Certainly whenever those men, who, by long exercise, have prayer as a habit, find in their praying greater sweetness and more burning desire, while that sweetness and ardor remain, it is good, therefore, that they not cease from their prayers. But when they cease—which often occurs on account of the corruptible flesh—they are able to engage in meditating on Holy Scripture or in doing some other useful thing. Thus, nevertheless, they do not permit their thinking to wander away from God, so that at once when they arouse themselves to prayer, they may be more ardent than they were before.

For we pray truly then when we do not think about anything, but our whole will is directed toward the highest things, and our soul is set ablaze with the fire of the Holy Spirit. Thus the wondrous running waters of divine goodness are found perfectly in us, because from the inmost marrow of our heart the love of God will rise up. And our whole prayer will be made with affection and effectiveness, so that now we do not hasten past the words in our prayer, but we even offer almost every syllable to our God with a powerful cry and an intense desire. For the intention in our heart, by means of burning love, also sets our very prayer ablaze, and from our mouth, it is consumed by fire in the sight of God, in an odor of sweetness, so that to pray is a great delight. For when ineffable sweetness is found in prayer, the prayer itself is transformed into a song of rejoicing.

Hence those certain people are to be rebuked who are pleased with meditation rather than with prayer. They do not know that the word of God can be fiery. By it the filths of sinners are cleansed and the minds of those praying are inflamed by love. They say that they formerly wished to meditate so that they might stabilize their heart, but they are led forth to this stability so much too late that they are not strengthened by it to pray continually. But although we are not strong enough to gather our heart into singleness as quickly as we wish to, we ought not, on that account, to cease. Instead we ought to desire to grow little by little, so that at length Jesus Christ may deign to make us whole. Meditation will help one to that end if he does not exceed in measure and manner.

CHAPTER EIGHT – *Concerning Meditation*

Moreover, meditation on the passion of Christ and His death is good, and it is good often to recall how great sufferings and miseries He underwent of His own free will for us and for our salvation—in walking about and in preaching, and in enduring hunger and thirst, cold and heat, reproaches and curses, so that it might not seem burdensome to a useless servant to imitate his Lord and Emperor. For it is fitting for the man who claims that he remains in Christ to walk as He walked.

But Christ says, through Jeremiah, "Be mindful of my poverty"—that is of my passage—"of wormwood and of gall"—that is, of sorrow and of bitterness—through which I have passed from the world to the Father. For this mindfulness (or meditation) confounds the devil and destroys his machinations. It extinguishes carnal temptations and inflames the soul toward the love of Christ. It raises up and makes the spirit shining, and by clarifying it, cleanses it.

I judge that this meditation is more useful than all others for those who are newly converted to Christ. For, as a consequence, the humanity of Jesus Christ is placed before them. In it a man may delight for a while; in it he may have matter for rejoicing and for lamenting. He has matter for joy because of the certitude of redemption; he has matter for mourning because of the shame of sin.

It is for the destruction of sin that so admirable a Victim has been immolated. For the rude and carnal soul is not snatched up in contemplation of the Godhead unless the spiritual soul is formed by the lifting of carnal impediments. For when he has already begun to possess a clean heart, and no image of a fleshly thing can delude him, then certainly a man is admitted to higher things, so that he may glory ardently in the love of the Godhead.

Certain men even meditate on the glory of the blessed angels and of holy souls rejoicing with Christ, and this meditation belongs to contemplation. Other men meditate on the miseries of the human condition and its worthlessness, which they examine in their meditations on the madness of men (because, for the sake of the vanity of the visible life, men forget invisible joys).

Still others arrange their meditations so that they sound nothing but the praise and desire of the Creator, in order that they may love Him as much as may be possible to pilgrims. But no one arrives at this meditation except the man who has been much exercised in the things previously discussed. Moreover, this meditation is more excellent than the others, and most greatly forms the contemplative man. Therefore, just as the works and exercises of the elect are diverse, so their meditations are diverse.

Nevertheless, all meditations which come forth from one fountain tend toward one end, and arrive at one state of blessedness, or lead to it, but by diverse roads through a single love, which is greater in one than in another. Therefore the Psalmist says, *"Deduxit me super semitas iustitiae."* ["He guides me by paths of virtue" (Ps. 22)], as if he said, "There is one justice, but many are the paths by which we are led to the glory of eternal life."

For all men, living in unity, are of diverse merits; in a single justice they are led by many paths to God. Some go by the lower path, others by the middle path, and still others by the higher path. But the higher path is given to the man who, so that he may love Christ more fully, is predestined from eternity for it, not because he works more than other men, or because he bestows more than they, or because he suffers more things, but because he loves more. Indeed, love to him is fervent and sweet and he seeks its rest in all things.

But no man can establish himself on any of these paths unless he accepts the one for which God has chosen him. Sometimes people who seem to us to be on the higher path are on the lower path, and vice-versa, for that condition only appears inwardly before God, within the soul, not outwardly before men, in any deed a man can do externally. But in truth men are directed according to their disposition, their meditation and their affection, to this path or to that one. By no exterior works can it be known who is the greater or who is the lesser in the sight of God.

Therefore it is foolish for people to make judgments concerning the chosen, and to say, "This man exceeds that one and this man's merits are far distant from that man's merits, when inwardly their minds are ignorant; they might judge them legitimately if they knew them. For certainly, God wills this to be kept secret for every creature, lest men hold this one too much in contempt, or honor that one too much. For without a doubt, if they could see the hearts of men, many whom they now honor as chosen, they would just as much despise as vile and fetid, and others, of whom they do not take care, and whom they are not moved to see, they would honor just as much, as the most beloved of God, and like the holy angels!

And thus the good thoughts and meditations of the chosen are from God, and He has poured into each of them such gifts, through His grace, as He sees are more suited to their state and condition. I might be able, therefore, to describe my meditations for you, but I do not know how to explain which kinds will be more fully effective for you, for I have not seen your interior affection. Certainly, I think that those meditations in you which God Himself pours into your soul through Himself will be more pleasing to God and will accomplish more for you.

Nevertheless you will be able to make a beginning from the sayings of others, which I have experienced in my very self. For if you hold the doctrine of the Doctors in contempt, and you imagine that you can discover something better than what these men teach you in their writings, know that you will not taste the love of Christ. For it is foolishness to say, "God taught them! Why, therefore, will He not teach me?"

I answer you, "Because you are not of the same caliber as those who have been Christ's! For you are proud and harsh, but they have lived as humble and gentle men, and they have acquired nothing from God by presuming, but, by humbling themselves beneath men, they have received the wisdom of the saints. Therefore, He taught them, so that we might be taught in their books!"

But if your meditations now desire the love of Christ, or now resound His praise, you have, as it seems to me, been well disposed. But exercise the meditations in which you experience the greater sweetness and delight in God, for these will more fully perfect you. For to meditate without sweetness produces little, except in that condition on account of which the sweetness is not felt.

Chapter Nine – *Concerning Reading*

If you desire to arrive at the love of God and to be set on fire with desire for celestial joys, and to be made resistant to the contempt of earthly men, do not be negligent in reading and meditating on Sacred Scripture—and mostly in those places where it establishes customs and teaches the snares of the devil to be on guard against, and, consequently, where it speaks about the love of God and about the contemplative life. (And the more difficult sayings should be left to academic debaters and to the more ingenious men, exercised for a long time in sacred doctrine.)

For Scripture helps us much to advance in goodness. In it we recognize our defects, and our perfections; in it we see in what things we sin and in which areas we do not sin; in it we recognize what we ought to avoid and what we ought to do, and in it the most subtle machinations of the enemy are perceived. The Scriptures set us afire to love, and they sting us to tears. They prepare us for a table of delights, if we have delighted in them as in all riches.

But let no greed for the honor and favor of men set us on fire for the knowledge of the Scriptures, but only the intention of pleasing God, so that we may learn how we may love Him. And let us teach this same knowledge to our neighbor, not so that we may be reputed as wise men among the people. On the contrary, we ought rather to hide our learning than to show it off for our own praise. As Scripture says, *"In corde meo abscondi eloquia tua."* ["In my heart I have hidden Your words so that I may not sin before You" (Ps. 118:11).] "I have hidden Your words"—that is, from vain ostentation.

Therefore the only cause for our speaking should be the praise of God and the edification of our neighbor, so that this word may be fulfilled in us: *"Semper laus eius in ore meo."* ["His praise shall be ever in my mouth" (Ps. 33:1).] This can only be when we do not seek our own praise, and do not speak against His praise.

CHAPTER TEN – *Concerning Purity of Spirit*

Through these nine steps, touched on previously, we are raised up to the purity of spirit by which God is seen. (I am speaking of that purity which one can possess on this pilgrimage.) For how is perfect purity acquired here, where a man is so often soiled by sins—at least by venial sins? The feet of the saints have to be washed because they drag up dust from the earth! Who indeed can say, "I am pure—free from sin"? Truly, no one in this life may claim such a thing! For as Job says, *"Si lotus fuero aquis nivis et effulserint velut munditiae manus meae, tamen sordibus intinges me et abhominabuntur me vestimenta mea."* ["If I have been washed with waters of snow, and my hands have glittered like cleanliness itself, nevertheless You will dip me in filths and my garments shall be abominated" (Job 9:30–31).]

"If I have been washed with waters of snow"—that is, by true penitence—"and my hands have glittered like cleanliness itself"—on account of deeds of innocence—"nevertheless You will dip me in filths"—on account of the venial sins which cannot be avoided—"and my garments shall be abominated"— that is, my flesh renders me abominable, and sensuality, which is so fragile and perishable and prone to love the delectable appearance of the world, often forces me to sin.

Therefore the Apostle says, *"Non regnet peccatum in nostro mortali corpore."* ["Let sin not reign in our mortal body" (Rom. 6:12)], as if he were to say, "Sin is not able to reign in us, but it cannot cease to exist!"

Therefore, what purity can a man have in this life? Truly, he can have great and praiseworthy purity if he has exercised himself rightly in the desire for reading, for prayer and for meditation, as has been noted before. For although he may sin venially sometimes, nevertheless the sin will be destroyed quickly, on account of his undivided intention directed toward God.

For the fervor of love existing in Christ consumes all the rust of sins as a drop of water is dispatched in a burning furnace. Therefore the virtue of the cleansed soul is to keep the spirit intently toward God, because in this state the whole thought is directed into Christ, and the whole memory is extended into Him, even when he seems to speak to other people.

For in the cleansed conscience, there is nothing bitter, nothing harsh, nothing hard, but all is sweet, all is smooth. From cleanness of heart there arises a hymn of glory, the most sweet-sounding song and a delightful joy. Then, for the most part, so much ineffable rejoicing is given by God that he is even filled with heavenly melody. In this condition a man can know that he is in the state of love, even in that love which can never be lost. He does not, nevertheless, live without great fear—not lest he incur torment, but lest he should offend his most dearly Beloved.

But I'll stop here, to speak more fully of something else, because I seem to myself to be exceedingly wretched. For often my flesh is afflicted and tempted.

Although, indeed, in these things which have been described, the love of God and the contemplative life are contained, nevertheless, there are other things which ought to be said about them, more spiritually, for our use.

O sweet and delectable Light, You Who are my uncircumscribed Creator, illumine my face and the sharpness of my inner eyes with uncreated brightness, and my spirit as well, so that, cleansed to its inmost marrow from filthiness and made marvelous by Your gifts, it may fly with agility into the height of the most delightful love. Set me ablaze with Your savor so that I may sit and rest quiet in You, O God, rejoicing in heavenly things, set on fire by their sweetness. Like one rapt, made stable in the contemplation of invisible realities, may I never be delighted except by Divine communication! O Eternal Love, inflame my soul to love God so that it may not burn except for His embraces.

O good Jesus, may You grant me that I may experience You, Who now may be experienced but not seen. Pour Yourself into the inmost recesses of my soul! Come into my heart and fill it with Your most brightly shining sweetness. Inebriate my spirit with the burning wine of Your sweetest love, so that, forgetting all evils and all limited sights, illusions, and images, I may exult, embracing You alone, and I may rejoice in God my Jesus.

By no means, O most sweet Lord, withdraw from me! Continually remain with me in Your sweetness because only Your presence is a comfort to me, and Your absence alone leaves me sad.

O Holy Spirit, Who breathe where You will, come into me and snatch me up to Yourself. Fortify the nature You have created, with gifts so flowing with honey that, from intense joy in Your sweetness, it may despise and reject all which is in this world, that it may accept (You giving them), spiritual gifts, and through melodious jubilation, it may entirely melt in holy love, reaching out for uncircumscribed Light.

Burn my inmost being with Your fire, and my heart will burn on Your altar forever.

Come, I beg You, O sweet and true glory! Come O most desired sweetness! Come my Beloved, Who are my whole consolation, to my soul languishing for Your sake and toward You, and slip into it with most sweetly flowing love. Set ablaze with Your heat the penetrable places of my heart and, by illumining its inmost places with Your light, feed the whole with the honey-flowing joy of Your love, in order to snatch up mind and body.

You ought to delight, still, in these and similar meditations, so that at some time or other you may rise up to the inmost part of love. Love, moreover, does not allow the loving soul to remain inside itself. Rather, love carries the soul outside itself toward the Beloved, so that the soul would rather be there, where it loves, than where the body (which feels and lives by it) is.

Indeed, there are three steps of the love of Christ; on them he who is chosen may advance from one to the other toward love. The first step is called "insuperable," the second is called "inseparable," and the third is called "singular."

Then, indeed, love is "insuperable," when it can be overcome by no other affection, and when it freely rejects all impediments for the sake of Him. It extinguishes all temptations and carnal desires, when, for the sake of Christ, it endures patiently all confining obstacles and is not overcome by any delectation or flattery. Every labor is easy to a lover, nor does he conquer that labor better than through love.

Love is, in truth, "inseparable" when the spirit, already set ablaze by the most vehement love and clinging to Christ by inseparable thought, at no moment indeed allows Christ to recede from his memory, but, as if he were tied to Him in heart, he thinks of Him and he sighs for Him. He cries out to be held by His love so that He might unchain the shackle of mortality, that he might arrive at Him Whom alone he has desired that he might see. And most greatly he honors and loves this name Jesus, in so much that It will continually rest in his spirit. When, therefore, the love of Christ works in the heart of the man who loves God and holds the world in contempt, so much that it cannot be overcome by another love, it is called the highest. But when it clings to Christ inseparably, by thinking of Him, and by forgetting Him in no action, it is called by the name "inseparable" and "everlasting."

And what love is able to be greater or higher than that love, if it is highest and everlasting? For this, the third step remains, which is called "singular" love. It is one thing to be alone, and another to be highest, as it is one thing to take the lead and another to admit no other as an equal. For we can have many associates and, nevertheless, hold a higher place before all of them.

Moreover, if you seek any present comfort, or receive any other than that of your God (even if, by chance, you should love most intensely), you do not, nevertheless, love "singularly." Therefore, you see by how much the magnitude of those who surpass you in growing may abound, when you may already be "the highest," and may even be able to be "alone."

Love ascends to the "singular" stage, therefore, when it excludes every consolation except the one which is in Jesus, and when nothing besides Jesus can satisfy it. In this step the established soul loves One—Him alone. He desires Him alone, namely Christ. He pants in a single desire, for Him. He sighs for Him; from Him he is kindled; in Him, burning, he rests.

Nothing is sweet to this man, nothing does he savor, except Jesus, the memory of Whom is made sweet as musical melody in a feast of wine. Whatever besides Him brings itself to mind is quickly rejected and at once trampled underfoot. If it does not serve his love or accord with his desire, he supresses violently every exercise which is not perceived as devoted to the love of Christ. On the contrary, whatever is done seems useless and intolerable unless it runs and leads into Christ, the goal of its desire. When he is able to enjoy Christ and all things with Him, he believes he has whatever he wishes. Without Him, all things are horrifying; everything grows filthy. But because he believes he will enjoy Him forever, he persists constantly. He does not fail in body, nor does he waste away in heart, but he loves with perseverance and suffers all things rejoicing. And the more fully a man lives in this fashion, the more greatly he will be set ablaze in love, and the more sublime it will be made for him.

Certainly, solitude is suited to such a man who does not admit of a fellow among men, for the more intensely he is seized inwardly by joys, the less he is absorbed in exterior things; he is not impeded by temptations or by the cares of the present life. And now he is even made as if unable to suffer in soul. Anxiety not obstructing him by any means whatever, he rejoices continually in God.

O my soul, may you break loose from the love of the world and be entirely melted in the love of Christ, so that it may always be sweet and agreeable for you to speak about Him, to read about Him, to write about Him, to meditate on Him, to pray to Him, and to praise Him unceasingly.

My soul, devoted to You, O God, desires to see You. It cries out to You from far away. In You it burns. It languishes from love of You. O unfailing Love, You have completely conquered me! O Sweetness and Beauty everlasting, You have wounded my heart, and now, conquered and wounded, I succumb. I am scarcely alive, for I die in the face of joy, because in my corruptible flesh I am not strong enough to carry the sweetness of such great Majesty. For my whole heart, fixed in desire for Jesus, is transformed into the fire of love, and is absorbed into another shape and glory.

O good Jesus, have mercy on this wretch. Show Yourself to me, languishing. Heal me, wounded. I do not feel myself ill—except for my languishing in Your love! He who does not love You has lost everything that is; he who does not follow You is mad. But in the meantime, be joy for me, be love and be desire, until I shall see You, the God of gods, in Sion.

Moreover, love is the noblest of virtues, the most excellent and the sweetest. We know that it joins beloved with beloved, and that it links Christ with the chosen soul perpetually. It re-forms in us the image of the Highest Trinity, and it makes the creature similar to the Creator. O gift of love! How greatly it is valued before all else. It claims for itself the highest rank, with the angels. For the more a man receives of love on this pilgrim-way, so much the more sublime will he be in the fatherland.

O singular joy of eternal love, which, binding its own with the bonds of virtues, snatches them up above worldly things and to heavenly things!

O dear love! He who does not possess you casts down on the earth whatever he has, but he who strives to rejoice in you is suddenly raised beyond earthly things. You enter the bedchamber of the King boldly, and indeed you alone do not fear to seize Christ. He is the One Whom you have sought, Whom you have loved. He is your Christ, Jesus! Hold Him, for He is not able not to receive you. You have desired to obey Him alone.

O love, without you no deeds are pleasing. You make all things savory. You are the heavenly seat, the angelic society, marvelous sanctity, the beatific vision and the life lasting without end.

O holy love, how sweet you are and how comforting! You make the broken whole again. You restore the ruin, you free the slave, you make man equal to the angels, you raise up those sitting and at rest, and you make sweet those you have raised up.

In this state or degree of love, love is chaste, holy and willing, loving his Beloved for His own sake, not for His gifts, and fixing himself totally in love, he seeks nothing outside Him, contented by Him. Burning and blazing fiercely, binding Him within himself, impetuous, ardent in a wonderful manner, exceeding all measure, stretching himself out to the Beloved alone, he holds all other things in contempt. Forgetting them, rejoicing in the Beloved, thinking of Him, remembering Him unceasingly, rising up in desire, falling down in delight, going on in embraces, he is overcome in kisses and entirely melted in the fire of love!

And thus, in truth, the lover of Christ, in loving, neither pays attention to any order nor desires any level, for in the present life, however much he has been burning and rejoicing in divine love, he aims at this—more and more ardently and joyfully to love God. And if he were able to live in this condition always, he would not at any time imagine that he might be able to stand still and not progress further in love. But rather, the longer he lived the more fully he would burn in love.

For the God of infinite magnitude, of inconceivable goodness, and of unspeakable sweetness which is incomprehensible to any creature, can, thus, never be comprehended by us as He exists eternally within Himself. But when the spirit has already begun to burn with desire for the Creator, it is given a capacity for uncreated light. And then, inspired and filled with the gifts of the Holy Spirit, it rejoices with such joy as is allowable to mortals, and, transcending all visible things, it is raised up to the sweetness of eternal life. And when, by the sweetness of the Godhead and the heat of Creating Light, it is poured out in a holocaust to the eternal King, offered and accepted, it is wholly consumed.

O delightful Love, strong, seizing, burning, spontaneous, powerful, inextinguishable! You bring the whole soul into Your service and do not permit it to think of anything beyond You! You claim for Yourself all that we live, all that we savor, all that we are!

Therefore, may Jesus Christ, Whom we love for His own sake, be the beginning of our love, and may He be its end. On His account we love whatever ought to be loved in orderly fashion, and to Him we refer all that we love and are loved by.

Here, at least, perfect love is shown when the whole intention of the spirit, the hidden works of the whole body, are raised up into divine love; the power of this love is as great as its purity, and so great is its joy that no joy of the world and no carnal commerce may be pleasing to it, even if it is licit.

O love inseparable! O singular love! Even if there were no torments for the impious, if there were no rewards for the elect in Heaven, you would not disengage yourself from your Beloved any the more swiftly! It would even seem more tolerable to you to incur inestimable humiliation than to sin mortally a single time.

Therefore, you truly love God and nothing else—not your very self—except for the sake of God. And from this it follows that in you nothing is loved except God. Besides, how shall God be All in all if anything should remain in man of human love?

O Shining Love, come into me and seize me within Yourself, so that I may be present before the Face of my Creator! For You are seasoning savor, You are the redolent odor, You are the pleasing sweetness, You are the purifying fervor, You are the consolation remaining without end!

You make men contemplatives; You open the door of Heaven. You close the mouth of accusers. You show God as visible and You hide a multitude of sins.

We praise You, we proclaim You through Whom we have overcome the world, through Whom we rejoice, through Whom we scale the ladder of Heaven! Flow into me in Your sweetness, to Whom I commend myself, together with what belongs to me, without end, that I may love You!

Chapter Twelve – *Concerning Contemplation*

Contemplation, or the contemplative life, has three parts, namely: reading, prayer, and meditation. In reading, God speaks to us. In prayer, we address ourselves to God. In meditation, the angels descend to us. They both instruct us lest we err and, ascending in our prayer, they offer our petitions to God, rejoicing in our perfection. They are messengers between God and us.

Moreover, prayer is a devout affection of spirit, directed into God; when it arrives at God, delighted, it does not withdraw from Him, except unwilling.

Meditation on God and on divine things is obtained through reading and prayer. This is where "the embrace of Rachel" is.

To reading belong reason and the seeking of truth, which is the pleasing light manifest above us. To prayer belong the praise of God, the hymn, speculation, digression, and wonder. And thus the contemplative life, or contemplation, consists in prayer—or, meditation looks to contemplation.

The inspiration of God, intelligence, wisdom, the sigh—if one asks what contemplation may be, it is difficult to define. Certain men say that contemplation is nothing other than that knowledge of hidden future things, or the freedom from all the occupations of the world, or the study of divine writings. Others say that contemplation is the free and sharp-sighted exploration of wisdom, raised with wonder. Still others say that contemplation is a book, the penetrating observation of the soul opened wide in every direction for the discerning of virtues. Still others say, and say well, that contemplation is rejoicing in heavenly things. And others say, and say best, that contemplation is the death of carnal affections through joy, by the raising of the spirit.

It seems to me that contemplation is the accepting of divine love in the spirit, with the sweetness of angelic praise. This is jubilation, which is the goal of perfect prayer and of the highest devotion on this pilgrimage. This is jubilation and exultation of spirit possessed forever! This is delight in spiritual song, breaking out at night! And this act, consummated, is the most perfect of all actions.

Whence the psalm says, *"Beatus vir qui scit jubilationem Dei"* ["Blessed is the man who knows the jubilation of God" (probably Ps. 89:15)]—"jubilation," that is, in the contemplation of God. For no one alienated from God is able to rejoice in Jesus, nor has he savored His sweetness at any time. But the man who continually sighs with the fire of eternal burning love, who by patience, humility, and mercy, sighs to be made beautiful with all cleanliness of spirit and of body, and to be saturated with spiritual perfumes, is raised up in contemplation of God. He seeks unceasingly the health-bringing virtues by which, in this life, he is burned clean from the misery of sin, and in the next life, free from all punishment, he glories in the blessed life forever. And thus in this exile we shall deserve to contemplate the joyful song of divine love.

Therefore, let it not disgust him to bind himself to prayers and vigils, and let him exercise himself in holy meditations. Having been perfected by spiritual labors of this kind, with the tears and sighs of eternal compunction, the love of Christ will be set on fire within him at the same time, and all virtues and gifts of the Holy Spirit will be poured into his heart.

Let him begin, therefore, through voluntary poverty, so that while he may desire nothing in this world, he may live sober, chaste, and devout in the sight of God and man. To have nothing is sometimes a matter of necessity, but to wish for nothing is a great virtue. Nevertheless, we can possess many things and yet wish for nothing (when those things which we have we do not retain for our pleasure, but as a necessity), just as sometimes a man who has nothing desires much.

Now, it is necessary for the most perfect man to accept the necessities, for, in another way, he would not be perfect if he were to refuse to take those things which he must have to live. Therefore, this measure ought to be kept in perfect men, that they despise the whole of the world for the sake of God, and nevertheless take for themselves food and clothing. And should these be lacking at any time, they should not complain but let them give praise! Altogether superfluous things they may entirely refuse, as much as in them lies.

The more intensely anyone begins to grow warm with the heat of eternal light, so much the more patient will he be in any adversities. Here, indeed, not in the future, is humility shaped, when a man, judging himself despicable and poor, is provoked neither by curses nor by shamings to wrath. Whence, submitting himself to continual meditation, it is given to him to climb to celestial contemplation, and, the penetration of his mind having been purified, to rejoice sweetly and ardently in interior joys, to the degree that he suffers the infirmity of the flesh.

But when he must now seek external things, he never descends, lest he go forth with a proud foot at any time, but he only rejoices in the delights of the spirit. First he is seized as if in ecstasy, by the sweetness of divine love, and then, snatched up marvelously, he is delighted.

Such indeed is the contemplative life, if it is taken up in the way it should be, for through the long exercise of spiritual works we ascend to the contemplation of saints. For the mental vision is snatched up above, and contemplates heavenly things through a mysterious and spiritual vision, not through a clear and penetrating sight, because when we see through faith we see "through a glass in obscurity" (1 Cor. 13:12). For if the intellectual eye rests in spiritual light to contemplate, it does not see that light as it is in itself. Nevertheless it feels itself to have been there, when it keeps the savor and fervor within itself in limited light. Whence it says in the Psalm, "*Sicut tenebrae eius ita et lumen eius.*" ["As is its darkness, so is its light" (Ps. 138:11).] For although the shadows of sins have vanished from the holy soul, obscurities have receded, and the spirit is purged and illumined in purity, nevertheless, while it is forced to remain here in mortal flesh, that ineffable glory is not perfectly seen.

Again, saints and contemplative men contemplate the glory of God with His face revealed, which is done for them either by their sense being opened (and so they understand the Scriptures) or by the door of Heaven being opened, which is greater (and so it is as if all obstacles between their spirit and God have been removed). The eye of the heart being purged, they may contemplate the heavenly citizens.

But indeed they have received both of these things. As, standing in shadows, we discern nothing, so in contemplation (which illumines the soul invisibly) we do not see the invisible light. And Christ takes his hiding place and from there speaks to us in a column of cloud, but what is felt is exceedingly delectable. And in this, indeed, is perfect love, when a man, walking in the flesh, does not know glory except in God, nor does he know how to wish for anything except God, nor how to love anything except for the sake of God.

To him it is plain that sanctity is not in the roaring of the heart, either in tears or in external acts, but in the sweetness of perfect love and heavenly contemplation. For many have been melted in tears and afterward have declined into evil, but no one ever polluted himself again with the worldly anxieties of business after he truly exulted in eternal love. To weep and to groan belongs to the newly converted, to the beginners, and to those progressing, but to rejoice and to go forth in contemplation belongs to none but the perfected.

Therefore, let the man who, although he has done penance for a long time, nevertheless still feels his accusations on his conscience, know that, without a doubt, he has not yet done perfect penance. In the meantime, there are for him "tears as his bread, day and night" (Ps. 41:3). For unless by tears and sighs he first afflicts himself, he knows that he will not be able to come to the sweetness of contemplation.

Contemplative sweetness is not acquired except by immense labors, but it is possessed with indescribable joy. Indeed, it is not a merit of man but a gift of God. Nevertheless, from the beginning even to today, one cannot be snatched up in the contemplation of eternal love unless he has perfectly relinquished in his soul every vanity of the world. Moreover, it is necessary to run to Christ by healthful meditation and devout prayer before one truly arrives at heavenly contemplation.

Contemplation is labor, but sweet, delectable and easy labor; it rejoices the laborer and does not aggravate him. In it he enjoys nothing but rejoicing. He is wearied, not when he comes to it, but when he leaves it. O good labor, to which mortals direct themselves! O noble and wonderful exercise which those who are sitting down do perfectly! For it requires that one whom the fire of the Holy Spirit has truly inflamed seize great quiet of spirit and body.

For many, not knowing how to keep the Sabbath in their spirit, nor how to expel from it vain knowledge and useless thoughts, cannot fulfill what is taught in the Psalm, "Vacate et videte quoniam ego sum Deus." ["Be still and know that I am God" (Ps. 45:10).] For they are "still" or "empty" from the body, but they are not "still" in heart; they have deserved to "taste and see how pleasant is the Lord" (Ps. 33:8), and how sweet the height of contemplation may be.

But every contemplative man loves solitude, so that there, impeded by no one, he is able to be exercised in his affections more frequently and more repeatedly. Whence, therefore, it is agreed that the contemplative life is more worthy and more meritorious than the active life, and that all contemplatives by the impulse of God, love solitude and, on account of the sweetness of contemplation, principally, they are burning in love. Certainly it is clear that solitary men, lifted up by the gift of contemplation, are the highest and have arrived at the greatest perfection, unless by chance, there are others in an equal state because by contemplation they have seized the high point of life, and nevertheless they do not cease to fulfill the office of preacher. It is allowed that these men outrank the solitaries highest in contemplation, and intent only on divine things rather than the needs of their neighbors, by this: that on account of their preaching they earn a crown for these other works.

But truly, the contemplative man is fastened by such great desire into that invisible light that he may be judged by all men as a kind of fool, or as almost insensible. This may occur because the spirit, inflamed at its foundation by the love of Christ, transforms his physical posture, separating even his very body from all earthly actions, even as it returns the divided man to God.

Thus, in truth, when the soul in a single delight of eternal love wholly collects itself unceasingly, keeping itself within, it does not flow out to seek outwardly for bodily things. And because it is delicately fed inwardly with delights, it is no wonder if, sighing, it should say, "Who will grant me, my brother, that I may discover you and kiss you?"—that is, may I deserve to discover You, freed from flesh, and, seeing You face to face, may I be joined to You totally, forever—"and now let no man despise me."

For the devout soul, bound to the contemplative life, filled with love of eternity, despises all the vainglory of the present world and, rejoicing in Jesus alone, desires to be dissolved. This soul is held in contempt by those who know the world, not heaven. It languishes grievously with love and it desires anxiously to stand with the choirs of angels in order that it may be given to loved joys; then worldly adversity will not be able to harm it.

Therefore, nothing is more useful, nothing more delightful, than the grace of contemplation which raises us from the depths. For what is grace except the beginning of glory? And what is the perfection of glory except perfection consummated? In it there is preserved for us a delightful happiness and a happy delight, a glorious eternity and an eternal glory, to live with companions, to stay with angels, and (what is above all) to know God truly, to love Him perfectly, to see Him in the splendor of His Majesty, and, with ineffable jubilation and melody, to praise Him eternally. To Him be honor and glory and the giving of thanks, forever and ever. Amen.

THE FIRE OF LOVE
(Incendium Amoris)

Prologue

I was more astonished than I can put into words when, for the first time, I felt my heart glow hot and burn. I experienced the burning not in my imagination but in reality, as if it were being done by a physical fire. But I was really amazed by the way the burning heat boiled up in my soul and (because I had never before experienced this abundance), by the unprecedented comfort it brought. In fact, I frequently felt my chest to see if this burning might have some external cause!

But when I had recognized that that fire of love had boiled over not from the flesh with its concupiscence (in which I continued to dwell), but solely from the spirit within, and that it was the gift of the Creator, I melted, rejoicing, in the experience of a love even more intense. This melting happened chiefly because of the influence of the love and the sweetness which, with the spiritual heat itself, inwardly and most pleasantly penetrated my spirit to the very marrow. Indeed, before that comforting heat was poured into me, flooding every devotion with sweetness, I had not thought such ardor could come interiorly to anyone in this exile, for it inflamed my soul in such a way that it was just as if elemental fire burned there.

This fire is in no way the fire that inflames others burning in love of Christ, as some have said it is because they see them bound to divine duties with diligence and contempt of the world. But just as when a finger is placed in the fire it experiences physical burning, so the soul set on fire by love in the way I have already described feels the most real burning desire. Sometimes that burning is lesser in intensity, and sometimes greater; when it is less it is in proportion to what the fragility of the flesh permits.

Indeed, who could bear in mortal flesh the presence of that

fire for a long time in its most intense degree—to the extent that this life could endure it without interruption? And then one would have to fail in the face of that sweetness and before the greatness of that feeling heated past the boiling point and of that inestimable burning; without a doubt it would be embraced with avidity and when one had been made glorious by these gifts of the spirit he would desire with the most burning sighs that, breathing forth his soul in this honey-sweet fire itself, he might delay there, departing from the world and immediately being held captive among the community of those singing praises to the Creator.

But certain things opposed to charity get in the way because the filths of the flesh take one by surprise and disturb one's tranquil times. In addition, the needs of the body, intense human affections and the difficulties of exile breaking in upon one change the shape of this burning love and lessen and disturb the "flame." (I have called this love "fire" as a metaphor, because it burns and illumines.) These things certainly do not steal what cannot be taken away because it wraps up the entire heart. For that most blessed glowing fervor, absent up to that time on account of such things, appears, and I, remaining as if frozen until it returns to me, seem abandoned while I do not have (as I have been accustomed to) that sense of inner fire to which the whole of body and spirit give applause and in which they know themselves secure.

Besides these things, sleep gets in my way like an enemy, because there is no time I must mourn as lost except that which I am forced to surrender to sleeping. In fact, keeping vigil, I try to warm my soul, made dark by the cold as it were; I have known it, undisturbed in devotion, to be set on fire, and to be raised by enormous desire indisputably above earth-dwellers.

For the fullness of eternal love has not come to me in idleness, nor have I been able to feel that spiritual burning desire while I have been too much fatigued in body on account of travel, nor, again, while occupied immoderately by the comforts of the world, nor even while given over, beyond reason, to theological debates. On the contrary, I have discovered myself growing cold in such activities until, having laid aside all those things by which I could be detained outside, I once again struggled to place myself exclusively in the presence of the Savior, and I once again remained in the ardors burning within.

Therefore, I offer this book for consideration not by philosophers, not by the worldly-wise, not by great theologians ensnarled in infinite questionings, but by the unsophisticated and the untaught, who are trying to love God rather than to know many things. For He is known in doing and in loving, not in arguing.

Moreover, I observe that those things that are considered by these questioners (who are superior to everyone else in knowledge, but are inferior in the love of Christ), cannot be understood. For this reason I have decided not to write for these people, unless, having put aside and forgotten all things which have to do with the world, they burn to be enslaved by single-minded desires for the Creator.

First, however, in order that they may flee all earthly rank, they must hate all the ostentation and empty glory of learning; then, conforming themselves most strictly to poverty, they must continually place themselves in the love of God by praying and meditating. In this way, without a doubt, a certain small interior flame of uncreated love will appear to them and, centering their hearts on the seizing of this fire (by which all darkness is consumed), it will raise them up in lovable and most pleasant burning ardor. Thus they will transcend temporal things and cling to the throne of tranquillity forever. Indeed, because these men are more learned, they may, by that fact, be better adapted for loving, if they truly despise themselves and rejoice to be rejected by others.

Accordingly, because I am rousing everyone here to love, and because I will try to show the superheated and supernatural feeling of love to everyone, the title *The Fire of Love* is selected for this book.

CHAPTER ONE – *Concerning the conversion of a man to God; what helps and what impedes this conversion*

Everyone lingering in this broken-down house of exile recognizes that no one can be filled with the love of eternity or be soothed with heavenly sweetness unless he is genuinely turned around toward God. He must be turned toward Him in fact, and be inwardly turned in spirit from all visible things, before he will be able to experience, at least in a small measure, the sweetness of divine love.

Indeed, this turning is brought about through well-ordered love, so that he loves what ought to be loved and does not love what ought not be loved, and he burns more intensely in love of things that ought to be more fully loved; thus, he loves less those things that ought to be loved less.

God ought to be loved most of all; the things of heaven ought to be loved a great deal; the things of earth ought to be loved little, and only in proportion to necessity. In this way, without a doubt, any person is turned to Christ while nothing besides Christ is desired by him.

A real turning away from these good things (which ensnare their lovers in the world and do not defend them), consists in the denial of carnal desire, and in the hatred of every kind of wickedness so that the one who has been converted does not taste earthly things nor, apart from strict necessity, does he seek again any of the earthly things for himself.

Indeed, those who accumulate treasures (and do not know for whom they are gathering them), taking comfort in these things, are not entitled to feel anything of delight in the pleasantness of heavenly love, and still less (in that they have shaped themselves not through holy but through simulated devotion) have they earned the privilege of tasting anything of future felicity in their affections, as they claim. On the contrary, because they have loved earthly rewards immoderately, on account of their shameful presumptions they fall away from the sweetness by which the beloved of God are caressed.

Certainly, all love which does not aim itself toward God is injustice and returns discontent to its possessors. For what other reason are those loving worldly excellence miserably inflamed by evil love, and kept farther separated from the fire of eternal love than the space which lies between the highest heaven and the lowest place on earth? Since indeed they are made similar to what they have loved because they are shaped to worldly concupiscence, keeping "the old man" on, they fully enjoy the vanity of visible life instead of fruitful fervor. Therefore they change the glory of incorruptible love into the lasciviousness of momentary beauty. In any case, they would not do this except that they are blinded by the fire of perverted love, which lays waste all sprouts of the virtues and brings an augmentation of all the vices.

Again, many are not fixated in the feminine figure, nor do they lap up licentious living, so they judge themselves, with pseudo-security, to be saved, and solely on account of the chastity which they exhibit externally they see themselves standing out among the rest as holy men. But they surmise thus worthlessly and uselessly, when they do not uproot cupidity, which is the root of sins.

And indeed, as it has been written, nothing is more wicked than to love wealth because when the love of temporal things seizes the heart of any man it allows him to have no devotion within. For the love of the world and the love of God can never exist at the same time in the same soul, but whichever love is the stronger will drive out the rest, so that it may appear openly who is a lover of the world and who is an imitator of Christ.

In fact, the glowing fervor of love breaks forth in the visible form of work, since indeed, just as the lovers of Christ hold themselves opposed to the world and the flesh, so the lovers of the world hold themselves opposed to God and their own souls. Indeed, the chosen eat and drink and, by total deliberateness, always direct these actions toward

God; they seek in all visible things not pleasure, but necessity. They speak of earthly things with brevity, and not unless they go beyond them, not making a delay in these things. But then, indeed, they are with God in spirit and devote the rest of the time to acts of divine obedience, not standing around in idleness nor running to spectacles or games (which is a sign of the reprobates), but, speaking more virtuously of those things which pertain to God, they are not sluggish either to speak or to act or to meditate.

In truth, the reprobates uselessly hold themselves altogether opposed to God. Indeed, they listen to the word of God with anxiety, they pray without affection, they ponder without sweetness. They enter the church—they fill its walls— they thump their breasts, they send out sighs, but because all these things have been done openly for the eyes of men, they do not reach to the ears of God. When indeed they are in the church of God in body, they have been drawn apart in mind toward the good things of the world which they either have or desire to have, so their hearts are far away from God. They eat and drink not for necessity but for pleasure, because except in sexual pleasures and also in foods, they cannot find relish or sweetness. They give plenty of bread to the poor and donate clothing to those suffering from the cold who are met by chance, but when their alms are given either while they are in mortal sin or for vainglory—or, certainly more accurately, from those things which are acquired unjustly—doubtless they do not please the Redeemer but provoke the Judge to vengeance.

Just as the chosen, when they concede to the world or the flesh, keep their thought attentive always to God, so the reprobates, when they seem to be subject to God, are continually carried off by the intention of the heart to the world, and to those things which pertain to the desire of the world and the flesh perpetually. And just as the chosen who relieve their necessities are not displeasing to God, so the reprobates are not pleasing to Him in the good deeds which they are seen to do, because they contaminate their good deeds by many evil ones.

And thus the devil possesses many whom we judge good. Indeed, he owns almsgivers, chaste men, humble men, and of course those confessing themselves to be sinners, clothed with hairshirts and afflicted by penance, for commonly mortal wounds hide under the appearance of sanctity. He even holds some fervent in toiling, importunate in preaching—but without doubt he goes without all those who are fiery in love and who are always avid for loving God and sluggish for all vanity.

The wicked, in truth, are both fervent toward shameful love and as if dead to spiritual exercise, or depressed by too much weakness. All the love of these people is out of order because they love temporal rather than eternal good things, and love their bodies more than their souls.

CHAPTER TWO – *That no one reaches the highest devotion nor is he refreshed by the sweetness of contemplation quickly*

Moreover, it is obvious to lovers that no one attains to the highest devotion in the first years, nor is he intoxicated with the sweetness of contemplation. On the contrary, one is with difficulty admitted, rarely and for a brief time, to any tasting of heavenly things, and progressing little by little, at length he grows strong in spirit. Next, when he has already taken to himself seriousness of behavior and stability of spirit, in proportion as present mutability allows, he rises; indeed, a certain perfection is acquired by great labors, so that joy in divine love is experienced.

Nevertheless, it does not seem that all who are made great in virtue both suddenly experience in a real way the burning of love, uncreated or created, and melting in the immense fire of love, sing the song of divine praise within themselves. Indeed, this mystery is hidden from the many and is revealed to the few and the most special. It is just because this step is more elevated that, therefore, it has fewer discoverers in this world.

Certainly, we rarely discover in this life any holy man, or indeed a perfect one, so greatly seized by love that he is raised into contemplation as far as the jubilation of song in this way—that is to say, so that he receives into himself the sound poured out from heaven, and resonates praise to God as if with a melody, making sweet melodies and putting together many sighs in heavenly praising, and so that he truly feels within his very self the very fire of the love of God—although, notwithstanding, one may have wondered if anyone might dare to be judged a contemplative otherwise.

Hence the psalmist, transforming himself into the person of the contemplative man, says, "I shall go over into the house of God in the voice of exultation and of confession" (Ps. 41:5), that is, of praise. This "praise" is "the sound of those feasting"—that is, it comes from the heavenly sweetness of rejoicing.

Moreover, the perfect who are lifted up into this fullness of surpassing eternal friendship, live in this magnificent chalice of love, already filled with this imperishable sweetness dripping with honey, and drink up fruitful burning ardor into their souls in this secret nourishing song of loveliness. For this reason these delighted people continually possess the inestimable comfort of the forever chosen. And in any case, this refreshment belongs to lovers for whom, having burst forth, it actually reaches in this exile the height of the eternal inheritance.

And in the meantime, this will not appear unsuitable to them—that they who will be raised up to dwell forever in heavenly seats should be afflicted here for a few years.

And thus they are chosen from all flesh that they may be most beloved in the sight of the Creator, and that they may be most brilliantly crowned, since indeed they have been set on fire in the manner of seraphim in the highest heavens. Their bodies sat solitary, and their spirits, walking among angels, panted for love. And most sweetly have they sung the divine announcement of eternal love, rejoicing in Jesus:

O love dripping with honey, sweeter than all delights, more delectable than all deeds! O my God, O my Love: flow into me with Your pierced love, with Your wounded beauty; flow into me, I say, and console me, languishing: with Your medicine, show Yourself to Your miserable lover. Behold, in You is all my desire, all that my heart seeks. To You my soul sighs; for You my flesh thirsts, and You do not open to me; on the contrary, You turn away Your face, You close Your mouth, You cross over, and You refuse, and You laugh at the sufferings of the innocent.

Nevertheless, You snatch Your lovers, in the meantime, from all earthly things, You take them up beyond all appetite for any earthly thing, and You make them capable of holding much of Your love, and powerful in loving. Breaking out from the fire in spiritual song because of such things, they offer You praises, and experience the dart of love with sweetness.

Ah, therefore, O eternal and amiable Love, Who has raised us up from the depths and brought us, snatched up so repeatedly, back to the face of Your divine majesty —come into me, my Love! Whatever I have possessed, I have given away for You, but I have spit out these ownerships so that You may have a mansion in my soul and console her, and may not leave me anymore. You see that I burn with Your very great desire, and cling to Your embraces continually, and attend You with most burning desire; permit me to love You thus, and also to rest in You, so that I may deserve to be seen by You in Your kingdom without end. Amen.

CHAPTER THREE – *That anyone who is chosen holds the position ordained for him by God*

Contemplative men who are burned beyond the ordinary by the love of eternity, in whatever way indeed they emerge as superior in burning ardor—most delightful, most worthy of love, eternal love—it is in such a way that never, or rarely, do they go forth into external ministries, nor do they accept the dignity of the prelacy and of honor.

Rather, on the contrary, keeping themselves within themselves, they always rise in spirit to Christ, harmoniously, with jubilant song. Indeed, in this the church imitates the angelic hierarchy, in which the highest angels, continually waiting on God, are not sent out for external tasks. In the same way, the men highest in the love and the contemplation of Christ concentrate on the divine presence alone, and do not assume ruling power among men. But this is reserved for other men, who are more greatly occupied with all human business and enjoy internal delights less fully.

Therefore any chosen one whatever has his state preordained by God. When such a one is chosen for a prelacy, he tries to leave it for God alone; for this God raises him interiorly, so that he lets all exterior occupations pass him by. Such, then, are the most holy men, and, notwithstanding, these men, who go forth rarely to work miracles, are judged lesser by men, in that they stay exclusively in that place by interior works.

In truth, to the others who subject themselves to divine service and rule their subjects discreetly, and also to the rest who live before the face of men in unheard affliction of the flesh, are commonly revealed signs granted either in life or after death—and also that they will be exceedingly tormented for a certain period of time harshly in purgatory.

Indeed, saints do not do all things, nor even have they all

worked miracles, either in life or after death—nor have all reprobate men lacked miracles either in life or after death. For in fact the judgment of God is hidden, so that the wicked may become more guilty of sins by means of the visible signs, and the good, having held in contempt those things which can equally be possessed by the good and the wicked, may burn more intensely in the love of their creator.

Of course, certain men have done good works, but they have sought from them not divine but human glory, and these men have perished after death, nevertheless having here what they have desired in this world.

For it often happens that less good and less perfect men work miracles; furthermore, the highest among those established in heavenly seats before the face of God commonly remain utterly quiet, having their rewards in any case among the highest choirs of angels. Just because the feast of Saint Michael is specially celebrated, nevertheless he is not believed to be one of the first rank of the angels!

Certain men, converted to God, doing penance and deserting secular affairs, rejoice in their thought that, after their deaths, their names may be honored by those who come after them. Indeed, the faithful servant of Christ will not cherish a consideration for this, lest he lose everything he has done.

Certainly those things which are common to good men and evil ones ought not to be sought after by saints, but love and spiritual virtues ought incessantly to be hammered into our hearts. For these not only guard the soul from the putridness of sins, but also, at the judgment, will raise the body into everlasting remembrance.

All those things that are done here flee quickly; there, however, they will continue without end, either in honor or in shame. In truth, active men and prelates made famous by virtue and knowledge ought continually to put contemplatives ahead of themselves, and judge them superior in the sight of God. They should not judge themselves capable of abandoning themselves to contemplation—unless, by chance, divine grace inspires them to make this judgment.

CHAPTER FOUR – *Concerning diversity among the lovers of God and their rewards*

The human soul which has not first perfectly abandoned all vanity of the world does not feel the fire of eternal love. It must also be continually busying itself to reach to heavenly things, to desire divine love without neglect, and to love in proper order every creature which ought to be loved. If indeed we love every being that we love for the sake of God, we love God in it rather than loving the being itself. Thus we delight not in the creature but in God, in whom we shall glory to delight forever.

Wicked men, in truth, delight in this world and they set the end of their delight in it; they desire incessantly only those things which pertain to the joy of the world. And who can act more stupidly, more miserably or more damnably than to cling to a transitory, failing thing for the sake of the thing itself?

Certainly only the Triune God ought to be loved for Himself. We ought to place our whole spirit in Him, we ought to try to bring all our thoughts back to that end so that He may be glorified in us forever. We ought to love ourselves and the others whom we love for His sake alone.

But the sinner who says that he loves God and nevertheless does not fear to serve sin is lying. For everyone who loves God is free, nor does he sin as a slave; he lowers himself, but he constantly persists in the service of justice.

When in truth we love earthly things and consolations for their own sake, without a doubt we do not love God. On the contrary, if we delight in creatures in this way, we shall be judged not as serving God but as hating Him, because we put aside our Creator and we do not take care to desire and follow those things which are eternal. Certainly it is exceedingly pernicious to the soul (and indicative of eternal perdition), when a man totally gives himself over to the world and wanders, as if at his pleasure, in diverse desires and errors of the flesh. Without a doubt when a miserable man lives delectably in this way, he is destroyed, and when he thinks himself to flow toward delights, he hastens toward punishment—unfailing and infernal.

Therefore, no one dares to presume concerning himself, nor to raise himself up through boasting. Indeed, when he is despised for his shame or when loud cries are thrown at him, he ought not defend himself or return an evil word for an evil deed, but he ought to bear all things with equanimity—that is to say, reacting to insult as he does to praise.

Certainly, acting this way, we shall rejoice forever with Christ—if we love Christ ardently and incessantly even in this life. His love, rooted in our hearts and steady in performance, transforms us to His likeness, and He openly pours into us another glory and divine rejoicing—into the spirits of those burning with love.

Indeed, His love is fire, making souls fiery, so that they may be shining and burning and that He may purge them from all the filth of sin. That fire, burning in the chosen ones, forces them always to look in spirit toward things above and unweariedly to hold back death in desire.

Just so, while we are in this place and able to sin, we ought to concentrate on fleeing the prosperities of the world and bearing adversities willingly. For the evil mind perishes when it rejoices, and kills itself as if with pleasant poison when it seeks enjoyment in creatures.

We try to avoid these contagions by concentrating on the internal feast that is arranged entirely for burning lovers in the highest heavens. And thus, Christ consenting, we are comforted in the song of love, and we delight in the most sweet devotion, while the impious fall asleep in horrid darkness and, filled with their wicked deeds, descend to their humiliations.

Without a doubt, it seems that mortal man is so strongly seized in divine love that he does not feel in his more secret substance anything except supreme solace, and, as if on a musical instrument, he rises on high to contemplate what he has desired as it reveals itself. He turns what has been inflicted on him by others from sorrow into joy, so that he seems even now to be, in a certain way, unable to suffer in soul. The fear of death will not be able to disturb him, nor at any time will he stagger from tranquillity into intemperance. Indeed, he is stirred up in assiduous love; in thought that is uninterrupted in Jesus, he quickly comes to detect his defects, and correcting them, he is thereafter on his guard against them. Thus he does justice continually until he is led back to God to sit on an everlasting seat with the Heaven-born. For this reason he stands shining in conscience and, standing firm, he is on good paths for all things; he is never afflicted with sadness for worldly things nor does he rejoice with the glory of a foolish thing.

Moreover, the obstinate do not know the love of Christ in spiritual works, because they are set on fire with carnal concupiscence, and they do not show requisite devotion for God because of the burden of riches by which they are pressed down to the earth. Further, they are not predestined for the delights to be enjoyed in Heaven, because they persist in their perversities even unto death. Therefore, their sadness will not be mitigated by merit, nor will the sorrow of damnation be ended, because they have wandered voluntarily in sensual delights and good things, and for the sake of deceptive love they have lost the love of the eternal Lover. Accordingly, they will plainly suffer in perpetual punishments, and, notwithstanding, they will never be cleansed of their crimes, but will burn without comfort in continuing fires.

CHAPTER FIVE – *Why greater attention ought to be paid to love of God than to knowledge of Him or debates about Him*

Among all the things we do or think, we ought to concentrate more on love of God than on knowledge or on debates. Certainly love delights the soul and makes the conscience tender, drawing it away from delighting in lesser loves and an appetite for its own excellence.

Knowledge without love does not build toward eternal salvation, but inflates one for most miserable damnation. Therefore our soul ought to be strong in laying hold of hard labors for God; it ought to be made wise by the taste of heavenly things, not by the world.

He who is made strong in loving and desiring the Creator alone and in the contempt of all transitory things ought to pant to be illumined by eternal wisdom and to be set on fire by that flame flowing with sweetness by which it is stirred up. Judging the greatest comfort in these things for himself to be that they do not last, seeing that he does not possess a mansion in the present time but a future one not made by hands, he prays and cries out unceasingly, "For me to live is Christ, and to die is gain" (Phil. 1:21).

Indeed, that one truly loves God who does not consent wrongly to any love. For a man is drawn exactly as far away from the love of Christ as he enjoys himself in any earthly thing. If, therefore, you love God, your work ought to show this fact, because a man is never judged to love God when he is driven to consent to evil desires.

Therefore I dare to declare this fact to all living in this exile—that all who will not love the Author of all things, who have not chosen to be burned here by the love of the Redeemer, will be cast out into unending darkness, and will experience forever the fire of infernal flame. Indeed, they will be excluded from the community of those singing in love of the Creator, and they will weep continually, having been cast out from the joy of those rejoicing in Jesus; they will lack the shining and glory of those who are crowned because they have preferred to delay for a short period of time in worldly voluptuousness rather than to do penance and suffer afflictions so that their sins might be purged and that, filled with piety, they might come before the face of the Protector of good men. Certainly, they were rejoicing on the broad and slippery road in this valley of tears, which is no place for rejoicing but for labors, and therefore they will lament in torments without any relaxation.

Sinners will lament when poor men are carried to everlasting peace where they will rejoice in the delights of the living Godhead, truly seeing the face of Christ. They were made beautiful by virtues and they have happily flourished exceedingly in spiritual fervor with those who are on high; they have in no way taken up the comfort of this world, nor have they disseminated insane pride among the wise, but they have protected their service to their Lord from evil deeds and they have driven away temptations from the throne of the Trinity, so that they might be held in tranquillity. Truly, they have rid themselves of the old age of a life filled with poison, praising spiritual sight clearly and most cheerfully; they have judged the games of levity (which youth accepts and foolish worldly men savor), as, in fact, worthy of damnation, meditating with continuousness on the loving song ascending to the Creator.

For this reason, having the capacity for the inward joy of love, and taking hold of the burning warmth which cannot be consumed, they run together into the song of shining music and of harmony full of love. They cherish the shadow poured over them in friendly delightfulness from Heaven, in opposition to all the mental commotion of sexual temptation and of spite. On this account they are lifted up in that most sweet fire of love to the face of the Beloved, and flowering through this most blessed flame, they remain in virtue and delight in the Maker. The spirit goes forth into melody, changed and yet remaining the same. After that their meditations are made by means of melody. Sadness having been sent away, the hall of the soul abounds with marvelous music, so that it destroys prior punishment within and, healthy in sonorous sublimity, it stands always, singing most wonderfully in sweet-sounding meditation.

Then when they take leave of these hard things and the anxieties which they are concerned with in the depths, the time comes that they are received without a doubt and are carried away to God without sorrow, and they receive seats among the seraphim. This is because, entirely set on fire by the flame of the highest love and burning ineffably within their souls so sweetly, they have loved God faithfully, so that whatever they have felt within themselves has become spiritual heat, a heavenly song and a divine sweetness.

It is on this account in any case that they die without bitterness, going forth, on the contrary, with joy—to so great a degree in eternal honors are they raised. They stand crowned in the fullest contemplation of the Creator, singing with the most illustrious choirs, and also pant the more ardently for that Essence governing all things.

And certainly, although they now manifestly look from afar in this way on the face of Truth and are without doubt intoxicated by the most delicate sweetness of divinity, after a little while they will certainly be exalted still more, when the bodies of the saints (which for a time are held in the earth) are raised up from their graves and their souls are united with them at the final judgment.

Then indeed they will take the place of sovereignty among the people and they will judge all men that are damned; they will show that ordinarily good men were approved for pursuing blessedness. Further, at the completion of the general judgment, they will be brought into everlasting jubilant song and they will ascend with Christ to the highest point of light, rejoicing forever before the face of God.

From these things it is a certainty that eternal sweetness will intoxicate these spirits, whom the bond of love links indissolubly. Just so, we ought rather attend to it that the love of Christ enkindles us inwardly, rather than concentrate on useless theological debate. Indeed, when we devote ourselves immoderately to inquiry, we certainly do not experience the sweetness of eternal softness. Because of this many burn with this kind of a fire of knowledge, not of love. For they do not know inwardly what this love is nor what taste it has, when they ought to reach for this end of all their desire so that they may be able to burn in divine love.

Alas, the shame! That a little old lady could be more experienced in love of God (and less experienced in the pleasure of the world!) than a theologian, whose study is empty because he studies for the sake of vanity—that he may learn and appear glorious—and so that he may acquire payments and dignities! Such a one deserves to be judged stupid, not learned.

CHAPTER SIX – Concerning the cause for heretics and faith in the Trinity

The fullness of truth shows itself to those who seek for it with integrity and holiness. Indeed, from what cause does the perfidy of heretics appear except from a disordered and undisciplined mind which is blinded by the appetite for its own excellence? Because indeed they do not cease to fight against God within themselves through foolish concupiscence, from their fault it comes that they also oppose the truth externally with open arguments. Although it may be the Christian religion to cut off all contradiction and to gather teaching together in the unity of faith and love, it belongs to heretics and proud men always to bring forth new opinions, to make public novel challenges to ecclesiastical teaching. Thus they rejoice to scatter, by means of their vanities, those things which faithful Christians hold undisturbed.

Of those men throwing out errors we say, indeed it must be believed and judged that the Son of God is utterly coeternal with the Father, because unless the Father begot Him from eternity, He truly cannot be full God in Himself. If, indeed, God existed at any time before, when He did not have a Son, then without a doubt He was less then than afterward, when He had generated the Son—and that no one sane in mind declares!

Unchangeable God, therefore, begot unchangeable God, and the One Whom He begot from eternity He does not cease begetting, even today. For the substance of the Begotten cannot at any time be called "unbegotten," nor can the essence of the Begetter ever know Himself without the Only Begotten, begotten from Himself.

It is for this reason, certainly, that the "beginning" of divinity will be discovered by no reason, by no intellect (because Godhead does not have a beginning), and thus the

Begetter of the Son endures unchangeably with the eternity of the Godhead. When, in fact, the admiration of God and the honor of omnipotence shine forth in infinity without a beginning, to what does human folly raise itself that it struggles to publish the ineffable sacrament to the ears of mortals? Moreover, he knows God perfectly who understands Him to be incomprehensible.

Indeed, nothing is known perfectly, unless its cause is known—whence and by what means it may be. In the present time, however, we understand in part and we know in part; in the future, truly, we shall understand perfectly and fully, as this is allowed to creatures and is useful to them.

Again, anyone who lusts to know anything beyond that which it is useful to know about the incorruptibility of the Creator, more foolish, falls away from the perfect knowledge of Him without a doubt.

You ask, "What is God?"

I answer you briefly, "He is of such a kind and so great that no one else is able to be of such a kind or so great."

If you wish to know for yourself, saying, "What *is* God?" I say that you will never find a solution for this question. I have not known, angels are ignorant of it, archangels have not heard! In what way, therefore, do you want to know what is unknowable and unteachable? Certainly God, although He may be omnipotent, is not able to teach you what He is! If, indeed, you knew what God is, you would be wise as God—a thing which neither you nor any other creature is able to be.

Therefore, stand in your tracks and do not seek higher things, because if you desire to know what God is, you desire that you may *be* God—a thing which is not proper for you, as you well know.

God alone knows Himself, and only He is able to know Himself. Moreover, it is not due to impotence that God is unable to teach you Himself as He is in Himself, but due to His inestimable magnificence, because such a One is not able to be other than He is, of such a kind is He. If in truth He could be plainly understood, He would not be incomprehensible! Suffice it for you, therefore, that you recognize *that* God is; it will hinder you if you wish to know *what* God is.

Thus it is praiseworthy to know God perfectly—that He is incomprehensible—by knowing this to love Him, by loving Him to rejoice in Him, by rejoicing to rest in Him, and by internal quiet to come to eternal rest. Don't let it upset you that I have said, "to know God perfectly," and that I have denied that you can know God, when, notwithstanding, the Psalmist says, "Extend Your mercy to those who know You" (Ps. 35:11). But if you do not wish to err, you must understand that quotation in this way: "those who know you," of course, means those who know You as God, to be loved, praised, adored, and glorified, and as the sole Creator of all things, above all things, through all things and in all things— You Who are blessed for endless ages. Amen.

CHAPTER SEVEN – *That in speaking of God we ought not say "three Lords" or "three Essences" as we say "three Persons"; that a man is judged great or small according to the quantity of his love*

If, therefore, people, erring, should wish to say "three Essences" because they say "three Persons," why indeed would they not say "three Gods," since for God it is the same thing to be God and to be Essence?

We say, moreover, "The Father is God, the Son is God, the Holy Spirit is God." Similarly, the Father is Essence, the Son is Essence, the Holy Spirit is Essence, and nevertheless we do not say "three Gods" nor "three Essences" but with firm faith we declare our God to be three Persons of one Essence. This is because the one Majesty of three Persons is full and perfect, and because any one of the Persons contains within Himself the full majesty, having indeed equality and identity according to the substance of Godhead, and not lacking the distinction of diversity, according to the property of names.

Thus there are three Persons and one God, one Essence, one Godhead—and however much "person" may mean "essence," notwithstanding, because there are three Persons, there are not to be understood three Essences! And in whatever way we say our God, Father, Son and Holy Spirit, is one Essence, not three Essences, so we say the same highest Trinity is three Persons, not one Person.

The Father is so named because He begets from Himself the Son; the Son is so named because He is begotten by the Father; the Holy Spirit is so named because, of course, He is breathed forth by both the holy Father and the holy Son.

The Father, in engendering the Son, gave Him life and all His Substance, so that the Father might be in the Son as much as He is in Himself; and the Son is not less in the Father than He is in Himself. But the Father draws from nothing that is, and, truly, the Son, in being begotten, draws what He has from the Father alone.

Again, the Holy Spirit, proceeding from the Father and the Son and existing with Them and in Them eternally, is not more in Himself than in the Two of Them. Certainly, He is equal and co-eternal with Them and from Them, since He is of the same Substance, of the same Nature, of the same majesty, and is the Third Person in the Trinity.

Now, the eternal Son of the Father is made man in time, born from a virgin that He might redeem the human race from the power of the devil. This is our Lord Jesus Christ; He alone ought to be fixed in our mind Who alone was fastened on a cross for our sakes.

Indeed, there is nothing so pleasant as to love Christ, and we ought not, on that account, to study too much those things which we are not able to understand as pilgrims here; certainly they will be made clearer by the light in the fatherland, if we offer our whole heart to loving God. We shall certainly be entirely docile to God and we shall rejoice in melody beyond the miraculous, and we shall praise our Creator in the highest delightfulness and with sweet ease, without anxiety or aversion, forever.

Certainly, he who loves much is great, and he who loves less is the lesser, because we are evaluated before the face of God according to the greatness of love which we have in us. This is not the case before the face of men; rather, for them, he who has most riches and possessions is weighed as greater and is chiefly feared—although they ought not act so, but always ought to honor and fear those whom they have judged to be the wiser. Furthermore, the powerful of this world cannot be in need of anything unless it is for the body or for temporal goods.

In truth, the saints have chosen a greater excellence. They will certainly have power to close Heaven to those who have injured them and have not chosen to repent for it, and to open it to those who have honored them in this exile—provided that they suffered misfortune through love and did not receive any empty glory in return. And therefore they ought to labor at acquiring, possessing and retaining love with all their strength and all their energies, so that in the day of temptation they will be able to stand like men against their enemies and, when they have been tested, that they may receive the crown of life.

In truth, love makes men perfect and lovers alone are allowed to ascend fully to the height of the contemplative life. And certain poor men, however much they may be overwhelmed by squalor and filth, ought not be held in contempt, nevertheless, because they are the friends of God and the brothers of Christ—if they have borne their burden of poverty giving thanks. Indeed, those whom you judge outwardly despicable you ought to honor inwardly as heavenly citizens. Increase your honor of these people for the sake of God as greatly as He has worked secretly—He Who, consoling them, said, "Blessed are you poor, for yours is the Kingdom of God" (Luke 6:20).

Great indeed are the tribulation and need which are visited in this life on a man who is purged of his sins, because while a poor man, he is afflicted in body by hunger, by thirst, by cold and nakedness, and by other deficiencies of this world, and he is purged in soul from his filthiness and earthly crimes. And certainly the poor, where in this present time they have endured the heaviest labor, shall experience there the sweeter rest of eternity in the future. One will say of them, "We have rejoiced for the days in which You have humiliated us, for the years in which we have seen evils" (Ps. 89:15).

Therefore, embrace the burden of poverty with joy, and sustain other miseries willingly; be mindful that you will deserve to attain to the glory of eternal peace through patience in tribulation.

CHAPTER EIGHT – *That the perfect lover of God would prefer to endure great punishment than to offend God a single time through sin; why God afflicts the just with the impious*

So much grace of virtue grows in the soul from the great fire of love that the just man would rather choose to incur all punishment than to offend God a single time, although, certainly, he might know that he would be able to rise again through penance and afterward please God more and be holier. That is because anyone perfect knows this—that nothing is dearer to God than innocence and nothing is more acceptable than goodwill. If indeed we would love God rightly, we ought to desire rather to lose a great reward in Heaven than to sin even venially. For the greatest justice is not to require a reward for justice except the friendship of God, which is God Himself. Therefore, it is sweeter to suffer torment forever than to be led away from justice to iniquity of one's own free will, and knowingly.

Nevertheless, since it is plainly established that those who love Christ so ardently do not choose to sin in any way, they will not only be free from punishment but they will rejoice with the angels eternally. In truth, those who are servants to evil actions, who judge filthy joy and fleshly solace as great and pleasant, and who strive after these things by clinging to them, will actually lose the good that they love and will incur the evil that they do not look for.

But one is used to being asked by certain people why the almighty God at the same time flagellates the just with the impious. You see that grain and chaff are under the flail at the same time, but in the exposure to the wind the chaff is thrown off and the grain is carefully collected for the use of men. If all lived justly, without doubt they would remain in tranquillity and peace, without discord and wars. But because

there are many evil men among a few good ones, many sufferings come so that the wicked may be punished, and these
sufferings also occur among the good because they will be
mixed in with the wicked until their death.

Furthermore, the just, because they are prone to sinning,
lest that proneness lead them on to that effect, are instructed
through the whip of the affectionate Father to accept the
easy present discipline, so that they may avoid a bitter future.
Therefore, if you suffer persecution, misery, and difficulty,
you have what is suitable for the place in which you delay.

Is it not, in fact, the valley of tribulation in which you are?
How then do you wish to rejoice in prison and to be prosperous in all things in exile, or to pass through your long
sojourning without sorrow? Keep in mind that Christ and the
Apostles have suffered torments—and you seek to attain to joy
through joy! But you will not do it!

Indeed, either in this life the fire of divine love will consume the rust of our sins and will make our souls shining, so
that they may be made fit for flying upward, or after this life,
the fire of purgatory will torment our very souls—if it happens
that we avoid infernal flames! Or, if there is not within us a
force of love great enough to strip us completely, it is proper
that we be purified by tribulations, infirmities, and difficulties.

Indeed, we hold this without uncertainty—that (unless by
an inestimable abundance of the grace of God), a young man
cannot become holy among the flatteries and sweet words of
beautiful women and among the abundance of delights where
so many and such great things draw him toward a fall, for
these things have often confused the holy man as well.
Therefore I judge it to be the greatest miracle when anyone,
through the grace of God and the love of Christ, perfectly
holds these allurements in contempt, and, among these ad-
versaries of the soul, however pleasant they may seem to the
flesh, ascends in manly fashion to the extraordinary sanctity
of heavenly contemplation. Without doubt, he is, on that account, holier and more fruitfully filled inwardly with the
solace of divine love. By means of this, placed in a fire he

does not know burns, he perfectly extinguishes the pleasures of a most seductive life offering themselves on the other side. This is without a doubt a thing which Christ does in certain of His lovers, though rarely.

Of these it is said, "He has spread out a cloud" (of course, the "shadowing" of divine grace), "for their protection" (from carnal concupiscence), "that He might shine for them" (inwardly, in spirit, by the fire of eternal love), "through the night" (of this life), lest they be seized by the inducements of vain beauty. In truth, the love of Christ burns in these people with so much sweetness that they count all illicit carnal delight as most vile excrement, and therefore crush it underfoot.

And therefore, you ought not touch deceitfully that which it is not lawful for you to desire, nor should you wish to have it. Remember also to restrain your hand, your tongue, and your belly, and do not upset yourself in regard to women.

Since the ornaments of men and women, and the warm potions and other foods inflaming the flesh too much by their heat (which the "physicians" of bodies and killers of souls labor to procure) are incitements to lasciviousness, they ought to be avoided by the pure.

Chapter Nine – *That God ought to be praised and loved in adversities; concerning the joyfulness and humility of good men*

If temporal honor is destroyed by disgrace and worldly glory is ended by shame, it is established without doubt that reproach is better than honor, shame is better than success and distress is better than praise. For through the latter one often slips into vainglory, but through the former (if he bears them patiently), one is instructed in humility. He will not suffer punishment in the future (for God will not twice confound the just!) and will be more sublimely crowned, for the patience of the poor will not perish in the end.

Now, these things pertain to sanctity: first, in no way to think, to speak or to perform what displeases God, and then to think, to speak and to perform what pleases Him. Do this according to your knowledge so that you may not fall into scandal nor feign excessive sanctity. For he is a fool who desires always to appear holy in men's regard, and he is morally crude who exposes himself as evil when he might be good.

In truth, there are certain things which, considered attentively, in accordance with themselves are neither good nor evil. For in pure naturalness there is neither merit nor demerit, and such things neither displease God if they are done nor please Him if they are not done. Indeed, we are able to see, to hear, to smell, to feel, to touch and nevertheless neither to earn merit nor to fail to earn it by doing so.

On the other hand, all sin is done either in contempt of God or with evil intent toward one's neighbor, or in detriment to one's very self, but many deeds can be found among men which in no way belong to these categories. Moreover, to be despised and confounded in the face of men makes a man ascend to the joy of the angels.

O good Jesus, here whip me, here cut me to pieces, here pierce me through, here burn me! By all means, do to me whatever may please Your Goodness, provided that I may not have evil in the future, but that I may experience Your love here and in eternity. For Your sake, to be the contempt, to be the shame and to be the reproach of all is sweeter to me than if I were to be called the brother of an earthly King, and were to be honored and praised among all men and by all men. O, that misery might rush in upon me from all sides in this life, so that You might spare me, O God, in the next!

I wish to be oppressed and reproached here, that Christ may grant me nothing in the present time, if I cannot avoid future punishment in any other way!

In truth, proud men and passionate men may seem glorious to themselves because they are able to endure nothing; they are moved often at a light word, and even without cause. Therefore, they are rather to be fled than to be conquered, because they are stubborn, and what they have taken up they will defend wholly, whether false or erroneous; neither by an authority nor by reason are they able to be overcome, lest they should seem to be beaten and to have produced an inconsistency. And although they may be untaught (and may know this well!), they wish nevertheless to seem inspired in all things which pertain to God, so that thus they may speak everywhere without the contradiction of anyone else. They would prefer to remain in their error than to be rebuked about it in the open.

Brothers, send away this proud insanity and this insane pride! Let us be deeply humbled while we are on the way, because it is better (and a great deal more worthy of love), that Christ say to us after our death, "Friend, go up higher" and that He may not say, "Rustic, go down lower" (Luke 14:10). Therefore no tribulation, no difficulty, no misery, no shame or objection should be feared by the just man, provided that he does not sin and that he progresses always in the contemplative life and in the love of God.

For before we will be able to arrive at that royal hall in

which we shall thoroughly enjoy complete sweetness with the angels of God and all the saints, it is necessary that we be tested here through flatterers and detractors, through blandishers and insulters, through praisers and vituperators, so that in all patience, humility, and charity, clinging to the precepts and counsels of Christ, we may be found everywhere tested (because he holds the fire on every part) as it is written, "As gold in the furnace he has tested them, and has found them worthy" (Wisd. 3:6).

Thus it may happen that we must travel through prosperity and adversity, through fire and water, until we arrive at the consolation of celestial life. And so, be mindful in all adversity and penury and poverty that you never murmur or say what is foolish or perverse, but in all things give thanks; then indeed you will rise more gloriously to the kingdom of the saints, for which you have suffered freely in this world the things just described.

O my soul, among all the things which touch you by delightful devotion, praise the Lord, in praising experience sweet songs, and in singing taste sweet honeys!

For I will praise the Lord in my life, whether I suffer or I prosper, whether I receive blame or honor, for so long shall I sing a psalm to my God. If I rest, I rejoice in Jesus, and if I suffer persecution, I do not forget the love of God. Suffice it to me, in truth, that I may love my God and come to Him. I am not able to do anything else nor do I see myself disposed for any other thing or act than the loving of Christ.

I am not reaching the point of such great love of God as my predecessors have reached: they also did many other useful things. On that account, I blush exceedingly and am confounded in myself.

Therefore, O Lord, open my heart that it may become more capacious for seizing Your love.

Indeed, the greater the capacity a man has, the more fully he seizes and knows love, and the less he cares about the flesh —though with discretion, so that it may be done by him according to the judgment of the wise man who says "I have labored for a little while, and I have found much rest for myself" (Ecclus. 51:35). For after a few years of this life the just man has found the rest of eternity. Moreover, in the habitation of this exile, the holy lover of God should not show himself too happy or exceedingly sad, but he should hold his joyfulness with maturity.

Now, some reprove laughter, and some praise it. Laughter which comes from levity and a foolish spirit is, in these circumstances, reprovable, but that which comes from joyfulness of conscience and spiritual happiness is laudable, for it occurs only in just men and is called delight in the love of God. For that reason, if we are joyful and full of delight, impious men call us dissolute, and if we are sad they call us hypocrites.

Certainly, it is with difficulty that anyone knows how to judge good in another which he has not found in himself, and he thinks another to have the vice in which he himself falls. This is the deed of the presumptuous man, because if a person does not follow the life he himself leads, he judges that the other deviates and is deceived. In this instance the judgment is so made because the judger lacks humility.

Now the steps of humility are these:

—To hold the eyes cast down, not raised up.
—To keep order in speech and not to talk too much.
—To listen willingly to those who are better and wiser.
—To prefer that wisdom be heard from others rather than from oneself.
—Not to anticipate the time for speaking.
—Not to draw back from the common life.
—To prefer others to oneself.
—To recognize one's weaknesses.
—To judge oneself as inferior to everyone else.

If indeed I should wish to come among men, I desire that I may sit as the last in the company and the least in their opinion. Thus, all my glory is in Christ and I heed neither the praise nor the blame of men, but burn with perpetual devotion for God.

For many who used to speak with me have been similar to

scorpions; flattering with their heads, they have fawned upon me, and backbiting they have persecuted me with their tails. From their wicked lips and grievous tongues God will free my soul, establishing her in the joy of tranquillity.

But whence comes such madness into the minds of men, so that none wish to be disparaged, none to be rebuked? On the contrary, all seek to be praised. They would rejoice for honors, they would laugh for favors, even those who bear the name of a holier life! Such people seem to me either holy beyond measure or as if they are irrational—even though they are called "wise men" and "learned."

In truth, who of sane mind abandons his very self unexamined, and takes joy in the foolish words of men? If, moreover, he would study himself diligently and take care to recognize what kind of person he might be, how he might be constituted in his thoughts and in his actions, he would quickly be able to understand himself and to discover whether he is worthy of praise or blame. Therefore, when he sees himself blameworthy in many areas and praiseworthy in few, he will not take up with pleasure either honor or favor where he is unworthy—unless, insane, he wanders in his wits.

But if, examining himself intensely, he discovers that he burns inestimably in the fervor and sweetness of divine love, that he is going forth eminently into the contemplative life, and that he is continually standing firm in that life as well, and if he should further consider in this examination that he has not committed grave sins or (should he have committed any) if he believes that he is absolved of them through true penitence, it is actually not fitting that he grieve himself for the honor of men, because he has deserved, of course, the better company of the angels.

In such a way, in truth, anyone so disposed will not rejoice more to sit with a King than with a pauper, because he respects not the riches and dignities of all men but the life and merits of the individual. He judges it to be nothing great to glisten with gold, to be surrounded by a great army, to process in royal purple, to rejoice at a banquet—but he prefers a holy and tender conscience to all these deeds and delights.

CHAPTER TEN – *That the lover of God rejects the world, boredom, and laziness; concerning hypocrisy and avarice*

It is said in the Canticle that love is stronger than death, and jealousy is harder than Hell. Death certainly kills the living—but Hell does not spare the dead. Thus indeed the love of God which seizes a man completely not only cuts him off from the love of this world at the foundation, but also greatly raises him, cut off from the world and united to Heaven, for the sustaining of tribulations and present miseries for God's sake.

Therefore, whoever you are who think you love Christ, pay attention to this. For if you attend to earthly things with delight, and you discover your spirit unprepared for bearing sufferings and even death itself, you actually show yourself not to be a true lover of God. Further, the true lover neither directs his eye toward the world nor fears to suffer, for the sake of God, anything which seems sad or difficult, but he is not held back from his meditation of love whatever seizes him.

Also, O you who either are a lover of God or wish to be one with your whole spirit, desire always, as much as you are able to, by the grace of Christ, not to be affected by boredom and not to be captured by laziness. And whenever a smooth facility in praying or meditating is not present to you, so that you are not (through the joyful song of holy contemplation) of such elevated mind and are not able to sing as you were accustomed to, you ought not cease to read or to pray or to do some other useful thing interiorly or exteriorly, lest you go to pieces in idleness or sloth. In truth, boredom drags many to idleness and idleness to negligence and wickedness.

Therefore, be fervent always, as much as in you lies, and do not hold your affections bent down toward anything which can be desired or gotten from this world. Nor indeed is anyone perfectly united to God while he is linked to any earthly creature by affection.

Further, there are certain people who seem externally to be joined to God, yet interiorly they are given over to the demons. These are simulators and deceivers who provoke the wrath of God.

These men are certainly simulators. They hold the world in contempt by their words, and are known to love it too much in their deeds. They want to be seen speaking about God and they are seized inwardly with so great a love of money that they even go to law for the loss of it on every occasion. Opening their mouths, they cry out to God and, although they have no fervor of faith and charity, nevertheless, devoid of devotion inwardly, they display themselves as the holiest of men in their walking, in their behavior, and in their speech.

Further, these people commonly throw themselves, as constant men, against easy enemies, but when they reach the point where they ought to resist more firmly, there they are shattered and fall the more quickly. At that point, what was previously hidden is openly laid bare.

And although these people flow with riches and are fed on delicacies, they nevertheless declare that they eat the very minimum because they have such a deep awareness that the whole world is nothing except vanity, and that they are able to subsist only with difficulty on account of their debility—they say!

These men are also deceivers, for they have secular knowledge and deceive with it, so that they are not caught by strange plots (in so much as they are on guard against the failure of temporal things), cloaking avarice under the appearance of spiritual quiet in contempt of eternal things. But however much such people may make merry for a time, without a doubt the kind of people they have been will appear long before the end, or suddenly at the end: they are men who have given alms, or done whatever other work they have done, in the sight of men, in order that all might be seen by men. And such men deservedly provoke the wrath of God, because, seeking to appear perfect, not to be perfect, and inwardly (where God sees), lacking true humility, they shout forth not God's glory but their own.

Moreover, it is exceedingly difficult to have riches and not to love them, and it is not less difficult to have a profession or hold a lucrative office and not be avaricious.

For this cause, priests are often defamed among the people in this way. For if they are chaste they are found to be avaricious, but if they become generous, they are judged spendthrifts! And commonly it happens that, having taken up the rank of priests, to the same extent that they run more deeply in crimes, they take higher rank unworthily. Indeed, some, inflamed by anxious cupidity, under the excuse of coming infirmity or poverty, say they are collecting goods so that they may avoid immanent misery. But they are deluded by demons because they are both losing the earthly goods and incurring the calamity which they fear. For God, Who frees His servants in His sight, will not provide for them.

And what is worst of all, although interiorly they are filled with earthly greed, they feign themselves to shine outwardly with the sign of sanctity.

But he who is a servant of the Lord trusts in the Lord, and distributes to the poor the goods he has beyond his necessities. But the servant of the world wickedly desires to keep all he possesses for his insatiable greed, so that he may even be so miserly that he does not dare to eat except of necessity and poorly—sparing to the extent that he has gathered much money. And these are they whom the Psalmist confounded, saying, "Your enemies lick up dirt" (Ps. 71:9).

CHAPTER ELEVEN – *That lovers of God will pass judgment with Him; concerning the love of acquired knowledge and the love of God; that the true lover does not err nor fail in fasting or abstinence, either through deliberations or presumption*

Nothing less than God can fill the human soul, which has a capacity for God alone, and thus the lovers of earthly things will never be satisfied. Rest for lovers of God, therefore, is when the heart is fixed in the love of God through desire and meditation, and, loving and burning, it contemplates Him with singing—since this quiet which seizes the soul is most delightful during the while that the sweet sound in which it delights descends from Heaven and the spirit is snatched up to singing the delights of eternal love in a supremely lyrical hymn flowing with joy.

Indeed, the praise of God and of the Blessed Virgin in which the lover glories inestimably already resounds in his mouth—and this occurs while the heart, from its singing, is being burnt up with heavenly fire at its very deepest part. The heart is shaped into the likeness of that in which the cherished sound exists, making his delightful affection drunk with the heavenly taste from which he flows with interior delights. He rejoices with singing meditation in the burning ardor of love.

This experience is certainly inestimable to all mortals, nor can anyone else imagine that a man existing in the body, which is being destroyed and is aggravated by the chains of mortality, could so pleasantly feel from this experience anything so flowing with honey. He wonders, even, at possessing it, but he rejoices on account of the ineffable goodness of God Who gives abundantly and does not taunt; he accepts from Him what he feels.

Again, when he has had that great experience—and it is

truly great because almost utterly unknown to mortal men—
he thinks he will never be happy if he is absent from it. He
will always languish in love, he will continually either sing or
meditate about love and his Beloved while he keeps vigil, but
he sings more certainly if he is alone.

Truly, from one who has accepted it, never thereafter does
the experience recede from that fullness, but indeed fervor, or
song, or sweetness always remains, even if all these things are
not present. However, all these things will remain at the
same time unless one is seized by too great an infirmity, or he
is strained in breast or side, or his flesh is shattered by too
much hunger or thirst or too much cold or heat, or he is impeded by a journey.

Therefore, it is necessary for him who wishes to sing in divine love, or, by singing, to rejoice and burn, to live in solitude. He must not live in too much abstinence, nor should
he deliver himself to any extent to superfluity. Nevertheless,
it would be better for him, if he were ignorant in a small
matter, to exceed the measure, as long as he acted with the
good intention of sustaining nature, rather than begin to fall
apart from too much fasting, and not be strong enough to
sing in the face of the weakness of the body.

But without a doubt, he who is chosen for this work will
not be conquered by the devil's fraud, either in eating or in
abstaining. Indeed, the true lover of Christ and the man
taught by Christ, because of this greater desire, need not be
on guard against the superfluous more than the diminished.
For with his melodious joy he will merit, incomparably more
by praying, by contemplating, by reading, by meditating, by
commending well but strictly, than if, without it, he were always fasting and ate nothing but bread or herbs, and were
continually praying and reading.

Therefore, I have eaten and drunk of those things that
seemed better, not because I loved delicacies, but that my nature might be sustained in the service of God and in the jubilant song of Jesus Christ. I conformed myself in a good way
to those people among whom I sojourned for the sake of
Christ, both lest I feign sanctity where there was none, and

lest men might praise me too much where I was less praiseworthy.

I also withdrew from many, not because they fed me more
commonly or in a harsher manner, but because we did not
agree in customs, or for some other reasonable cause. Nevertheless, I dare to say with blessed Job, "The foolish despised
me and, although I withdrew from them, they dragged me
down" (Job 19:18). Nevertheless, they will blush with shame
when they see me, they who have accused me of wishing to
stay in no dwelling unless it were one where I could be dain-
tily fed! For it is better to see what I hold in contempt than
to desire what I do not see.

Certainly, fasting strengthens one to rebuke the desires for
fleshly pleasures, and to command the unruly petulance of
the spirit. But in him who climbs the path of contemplation
through joyful song and the ardent fire of love, it is as if the
carnal concupiscences lay already extinguished. For the death
of evil affections belongs to him who devotes himself to contemplation, and his inner man is already transformed into another glory and another shape. He lives, not now he, but
Christ lives in him, so he melts in His love and languishes
within himself; he almost dies for the sweetness, he scarcely
subsists for the love! It is the soul of such a one which says:

> "Say to my Beloved that I languish for love" (Cant.
> 5:8), I desire to die, I want to be dissolved, I burn to
> take my leave. Behold! I am dying from love! Descend
> O Lord! Come, my Love, and lift me from my languor.
> See! I love, I sing, I burn, within myself I am boiling
> hot! Have mercy on me, a miserable one, command me
> to be presented before Your Face!

He who possesses this joy and is thus glorified in this world
has been inspired by the Holy Spirit. He cannot make a mistake; he may do whatever he wishes—he is secure! No mortal
man can give him such salvific advice as is that which he has
in himself from Immortal God. Truly, others, if they want to
give him advice, will doubtless make mistakes, because they
have not known this love. But he himself will not make a mis-

take because, though he might wish to give assent to the persuasion of others, he is not permitted to do so by God, Who constrains him to His Will so that he might not lose Him. For this reason it is said of such a man, "The spiritual man judges all things and he is judged by no one" (1 Cor. 2:15).

But no one ought to be so greatly presumptuous that he readily suspects himself to be such a person, even though he may have left the world completely and have gone forward in contemplation of heavenly things. This grace of contemplation is not, in truth, granted to everyone, but rarely and to the extremely few, who, taking on the deepest quiet of mind and body, are chosen exclusively for the work of divine love.

It is difficult to find such a man, and because they are rare, they are therefore held as dear, and they are desirable and beloved before God and men. But the angels rejoice at their exit from this world—these men for whom angelic society is fitting! There are many, certainly, who frequently offer their prayers to God in great devotion and delight, and who are able to taste the sweetness of contemplation by praying or meditating, who do not run back and forth, but remain in quiet.

CHAPTER TWELVE – *Concerning not judging others but giving thanks; concerning eight affections of the love of God; concerning avoiding the company of women*

If any man should live justly or in a holy way, he would not hold sinners and those who do much worse than he in contempt. For, having been tempted, they fall because they do not have the grace of resisting, although they have turned themselves from good to evil through their own malice. A man cannot work well and love God, and continue to do so, unless God should give him this gift.

And so, O you who swell with pride because you behave properly, because you have restrained yourself from carnal voluptuousness and have sustained harsh penance—for which you have accepted praise from man's mouth—remember that unless the goodness of Christ had protected you, you would have fallen into evils equally as great as—or worse than—that fall is. Nor, in truth, do you possess the strength of resisting, except from Him to Whom it is said, "I love You, O Lord, my strength" (Ps. 17:2).

If, therefore, you have nothing that you have not received, why do you brag as if you had not received it? But I give thanks to my God, Who, without my merits, has thus chastised His son, has thus terrified His servant, for my good and His honor, so that it might seem sweet to me to flee the delights of the world, which are few and quickly failing, and so that I might deserve to avoid the pains of Hell which are many and never to be ended.

And again, He Who has taught me in this way, by teaching, has brought forth virtue so that I might willingly bear present penance and tribulation in order that I might arrive at eternal delight and the fullest prosperity easily. For if we wish, we can, easily and without great harshness, repent in this life and purge ourselves, while we destroy all vices, as much as we have the strength to do. But in the future, if we have not been purged here, we shall discover that the Apostle was truthful saying, "It is a horrendous thing to fall into the hands of the living God" (Heb. 10:31).

> O Lord God, have mercy on me! My infancy has done stupid things, my childhood has done foolish things, my adolescence has done unclean things. But now, Lord Jesus, my heart has been inflamed by holy love and my inner depths have been transformed, so that my soul does not wish even to touch, for their bitterness, those things which have previously been the sweetness of my food. And my affections have become such that I hate nothing except sin, I fear nothing except to offend God, I rejoice at nothing except in God. I do not mourn except for sin, I do not love except for God, I do not hope except in Him; nothing makes me sad except for faults, nothing delights me except Christ.

A long time ago, nevertheless, I deservedly received worthy rebuke from three women.

The first blamed me because, desiring to correct women's insanity in their superfluity and softness of clothing, I inspected their adornment immoderately. She said that I ought not pay enough attention to them to know whether they might be wearing horned headdresses or not! It seemed to me that she had answered me well, and she made me blush with shame.

The second scolded me because I spoke about her fat breasts as if they delighted me. "What does it concern me if they are large or small?" she demanded and, similarly, she spoke rightly.

The third teased me in a joke because I threatened her as if I wished to touch her with a rod (or because I did touch her). "Quiet down, brother!" she said. It was as if she had said, "It doesn't suit your state (the hermit's state, of course) to play with women!" And so she confounded me—and not undeservedly.

Indeed, I ought to have held up better, than for anything of this kind to have carried me away. For, coming back to myself, I gave thanks to my God because, by the words of these women, He taught me a good thing, and showed me a smoother road than I had known before, so that I might be busy with the grace of Christ more fully, and might not be found reprehensible in the presence of the women in this part.

A fourth woman, to whom I acted in the manner of a friend, did not rebuke me, but, as if I had held her in contempt, she remarked, "You have nothing except a beautiful face and beautiful talk! You have no performance!"

And therefore, I judge it better to do without women's peculiarity than to fall into their hands—those who do not know how to hold a limit, whether in love or in contempt. Moreover, those things were my business because I was procuring their salvation, not because I desired anything illicit in them, when for a certain time I accepted physical sustenance from them.

CHAPTER THIRTEEN – *That the solitary or hermitical life is superior to community life and the mixed life; how it reaches the fire of love; concerning the sweetness of joyous song*

Certain people have emerged and there are perhaps still survivors, who place the common life entirely ahead of the solitary life in importance, saying that we ought to hasten to a community if we desire to reach the highest perfection. There is not much use arguing against such people because they set forth with praise only that life which they desire to live, or the one that they at least know a little bit about. But they do not praise the solitary life because they are ignorant of it.

The solitary life is, indeed, one which no one living in the flesh can know, except the man to whom God has given it to live, and no one can judge with certainty concerning this life (of which he is still uncertain) either what it does or how it works. Without a doubt I know that if they knew this life well, they would praise it more to other people.

Some people make a worse mistake. They do not stop blaming and defaming the solitary life, saying, "Woe to him who is alone," not understanding that that "alone" means "without God" not "without companions." He is indeed "alone" whom God is not with! For when he shall have fallen into death, he is seized at once for torments, and is separated from the vision of the glory of God and His saints forever. But he who chooses the solitary life for the sake of God, and leads it in an upright manner, will not have "woe," but "beautiful virtue" will come to him and the remembrance of the name Jesus will continually delight him.

And where they do not fear to accept, for the sake of God, a life without human solace, there they will be given the gift of rejoicing more fully in divine consolation. Indeed, they will receive frequent spiritual visitations which those placed in religious communities will be inwardly ignorant of. That is why "I shall lead her into solitude and I shall speak to her heart" (Hos. 2:14) is said for the loving soul.

Indeed, certain people have been taught from Heaven to desire solitude for the sake of Christ, and to hold to this single intention. At once, in order that they may serve God more freely and more devotedly, when they have left behind the common life, they transcend temporal things by sublimity of spirit—the transitory things of this world which they reject and despise. They desire eternal joys alone, they abandon themselves to devotion and contemplation and they do not cease to occupy the whole of their time with the desire for loving Christ. Although many of these people sojourn separately among men, they nevertheless do not falter from celestial desires because their minds stand a long way off from the conversation of impious men.

And thus they hold to the way of life of a solitary hermit in an upright manner. They live in the love of God and of their neighbors, they despise temporal praise, they flee the sight of men as far as they can, they judge all men as worthier than they, they give their minds continually to devotion, they hate idleness, they resist carnal pleasures manfully, they know heavenly things and ardently seek them, they do not desire earthly things but abandon them, and they are delighted by the pleasantness of prayers.

But certain of them experience the sweetness of the eternal. Rather, I should say, chaste in heart and body, they examine God and the heavenly city, because they have loved through the bitter cup of penance and through great labor. And, already raised upward by the love of contemplation, they have deserved to abandon themselves to God alone and to await the kingdom of Christ.

And therefore the life of the hermit is great, if it is lived generously. For blessed Maglorious who was filled with miracles and from his childhood was made glad by angelic visitation, when, according to the prophecy of his predecessor, the blessed Sampson, he was created archbishop, ruled the

Church of God for a long time and in a praiseworthy way; having been warned by an angel visiting him, he put aside the archbishopric and chose the life of the hermit, and in the end of his life the death that would be his was revealed to him. Similarly, blessed Cuthbert crossed over from a bishopric to the life of an anchorite.

If, therefore, such men, pursuing greater merit, behave in this fashion, who of sane mind would dare to place any other state in the church ahead of the solitary life? For in this life they occupy themselves with no external things, but abandon themselves exclusively to heavenly contemplation, so that they continually burn in love of Christ and perfectly put behind them the cares of the world.

Because of this, heavenly music resounds within them, and sweetly flowing song delights the solitary. The tumult drags him from this delight when he is placed among many people, and it does not allow him to meditate or pray except rarely.

The Psalmist is talking about this solitary in the hymns of the loving man, saying, "I shall travel into the place of the admirable tabernacle, even up to the house of God" (Ps. 41:5). He describes the manner of traveling in jubilant song and singing praise, setting this down: "In the voice of exultation and of confession is the sound of the banqueter" (Ps. 41:5). And he indicates openly in another place that it is necessary for whoever would seize the joy of those melodies and would retain it in rejoicing and singing, to be solitary, beyond the reach of the din and of physical song, for that kind of music. He says, "I have gone far away, fleeing, and I have remained in solitude." For he tries to burn continually in this life with the fire of the Holy Spirit and to exult, captured in the joy of love and divinely comforted.

Certainly the perfect solitary burns intensely in divine love, and while he is snatched away, beyond himself, in the going forth of his spirit through contemplation, he is lifted up, rejoicing, to the jubilant sons of the singers and their heavenly music. And certainly, such a man is made like the seraphim, burning especially within himself with incomparable and most constant love. His heart is transfigured by divine fire burning and shining with extreme fervor, he is carried into his Beloved. And if indeed he is raised up suddenly after this to the highest seats of the heaven-dwellers, so that he sits serenely in the place of Lucifer, it is because, burning so greatly with love, beyond what could be made apparent, he has sought the Creator and His glory alone and, advancing humbly, he did not exalt himself beyond sinners.

CHAPTER FOURTEEN – *Concerning commendation of the solitary life and its chief lovers; that the love of God consists in glowing fervor, song, and sweetness, and that quiet is a necessity; that such lovers are preserved from illusions and are not appointed as prelates*

Blessed Job, led forth among whips by the Holy Spirit, embraces in one commendation the multi-layered holiness of the hermits, saying, "Who has set the wild ass free . . . ?" [The full text, which Rolle explicates below, reads:

"Who gave the wild donkey his freedom,
  and untied the rope from his proud neck?
I have given him the desert as a home,
  the salt plains as his own habitat."

(Job 39:5–6)]

First, therefore, the freedom of grace is commended when he says, "Who has set the wild ass free?"

Second, the freedom from the disposition for carnal affections is indicated, when he says, "and He has unlocked his shackles."

Third, Job praises freedom for solitary conversation when he adds, "He has given him a home in the wilderness."

Fourth, he praises the freedom for the desire for eternal beatitude when he says, "And his tabernacle in the salt flats." For in the salt flats thirst is not quenched, but rises more intensely. And thus, where they have perceived something about the sweetness of eternal life, they burn more intensely to understand and taste of it.

Further, Saint John the Baptist, the chief of the hermits (after Christ), slowing his affection in no way, chose the solitary life, and others chose in similar fashion. Such a man, as Solomon says, is like the lobster: he does not have a leader and a prince, and a commander, yet he excels through crowds of virtues and of gifts. Moreover, there are the chains of nature and sin which God unlocks in these people as He strengthens the chains of love.

In the same way, the home of solitude can be called the quiet of the heart, because holy hermits, separated from the tumults and vices of the world, receive the smoothness of a clear conscience which Christ dispenses, and, singing the joy of eternal love, they rest refreshed in most agreeable fervor. And however often they are attacked by asperities and adversities in the flesh, they nevertheless retain the song and the burning ardor firmly in their souls.

There is an evil solitude—that of pride, of course—which occurs when a man either prefers himself alone to others, or ascribes what he has to the energies of unshackled free will. Of such a one is it said, "Woe to those who are alone! If they should fall, they have no one to raise them up" (Eccles. 4:10).

In the beginning of their conversion, certainly, hermits (I'm not talking about vagabonds, who are the scandal of hermits), are wearied by many and diverse temptations. But after the tempest of wicked impulses, God pours in the serenity of holy desires, so that if they have worked manfully in weeping, in meditating and in praying, in seeking the love of Christ alone, after a short time they seem to themselves rather to live in delights than in tears or in the anxiety of labor.

For they will have Him Whom they have loved, Whom they have sought, Whom they have desired. And then they will rejoice and they will not mourn. Indeed, what is it to rejoice but to obtain the good one has loved, to meditate upon Him, to rest in His very Self? Sweet, certainly, is the joy where lovers truly come together, and the mutual comforts of touching lovers are present! For the desire of those who love burningly is inexplicable, and their mutual sight and conversation is sweet to them beyond honey and the honeycomb.

Moreover, Jeremiah, commending the solitary life, says, "Good is the man when he bears the yoke of the Lord from his youth. He will sit alone and he will be silent, and he will raise himself above himself" (Jer. 3:28)—of course through the desire for and contemplation of eternal things. For this reason it says in Ecclesiasticus, "There is not born on earth a man like Enoch" (Ecclus. 49:16).

For he has been snatched away from the earth, because contemplatives are superior to others both in the excellence of their work and in the fervor of their love. For love inhabits the heart of the solitary if he seeks no part of empty lordship. Hence he burns from his very deepest part and languishes for light, when he savors heavenly things thus sincerely. And he sings sweetly without grief, bringing forth the shout for his noble Love as does a seraph, because he is reshaped in a most loving spirit, as it is said, "Ah! Loving, I burn, panting avidly!"

Thus, the soul of the lover burns with inestimable fire, and the penetrating flame which gladdens him shines in a heavenly manner. (Nor, burning blessedly, do I make an end, but since I am ever hurrying toward that which I love, death is to me smooth and safe.)

Indeed, the holy solitary, because he endured sitting in solitude for the sake of the Savior, will receive a golden seat among the inhabitants of Heaven, an excellent place among the ranks of the angels. Because he was clothed in vile garments for the love of his Author, he will don an ankle-length and eternal tunic prepared in the light of the Creator. In the same way, he will receive a supremely wonderful splendor in face because, conquering his flesh, he did not blush to have a pale and wasted face. He shall wear forever among the heaven-dwelling powers a most beautiful robe interwoven with precious gems in place of his despicable clothing. But because he abandoned vices and did not live in the loveliness of a visible life, he has utterly cast away the outward appearance of filth. He has taken up within himself the most sweet and heavenly melody in the fire of omnipotent love, and he has deserved to have the melodies of singers in love-filled song poured sweetly into his mind.

Therefore, he goes forth from this exile bravely and without horror, hearing in his last moments angelic harmony. Stepping forth with joy, the man who has loved most ardently is more honorably lifted up into the eternal hall, to a most glorious place, so that, of course, he may dwell with the seraphim in the highest seat.

Further, as I have been able to investigate in the Scriptures, I have discovered and recognized for certain that the highest love of Christ consists in three things: in burning fervor, in song, and in sweetness. And I, who am an expert, have found that these three are not able to persist for a long time without great quiet in spirit. So that if I should wish to contemplate standing or walking around or prostrating myself, I found that I had greatly withdrawn from these three and passed judgment as if I were desolate. From this circumstance, compelled by this necessity, I have chosen to sit down in the highest devotion which I can possess and stick to.

I am not ignorant of the cause of this reaction. For if a man should stand or walk around a great deal, his body becomes tired, and thus his soul is impeded, and, in a certain way, he grows bored in the face of the burden. And he is not in his deepest quiet, and, as a consequence, he is not in perfection, for, according to the philosopher, by sitting and being quiet the soul becomes prudent. Therefore, let a man, who has delighted thus far in divine things by standing rather than by sitting, know himself to stand far distant from the peak of contemplation.

And when, in truth, in these three things, which are signs of the most perfect love, the highest perfection of the Christian religion is found without any ambiguity, and I, already, for the small measure of my capacity have received these three (because Jesus has lavished them on me), I shall pursue this course up to this point by virtue as far as I am able, so that I may love more ardently, sing more liquidly and experience more fully the sweetness of love. (Nor, notwithstanding, do I dare to equate myself with those saints who have shone forth in these three things, because they perhaps have seized upon them more perfectly.

Indeed, brothers, you are making a mistake if you think that there are now no saints such as the prophets or apostles were. Moreover, I call it "fervor" when my spirit truly burns with eternal love, and my heart is felt to burn with that kind of love, not just in my judgment but in reality. For the heart, transformed in fire, causes the sensation of the fire of love.

I call it "song" when already in the soul, burning fervor abounding, the smoothness of eternal praise is taken up and meditation is transformed into song and the mind lingers in honey-flowing melody.

These two things are not experienced in idleness, but in the most intense devotion, and from them the third, that is to say, inestimable sweetness, becomes present. For burning fervor and song cause marvelous sweetness in the soul, and furthermore, these are able to be caused on account of that excessive sweetness.

For there isn't any deception in that flowing forth, but rather the most consummate perfection of all actions, however certain people, inexperienced in contemplative life, may be betrayed in certain false and feigned devotion by the noonday devil, because they think themselves highest when they are lower! But the soul in whom the three things mentioned above run together inwardly remains impervious to the arrows of the enemy while, meditating on love with an unchanged intention, she raises herself to the heavens and stirs herself to loving.

And do not marvel if melody is commanded of the soul thus ordered in love, and she continually seizes the consoling song from her Lover. For she lives as if she were not subject to vanity, supported from Heaven, so that she may burn without fail in eternity in uncreated heat, so that she may never fall. When she loves in this way, incessantly and ardently, as it has been said above, she may experience within herself the most blessed fervor and she may know herself to be subtly burnt up with the fire of eternal love. Deeply feeling her very greatest delight in desired sweetness, her meditation is transformed into a song of glory and her nature is wrapped up in the pleasantness of renewed sweet song.

Because of this, the Creator has granted to her what she has desired with her whole heart, to depart without fear and sadness from a corruptible body so that she leaves the world without the bitterness of death, for this friend of light and enemy of darkness loved nothing except life.

Moreover, in this manner men who are raised up so greatly on high to love ought to be chosen neither for offices nor for prelacies, and they should not be called to other secular business. They are similar to the topaz gem, which is found rarely and therefore is held as exceedingly precious and rare. Within this gem there are two colors. The first is very pure and like gold, and the other is clear, like the sky when it is serene. The topaz surpasses the clarity of all gems, nor is there any other thing more beautiful to see. If anyone would want to polish it, it would be dulled, but if it is left by itself, its beauty is retained.

The holy contemplatives, concerning whom we have been told before, are like this—most rare and therefore most beloved. They are like gold because of the eminent fervor of their love, and like the sky because of the clarity of their heavenly conversation. They surpass the life of all the saints and therefore they are more beautiful and more shining among the gems—that is to say, among the chosen. Loving and holding onto this life alone, they are more shining than all other men who are, or who have been. Moreover, those who would wish to "polish" such men, that is to say, to honor them with dignities, strive to diminish their burning ardor, and to "dull" their beauty and clarity in a certain measure. But these men, if they seek to receive princely honor, would really become more vile and of lesser merit. Therefore, they ought to be left to give themselves to their own works, so that their clarity may be increased.

CHAPTER FIFTEEN – *In what manner and for how long a time the writer has been carried toward the solitary life; the joyous song of love; concerning the changing of dwelling places*

When I was flourishing unhappily, and the youth of a wakeful adolescence had already come over me, the grace of the Creator poured forth. He restrained the petulance of temporal beauty and turned me toward the desiring of incorporeal embraces. Raising my soul from the depths, He carried it over to the heavens so that I might burn especially for the delight of eternity, more fully than I was ever delighted before in certain fleshly embracing or even in worldly voluptuousness.

Indeed, if I want to publicize the favorable outcome, I would have to praise the solitary life, for the Spirit, breathing, bent my intention toward following and loving this life which I then took care to lead, according to the small capacity of my infirmity. Nevertheless, I have remained among those who have flourished in worldly things, and I have accepted from them foods, and I have also heard flatteries which have often been able to drag celebrated warriors down from the heights to the depths. But casting away things of this kind for the sake of One, my soul has been lifted up to the love of the Author, and desiring to be delighted in eternal sweetness, I have given my soul that I might love Christ in the devotion which He accepts especially from His beloved, in order that the most delightful solitude may become visible to her and in order that she may count for nothing the fulfilling comforts for which the error of men abounds.

Actually, I was accustomed to seek for quiet, however much I used to travel from one place to another. For it is not wicked for hermits to leave their cells for a rational cause and to return to them again, if it seems appropriate. Indeed, cer-

tain of the holy fathers acted thus, although they suffered the
murmur of men (but not of good ones!) for doing so. But
evil men spoke evil because it had become customary for
them—for they would have done the same thing if the hermits had remained in the same place. When the lid is lifted
from the latrine, nothing comes out but a stink! And evil-
speaking men speak from the abundance of the heart in
which the venom of asps is hiding!

This I know because the more fully I have stirred in spiritual progress, the more greatly men have raved against me with
detracting words. For I have those worst detractors, the people
whom I formerly thought faithful friends. And then, I have
not ceased from doing those things which were useful to my
soul on account of the words of those men. On the contrary,
I have followed my desire, and I have always found God
befriending me. I have recalled what is written, "They shall
speak evil and you shall bless" (Ps. 108:28). And by the passing of the times the progress of spiritual joys has been given
to me.

For from the beginning of my alteration of life and spirit,
up to the opening of the door of heaven (allowing the eye of
my heart to contemplate heavenly beings with their beauty
revealed, to see by which road it might seek its Beloved and
to sigh continually for Him), there flowed past three years,
except for three or four months.

Almost one year passed with the door remaining opened,
until the time in which the heat of eternal love was felt in
reality in my heart. In fact, I was sitting in a certain chapel
and while I was greatly delighting in the smoothness of
prayer or meditation, suddenly I experienced within myself
an unaccustomed and joyous burning ardor. But, although at
first doubting from where this might be coming, I have
proved through a long period of time that it comes not from
a creature but from the Creator, because I have found it
more burning and more agreeable.

Moreover, from that inestimably delightful heat blazing in
my senses to the infusion and perception of the celestial or
spiritual sound which belongs to the canticle of eternal praise

and the smoothness of invisible melody (which cannot be known or heard except by him who receives it—who must be cleansed and separated from the earth), there flowed past nine months and several weeks.

For when I was sitting in that same chapel and I was singing the psalms in the evening before supper as well as I was able, I jumped as if at the ringing, or rather, the playing of stringed instruments, above me. And further, when I strained toward these heavenly sounds by praying with all my desire, I do not know how soon I experienced the blending of melodies within myself and drew forth the most delightful harmony from heaven, which remained with me in my spirit. For my meditation was continually transformed into the song of harmony, and it is as if I have odes in meditating. And further, I have enjoyed that same sound in psalmody and in the prayers themselves. Then I have hastened before the flowing forth of that inward, indeed hidden, sweetness, to that singing I have described previously, because I have been hastening into the presence of my Creator alone.

I had not been recognized by those who examined me, lest they might have honored me beyond measure if they had known, and thus I might have lost part of this most beautiful flower, and might have fallen down into desolation.

Meanwhile, wonder seized me because I had been raised up to such great joy while I was in exile, and because God had given me gifts which I did not know how to ask for; nor did I think that even the holiest man could receive such a gift in this life. Just so, I judge that this gift is given to no one because of merit, but gratuitously, to whomever Christ shall will. Nevertheless, I think that no one would receive it unless he loved the name of Jesus especially, and also honored it, so much that never, except in sleep, would he allow it to fade from his memory. I judge that the man to whom this has been given to do will reach that state.

Now, from the beginning of the change of soul up to the final degree of love of Christ which I had the God-given strength to attain—the step in which I resounded divine praises with the melody of jubilant song—I lived through four years and around three months.

Here, certainly, for men disposed for it by previous experiences, the state will persist even to the end. And it will become even more perfect after death, because the joy of love, or this fire of charity, has been started, and in the kingdom of Heaven it will receive its most glorious consummation. And indeed, a person in this life, disposed in these steps, will profit not a little, but he will not ascend into another state; on the contrary, as if he were confirmed in grace, he will rest (as a mortal can).

For this reason, I desire to bring back thanks to God, praises to Him, incessantly. In my anxieties and vexations and persecutions, He has given me comfort, and has caused me to look for an eternal crown with security amid prosperities and flatteries.

From this place, O Jesus, I continually loose praises to You, Who have deigned to intermingle me, the wretched and least, who send forth small measures of melody from my spirit (but from heaven) among Your mellifluous ministers. "Assiduously I shall give thanks with joy, because You have brought it about that I have shaped myself excellently to the singing, through clarity of conscience, in a soul burning with eternal love, while it loves and boils, sitting in fire. My spirit is transformed, burning with heat and vehemently dilated with desire. And its true beauty of delightful virtue blooms without a blemish in the sight of the Creator; jubilant song pours itself forth so, when He rejoices the languishing soul with joyful singing and relieves its labors.

Many are the wonderful and great rewards, but there are none such among the gifts of life which so preciously confirm hope by a kind of invisible life in the loving soul, or which thus delightfully console the sitting man and snatch him up to the peak of contemplation, or to the harmony of angelic praise.

Behold, brothers, I have told you how I have reached the

fire of love, not so you will praise me, but that you may glorify my God, from Whom I have received whatever good I possess, and so that you, judging everything under the sun as vanity, will be encouraged to imitation, not detraction.

The devout poor man, when he is tormented in the face of his weakness, if he wishes, can pray and say,

O Lord, my God, Jesus Christ, have mercy on me and deign to examine the heavy yoke which has been placed upon my body, that it may not linger to weigh down my soul. For my flesh is weak in the struggles of this life, because of which even spiritual virtue is thought to be wearied. For I have consumed all of what I had concerning this world and in this world, and nothing is left except that You may lead my soul to the other world where is my most precious treasure, and my richest substance, and where it remains unfailing. For this reason I shall live without sin, I shall rejoice without grief, I shall delight without disgust, and loving You, living You, rejoicing in You, I shall be satisfied eternally. For You are my treasure.

O death, why do you delay? Why do you come so tardily to the living man? But why do you not embrace the mortal desiring you? Who would be sufficient to imagine so much sweetness? You are the goal of the sigh, the principle of desire, the gate of the unfailing joy of the chosen! You are the end of lamentation, the limit of labor, the beginning of enjoyments, the door of joys. So I rage, I pant for you; if you will come, suddenly I shall be saved. For, seized by love, I cannot fully enjoy what I desire, until I shall have tasted the joy which you are about to give.

Since it is necessary—or rather, *because* it is necessary —for me as a mortal to pass away through you, in the way all my fathers have died, I ask you not to make me much different, not to remain distant from me for a long time. For behold, I am languishing with love, I desire to die, I burn for you—but certainly not for your own sake, but for the sake of my Savior, Jesus, Whom afterward I shall have the gift of seeing, for eternity, I hope.

O death, how good is your judgment for the indigent man, whose soul nevertheless is made mellifluous with love—if only for the man loving Christ, gazing at the Heavens, delightfully burning up with the fire of the Holy Spirit!

Certainly after death he is taken up to the angelic melody because, having been purged in his traveling, he also lingered in music from the Spirit. For he who, while living, meditated to his very marrow on the honey-dripping Name, will die in supremely marvelous melody and, the heavenly hosts meeting him with hymns, he will be raised up with honor into the hall of the eternal Lord, standing among the heaven-dwellers in the blessed abode.

But love has conducted him to this condition so that he might live inwardly so luxuriously and so that he might joyfully endure everything that might befall him, and so that he might consider death not with horror but with sweetness. Then, on the contrary, when it has been given to him to pass from this light, he judges himself truly to live.

O sweet love, you are plainly the most dear in delight, you who seize the mind with your love as clearly as you inebriate it, because you quickly make it despise all transitory things and vain joys, and pant marvelously in your desires alone. You have come to me and, behold, the whole inner heart of my soul is filled by the delights of sweet-sounding pleasantness, and abounds with a fervor for spiritual joy. Thereupon indeed I languish with love, the brightest of flowers, and I burn inwardly with a flame of fire. Oh, that I might go forth from the habitation of this exile!

For truly, he burns in a way one cannot imagine unless he has experienced the comfort within himself—the heart singing a song and seized by the anxiety of love. For certainly it is this greatest delight that I receive here, and I all but die when it becomes utterly thus with burning love, already most dearly beloved as when I shall die. Because death, which many men fear, might be like a melody of music to me, although already I abide as if placed in paradise, sitting in solitude, there sounding the loving canticle smoothly, in the delights which my Beloved has given to me.

CHAPTER SEVENTEEN – *How perfect love is acquired by purity and love; concerning beauty; concerning the threefold power of divine love; concerning rich people, poor people, and alms*

From cleanliness of conscience and from the abundance of spiritual joy and of inward rejoicing there rises inwardly in reality the song of glory and the flame of love in the loving mind. Certainly in this manner the loving man possesses love as a perfect habit, great in fervor, directed in its movement entirely to God, separated from its Beloved by no obstacle, clinging to Christ without the contradiction of empty thoughts, rejoicing in Jesus perpetually, never distracted from Him, never allured by evils—a love which dying flies never beguile nor drive away from the sweetness of the ointment [cf. Eccles. 10:1].

The world, the flesh, the devil in his own person, have no effect, however much they attack such a lover, but he grinds them under his feet; reckoning their strength for nothing, he burns without conflict, he loves with force, he sings with sweetness, he glows with warmth, he delights in God without resistance, he contemplates with his ascent unrepelled. He conquers all things, he overcomes all things, nothing of all he aspires to seems impossible to him. Certainly, when a man tries with all his strength to love Christ, he experiences the great delightfulness of eternal life within himself in reality.

We are indeed converted to Christ if we try to love Him with our whole mind. For so admirable a Being is God and so delectable to behold that I am stupefied that anyone, nevertheless, is able to act foolishly and to turn away, because such a one does not strain in soul toward his vision.

Indeed, it is not he who does many and great deeds who is great, but the man who loves Christ a great deal is the great one, and is beloved of God. For philosophers have labored very much and nevertheless they have vanished without fruit, and many people who seemed to be Christians have done great deeds and have shown wonders, and they have not merited to be saved. For the fullness of the heavenly crown belongs not to those doing deeds but to those loving God.

I ask You, Lord Jesus, to impart to me in Your love, motion without measuring, affection without limit, languishing without order, burning ardor without discretion. For here Your love is more noble where it is more impetuous, because it is not restricted by reason nor shaken by counting, nor tempered by judiciousness.

No man will ever be happier than he who could die on account of the intensity of his love, for no creature can love too much. In all other things, anything which becomes too great is transformed into vice, but in the case of the virtue of love, the more it exceeds, the more glorious it will be. For the lover languishes if he does not have what he loves next to himself, through an image. Therefore, it is said, "Tell my beloved, because I languish for love" (Cant. 5:8), as if he were to say, "because I do not discern what I love, for the sake of love I am also wasting away in body."

Certainly the man turned with his whole heart to Christ is first influenced through true penitence, and thus, leaving behind all things that pertain to vanity, after a taste of internal delight, he will be snatched up by heaven to sing in resounding rejoicing. Whence Isaiah says, "I shall sing to my beloved" (Isa. 5:1), and the Psalm declares, "In You is my song always" (Ps. 70:6). Therefore, those who have conquered in the love of the divine and burned delightfully with inner flaming, certainly pass over in death without fear. On the contrary, they depart from this light with joy, and after death they ascend happily to the heavenly kingdoms.

Therefore it is the property of the fire of divine love to wound the mind that it seizes (so that that mind may say, "I have been wounded by love,") and, further, to cause languor on behalf of love (whence is said, "I languish with love") (Cant. 2:5), and to inebriate, so that the mind may lean toward its Beloved, because it has become oblivious of all things and of its very self on account of Christ. For that reason the mind says, "Place me as a signet upon Your heart" (Cant. 8:6).

For what is love but the transformation of the affections into the thing beloved? For love is a great desire for the beautiful, the good and the lovable, with a continuation of meditations leaning into that which it loves. When it possesses its beloved, then it rejoices because its joy is caused only by love.

Moreover, every lover is made similar to his beloved, and love makes him who loves similar to that which is loved. But neither God nor any other creature scorns to be loved, or spits it back; on the contrary, all men joyfully acknowledge themselves to be loved, and to be delighted by love. Moreover, they are not made sad in loving unless they have loved an unreceptive person, or if they despair of being able themselves to attain that which they had sought by loving. Such situations never occur in the love of God, but they often touch on the love of the world and of women.

I do not dare to say that every love is good, because that love which is delighted more in creatures than in the Creator, and prefers the delectability of visible appearances to intellectual clarity, is evil and hateful, because it has turned away from eternal love and turned toward temporal love, which cannot endure. Nevertheless, perhaps it is punished less because it intends and rejoices rather to love and be loved than to pollute and be defiled.

The more beautiful a creature is, the more lovable it is in the eyes of all people. Therefore, certain people were accustomed to care more diligently for the salvation of the person with the most beautiful body than of the person with the contemptible one, because the beautiful person has in his beauty more occasions for leading him into evil. And nature teaches that the more beautiful person is to be loved more agreeably; nevertheless, regulated charity says that the man of greater goodness should be loved more greatly. For all carnal beauty is an easily vanishing advantage, but goodness remains, and often God chooses the infirm and despised of the world and abandons the strong and the beautiful. Whence in the psalm is said, "He has betrayed your virtue into captivity and your beauty into the hands of the enemy" (Ps. 77:61), and in another place, "Having fidelity in your beauty, you have fornicated" (Ezek. 16:5).

It is also the property of love to melt the mind, as it is written, "My soul has been melted as my Beloved has spoken" (Cant. 5:6). For sweet and devout love so releases the heart in divine sweetness that the will of man is joined with the will of God by a marvelous friendship; in this union, so great a delightfulness of sweet fervor and loving singing is poured out in the soul that the man who experiences it is not able to speak it clearly.

To be sure, love has diffusive, unifying, and transforming power. It is diffusive because it pours forth the rays of its goodness not only on friends and neighbors, but even on enemies and strangers. It is unifying because it makes lovers one in affection and will, and unites Christ and every holy soul. For the man who clings to God is one with Him in spirit—not by nature, but by grace and by identity of will.

Love also has a transforming power because it transforms the lover into the beloved and brings the one into the other's very self. Whence the fire of the Holy Spirit, because it really seizes the heart, burns it up entirely and changes it, as if in a fire, and brings it back into that form which is most like God. It cannot be described in any other way. "I have said that you are gods and all sons of the Most High" (Ps. 81:6).

For certain men have so loved one another that they almost might believe nothing except that the soul of each is in the other. But the man poor in the things of this world, however much he might be rich in spirit, stands at a long distance from such love. For it would be a wonder if the man who must always receive, and rarely or never is able to give, might have a friend in whom he could confide in all things. Therefore, judged by other men to be unworthy of faithful love, he possesses Christ, the faithful friend, from Whom he faithfully asks whatever he wishes. For where human aids are absent, divine helps are present without doubt.

Nevertheless, it would be more useful to a rich man if he

would choose a holy poor man for himself as a friend and special companion with whom he might wish to share everything he might have, and give it willingly (even more than the poor man might wish), and that he might love him affectionately—as much as he loves his best and most pleasing friend. Therefore Christ has said, "Make for yourselves friends . . ." (Luke 16:9), especially holy poor men (understanding "who are friends of God"), and God gives freely to true lovers of such poor men, for love of them, the joy of paradise.

Indeed, I judge that such rich men ought to be well pleased with their friendship, but now—true is the proverb that says, "The sea will be dry when the poor man has a friend!" For I have found certain rich men who, giving holy poor men the food that they themselves have thought of, do not wish to give them clothing or other necessities, judging it to be enough if they have given them food. Thus they make for themselves half-full friends, or friends for a certain part, caring no more for the friendship of good men than of bad men. And all which ought to have been given away of certain wealth, they have reserved for themselves and their sons.

And thus holy poor men are held only as closely to them as they are to their other benefactors who have given them clothing or some such other thing—and what is worse, very frequently the poor seem a heavy burden to the rich.

Chapter Eighteen – Concerning the praise and efficacy of love; concerning renouncing of the world and taking hold of the road of penitence

Love, the queen of the virtues, the most beautiful star, is the beauty of the soul which does all these things in the soul —that is to say, it wounds the soul, causes languor in it, makes it drunk, melts it and adorns it, makes it happy and enflames it; its action is ordered and its behavior is lovely.

All virtue, if it is truly called virtue, must, without a doubt, be rooted in love. For no one can hold any virtue who has not planted his very self in the love of God. But anyone who, without the love of God, multiplies virtues or good works—it is as if he threw precious jewels into a latrine without a bottom. For it is obvious that all that men may do will not, in the end, help them to the attainment of salvation if their deeds do not stand firm in the love of God and of neighbor. When, therefore, love alone may be what makes us blessed, we ought sooner wish that our life might depart than to violate love in mind, or mouth, or deed. In this the contenders rejoice; in this the triumphant are crowned.

Moreover, every Christian is imperfect who clings to earthly riches with love, or is cemented by any worldly solace, because he has not renounced everything that he possesses— without which he will never attain to perfection.

But when anyone intends to love God perfectly, he studies to remove all those things—as much the interior as the exterior—which are contrary to divine love and impede him from His love. And so that he may do this truly, he has great diligence because he will sustain great conflicts in the doing. But afterward he will find the most delightful rest in that which he has sought.

But we have heard that narrow is the road that leads to life. This is the penitential road which few have discovered, and which therefore is described; for if it is ruled through penitence, the flesh is stripped of the allurements and the solace of the world, and the soul is restrained from depraved delight and unclean thinking, and the man is freed for divine love alone. But this is rarely found among men, because no one savors often the things which are of God, but they seek earthly joy and are delighted in that. Whence, frequenting the appetite of the senses and neglecting that of the intellect, they detest and abhor every salvific road of their soul—as narrow and harsh and intolerable to their voluptuousness.

Notwithstanding, mortal man ought to consider carefully that he will never arrive at the heavenly kingdom through the road of riches and of luxuriousness and of fleshly pleasures, since indeed it is written concerning Christ, "That it belonged to the Christ to suffer, and thus to enter into His glory" (Luke 24:26). If we are members of our head, Jesus Christ, undoubtedly we shall follow Him, and if we love Christ, we ought to walk as He Himself has walked.

Yet in another way, we are not His members, because we are divided from that Head. If, moreover, we are separated from Him, it ought greatly to be feared, because then we are joined to the devil and, when the general judgment has been completed, Christ will say, "I do not know you" (Matt. 7:23).

But He entered into Heaven through a narrow doorway and a strait road; how should we, who are wretches and sinners, wish to be made into wealthy men from being poor men, to feed ourselves with the enticements and flatteries of this world for the sake of pleasures, and to lust for every vanity and the wantonness and delectation of the flesh—and nevertheless to reign with Christ in the future life? Christ, when He was wealthy, for our sakes became a poor man—and we, although we are poor men, desire nothing so much as to be, or to appear to be, opulent.

Christ, although He was God of all, was made slave of all—and we, although we are unworthy and useless slaves, do we wish, nevertheless, to have dominion over all men?

He, although He was mighty God, was made a humble

man—and we, although we are infirm and exiled men, to what degree do we extol ourselves for the sake of pride, as if we were gods?

Although He dwelt with men so that He might lead us up to Heaven, we desire earthly things through our whole life! Accordingly, He suffers that we do not love Him, because we do not conform our will to His will, nor do we bustle about to fulfill what we ask for daily, saying, "Thy will be done, on earth as it is in Heaven."

It is in vain that men of this kind assert that they will take possession of an inheritance with the chosen ones, because they are not sharers of the redemption of Christ. Through their sins and unclean activities, these men despise the Blood through which we are redeemed, and submit themselves of their own free will to the service of the devil.

CHAPTER NINETEEN – *Concerning beauty of mind, the vanity of the world and the love of God and of neighbor as connected together; whether perfect love can be lost and prepared for in this life*

If you would delight in beauty, know that the appearance of your spirit will make it deeply loved by the Highest Beauty if you conserve it intact for the love of Him alone. Indeed, all the beauty of corruptible flesh is frail and contemptible because, quickly passing away, it deceives all its lovers. Therefore, the virtuousness of our lives consists in this, that when we have condemned vanity and trampled it underfoot, we should adhere inseparably to truth.

Vain are all those visible things that are desired on earth. True indeed are those things that cannot be seen—the celestial and eternal. But every Christian shows himself chosen by God in this: that, judging these earthly goods as nothing, he is wholly enlarged in divine desires. Thence he receives the sweet-sounding secret of love which no one ever learns from earthly things, because while a man is involved with earthly concupiscences, he is unhappily placed at a distance from the savor of celestial joy.

But without a doubt, the emptiness of the soul of the man resting on the love of eternity with absolute earnestness, and of the heart choosing Christ indefatigably, is accustomed to be filled again with an abundance of delight, so that, full of joy even in this flesh, it may be engaged in the melodious loveliness, as it were, of the life of the angels.

Therefore, if our love is pure and perfect, whatever our heart may love, God emerges. But if we do not love ourselves and all other creatures that ought to be loved, except in God and for the sake of God, what else do we love in ourselves and in them but Him? For when God is loved by us with our whole heart and our whole spirit, then without a doubt our neighbor and everything that ought to be loved is loved rightly. If, therefore, we pour out our whole heart in the sight of God and in love of God, having bound and detained it close to God, what remains besides by which we may love anything else? In true love of God is love of neighbor. Therefore, just as he who loves God does not know how not to love man, so he who truly knows how to love Christ is proved to love in Him nothing except God.

And thus, all that we are loved by or that we love we bring back wholly to God, the fountain of love. Because He Who commands that the human heart be yielded wholly to Himself also desires that all its affections and all the motions of the spirit be fixed in Him. Again, the man who truly loves God experiences in his heart nothing besides God, and if he feels nothing else, he has nothing else. But whatever he has he loves for the sake of God and he loves nothing except what God wills him to love. Therefore, he loves nothing except God, and thus his love is entirely God.

Indeed, the love of such a man is true because he conforms himself to his Creator, Who has formed all things for Himself; thus, such a man loves all things for the sake of God. Certainly, when the love of eternity is really kindled in our souls, without a doubt all the vanity of the world and all carnal delight is judged as nothing but the vilest excrement. And when the spirit, entirely given over to continual devotion, desires nothing except pleasing its Creator well, it burns wonderfully in itself by the fire of love, until, advancing and kindling little by little in spiritual goods, it does not in any way sink into that slippery and wide road which leads to death, but rather, raised up by heavenly fire, it goes forth and ascends even into the contemplative life.

For the contemplative life (even a small portion of it) is not completely acquired by anyone in this valley of tears unless his heart is first set on fire at its foundation by the torches of eternal love, so that he experiences his very heart burning with the fire of love and recognizes his conscience being melted by that honey-like delight. Thus, without a doubt, the contemplative is formed properly with difficulty, the while; by tasting the sweetness and experiencing the burning ardor, he may many times be almost dying on account of the intensity of his love. Whence he is continually pierced, as it were, in the physical embraces of eternal love, because in contemplating incessantly, he tries to ascend to the seeing of that uncircumscribed light with his whole desire.

And then, such a man knows how to admit none but divine consolation into his soul. Already languishing in His love, he thinks to sigh to the end of the present life, crying anxiously with the Psalmist, "When shall I come, and when shall I appear before the face of God?" (Ps. 41:3). He is perfected for love, but whether or not this state of love, once possessed, can ever be lost, it cannot be sought unsuitably.

Moreover, while a man is able to sin, he is able to lose love. But to be unable to sin does not exist in this state of life, but in our Fatherland. Therefore, every man, to whatever degree he has been made perfect in this life, is able to sin in this world, even mortally, because the kindling-wood of sin has not been fully extinguished in any pilgrim, according to the common rule.

If, moreover, there were any such man, who could neither lust nor be tempted, according to this condition he would belong rather to the state of heaven than to that of earth. Nor would it be much credit to him not to fail, when he was not able to sin! I do not know inwardly whether there is anywhere such a man living in flesh, for (I speak for myself), "the flesh lusts against the spirit and the spirit against the flesh" (Gal. 5:17). And I delight for the law of God according to the interior man, but I do not know how to love here so intensely that I am able to extinguish the concupiscence within.

Nevertheless, I judge that there is one level of perfect love which the man who shall have attained it will never thereafter lose. For it is one thing to be able to lose a thing, but it is another thing to hold always what one would not wish to lose even if he could. But perfect men hold themselves at a distance, as much as is in them, from anything by which their perfection could either be destroyed or even be hindered. They have been filled with freedom of decision by divine grace, by which they are stirred assiduously to love, speak, and do good, and they are drawn back from evil of heart, mouth, and deed.

When, therefore, a man perfectly turned to Christ has despised all transitory things and has fixed himself as immovably in the single desire of the Creator as is permitted to mortals on account of the corruption of the flesh, then, without a doubt, exercising his spiritual powers in manly fashion, first he will see with his intellectual eye, as if by means of an opened door, the heavenly citizens. Afterward he will experience the most delightful warmth, as if it were a burning fire. Thereupon he will be imbued with wondrous delight and then he will glory in jubilant song.

This, therefore, is perfect love, which no one knows unless he receives it. And he who receives it never loses it, lives sweetly, and will die securely.

Chapter Twenty – *Concerning the usefulness and worthiness of prayer and meditation*

Ever-flowing prayer greatly assists one in acquiring and retaining this stability of spirit, for if it be poured out by the intention, it weakens the power of the demons. For however much God may know all things, and further, though He may know what we wish to ask perfectly even before we ask for it, nevertheless we ought to pray for many reasons. For Christ has offered an example of praying when He watched through the night alone on the mountain, in prayer, and this is the precept of the Apostle: "Pray without intermission, for it is necessary to pray and not to fail" (1 Thess. 5:17).

Again, we ought to pray so that we may merit grace in the present time and glory in the future, as the gospel says, "Ask and you shall receive. He who asks receives and to him who knocks it shall be opened" (Luke 11:10).

And again we ought to pray because angels offer our prayers to God so that they may help toward their fulfillment. But meditations and desires are laid bare and open to God alone. Nevertheless, the holy angels know them when they meditate on worthy and holy things, and they are intensely set on fire with the love of eternal life through the revelation of God and the experience of external actions, because they see them zealously serve God alone. For this reason the angel said to Daniel, "You are a man of desires" (Dan. 9:23).

Another reason we should pray is because through continuous prayer the soul is set aflame with the fire of divine love. For God says through the Prophet, "Are not my words like to a burning fire and a hammer crushing rocks?" (Jer. 23:29). The Psalmist also says, "Your word is intensely fiery" (Ps. 118:140).

But now there are many people who quickly recite the

word of God from their mouth and by heart, not allowing it to rest there within themselves. And therefore they are not set on fire by the heat of consolation, but remain frigid in torpor and negligence, even after uncountable prayers and meditations on Scripture, because they neither pray nor meditate with a perfected spirit, when others, who drive out all sloth, are powerfully set on fire and burning with love of Christ within a brief time. Whence, rightly, the Psalm continues "and Your servant loves it" (Ps. 118:140).

Certainly, therefore, he has been raised up, because he has loved Your word, O Lord—obviously to be meditated upon and, following that, to be put into action. He has sought You rather than Your gifts, and he receives from You both You and Your gifts. Some people are servants to You so that they may possess Your gifts, and they care too little about You. But they make themselves wish to submit to Your service so that they may acquire the honor of the world, and so that they may appear glorious among men. But while they rejoice to have discovered a few things, they have lost many. For they have lost You and Your gifts, and themselves and their own gifts.

Again we ought to pray so that we may be saved. Hence St. James urges us, saying, "Pray for one another that you may be saved" (James 5:16).

And then again we ought to pray lest we be slack, and so that we may be occupied continuously in good. Whence it is said, "Keep watch and pray lest you enter into temptation" (Matt. 26:41). For we ought always either to pray or to read or to meditate, with other useful deeds, so that our enemy may never find us slothful. But we ought to pay attention with all diligence as we keep watch in prayers—of course, by means of our bodies and our meditations, so that we are not lulled to sleep—to those things which distract the spirit and make it forget where it was going, and to all things that block it, if they come before it to overcome the effect of the devotion that the mind of the praying person perceives, if he prays with vigilance and solicitude and with affection.

CHAPTER TWENTY-ONE – *That the contemplative life is worthier and more meritorious than the active life; concerning each of them; concerning preaching and prelacies*

Moreover it is doubted by certain people that this life—the contemplative life, of course—may be more meritorious and more noble than the active life. To some it seems that the active life may be more meritorious on account of its more numerous works and the preaching which keeps it busy. But these people, not knowing, err, because they are ignorant of the power of the contemplative life.

Nevertheless, there are many living the active life who are better people than some contemplatives. But the best contemplatives are superior to the best of those leading the active life.

Therefore we say that the contemplative life is simply more delightful, more noble and more worthy, and that it is more meritorious as far as concerns the essential reward, for this is the joy from Uncreated Good. For, if the contemplative life is properly led, the contemplative loves God more ardently and is rewarded by greater grace.

The cause for love being more fervent in the contemplative life than in the active life is that contemplatives are in quiet of mind and body, and therefore they taste the delight of eternal love through all mortal things. But men leading an active life serve God in work and external discourse, and they remain but little in internal quiet. Whence they are not able, except rarely and briefly, to be delighted. Contemplatives, certainly, enjoy continually the embraces of their Beloved.

But certain men oppose this opinion, saying, "The active life is more fruitful" because it performs works of mercy and preaches and does other things of this kind, and therefore it is more meritorious. But I say no to this, because such activities arrive at the non-essential, or accidental, reward which is joy from created good.

Whence, one who is raised up into the rank of the angels can thus have something that he who will be in the rank of the cherubim or of the seraphim will not have—that is, joy from some created good which he did in his lifetime. For the latter, who excelled in the love of God, as it were, incomparably, did not do that work. Often it happens that as someone of lesser merit is good and preaches, another who loves much more does not preach. That one who preaches is not, therefore, the better man, is he? No! But that man who loves more is higher and better, however much merit that lesser man will have for his preaching—a merit that the greater man will not deserve because he has not preached. It is obvious, therefore, that a man is not holier nor more excellent because of the external deeds he performs. For God, Who is the Examiner of the heart, rewards the will rather than the work.

Indeed, the works depend upon the will, not the will upon the works, for the more ardently a man has loved, the higher the reward to which he will ascend.

There is, moreover, in true contemplative men, a certain fervor flowing with honey and the abundance of divine delight. Jubilant song is sent forth from these abiding sources into these people with inestimable delightfulness. And these things will never be found in men leading the active life in this present time because they do not exert themselves for heavenly things so greatly that they deserve to rejoice in Jesus this way. And therefore, the active life is esteemed less in merit and the contemplative life is preferred in the present and in the future.

Whence, in the litter of the true Solomon, the columns are of silver and the couch-back is of gold. The "columns of the chair" are the strong sustainers and the good rulers of the Church. These are "of silver" because they are brilliant in conversation and sonorous in preaching.

The "couch-back of gold" are the contemplative men existing in the most intense quiet, in whom Christ especially rests

His Head, for these men rest particularly in Him. These men are "of gold" because they are purer and more careful in living honestly and they are more ruddy in the fervor of their loving and their contemplation.

Again, God preselects His chosen ones for fulfilling diverse ministries. For it has not been given to any single man to superintend all the offices, but each man has what best accords with his state. Whence the Apostle says, "To each of us is given grace according to the measure of the gift of Christ" (Eph. 4:7). For some give alms from goods justly acquired. Others defend the truth even to death. Still others preach the word of God clearly and strongly. Others again endure great penance and suffering in this life for the sake of God. And others through the gift of contemplation have time for God alone, and to loving Christ they bind themselves utterly. But without a doubt, among all the states that exist in the Church, they rejoice in extraordinary reward who, as contemplators perfected in divine love, have already deserved to rejoice by singing.

If, moreover, a man were able to acquire each of these two lives—that is, the contemplative life and the active life—to keep them both and to fulfill them both, great would he be, so that it is easy to see that he might fulfill a bodily ministry, and experience within himself nothing less of the heavenly harmonies, and that he might melt singing in the joy of eternal love. I do not know if any such mortal has lived here on earth; to me it seems impossible that both could be done at the same time.

But Christ is not to be included among men in this category, nor is His Blessed Mother to be included among women. For Christ did not have whirling thoughts, nor did He contemplate in the common manner by which the saints contemplate in this life. For He was not unworthy to labor in the way that we are unworthy, because from the very start of His conception He saw God. Certainly through the greatness of His spiritual works there came into us the jubilant song and we received the most delightful sound from the Heavens, and then we desired to continue in quiet so that we might rejoice in perpetual sweetness.

Therefore the man who serves the active life nobly should try to ascend to the contemplative life. He who is raised up by the true gift of heavenly contemplation in the manner described above does not descend to the active life unless, as it happens, he is compelled to accept the governing of Christians, which, nevertheless, I judge happens rarely or never. But some contemplatives are well able to be chosen for this work, because they have been less filled with the fervor of love. For less holy men are sometimes better suited to the office of prelate than are more holy men, because those who are not the more perfectly able to rest quietly in interior desires will handle themselves more harmoniously around exterior things.

CHAPTER TWENTY-TWO – *That the fire of love purges vices and sins; concerning the signs of true friendship*

The fire of love, truly accepted into the soul, purges it of all the vices together, empties out the diminished and the superfluous, and plants every beauty of the virtues. Although it never remains with mortal sin, yet with venial sin it does remain.

But nevertheless so burning is the motion and affection of love toward God that it even consumes all venial sins even without actual thinking of these venial sins, because when the true lover is carried into God by vehement and fervent desire, all things that block him from the vision of God are displeasing to him. Indeed, when he rejoices in jubilant songs his heart is not strong enough to express what he tastes of heaven; on this account, he languishes with love.

For perfect men never carry combustibles with them to the future life—because all their sins are consumed in the burning ardor of the love of Christ. But, lest anyone in vain judge himself to be perfect when he is not so, let him listen to a description of when he has perfection in himself. This, certainly, is the life of perfect men:

–to cast from them every care of secular business;
–to leave behind for the sake of Christ parents and every thing of one's own;
–to hold all transitory goods in contempt, for the sake of eternal life;
–to destroy carnal desires by means of lengthy labor;
–to refrain from petulance and all illicit reactions, as far as this is possible;
–to burn in love of the Creator alone;
–to experience, after bitter tears and the immense exer-

cises of spiritual works, the sweetness of heavenly contemplation;

and thus, to the extent that I may speak concerning these privileged ones

—by contemplating, to be caught up for joy of divine delight into spiritual song or into the Heavenly harmony

and

—to linger delightfully in interior quiet, with disturbances far removed

to the extent that when it is permitted to the man of God to do nothing else externally, he is seized interiorly to resound the delights of eternal love in singing melody and ineffable jubilation.

Thus, without a doubt, he will have the same kind of delight in spirit that the angels in Heaven have, though he is not permitted so great a delight. Certainly in this way is made the perfect man who will not need to be cleansed by fire after this life—so ardently does the fire of the Holy Spirit burn him while he exists in flesh.

And nevertheless that perfect love does not bring it about that a man entirely does not sin, but only that no sin remains in him that is not immediately annihilated by the fire of love. Indeed, such a lover of Jesus Christ does not say his prayers according to the custom of other men, even of just men. For, placed in sublimity of spirit and rapt by the love of Christ beyond himself, he is caught up in wonderful joy. And, by harmony divinely infused into himself, as it were, singing prayers with a certain Breath, he sings more than orally, offering them in melody hidden from human senses, but clear to himself and to God. Indeed, the spiritual vigor or virtue has already overcome in him the heaviness of the flesh insomuch that he is able to delight assiduously in Christ. His heart, transformed in the fire of love, experiences heavenly heat in a way accessible to the senses, so that his strength suffices to sustain so great an intensity of the fire of love and is not dis-

solved. But the goodness of God preserves it even to the appointed time which He gave him so that he might love so
greatly. And truly it is said, "I languish from love." Set on
fire like the Seraphim, he burns and loves, he sings and
rejoices, he praises and is aflame. And the more fervent he is
in love, the more worthy he becomes. It is not only that he
does not fear death, but he rejoices to die, saying with the
Apostle, "For me, to live life is Christ and to die is joy"
(Phil. 1:21).

CHAPTER TWENTY-THREE – *That perfect love mixes nothing else with God; why and what it is necessary to love; concerning the blindness of carnal love*

If we perfectly relinquish the filth of evil deeds and the vices of the world, there is nothing that we love besides God. For what are we seen to love in our neighbor other than God, when we do not wish to love him except for the sake of God and in God? But how may God be All in all if anything of an alien love should remain in a man?

Moreover, no one has joy except from a good beloved. Therefore, however fully anyone has loved God, so much the more abundantly without a doubt, shall he rejoice in Him, because where we desire anything more vehemently and more fervently, having acquired it, we rejoice in it the more intensely. But therefore a man has that joy because he has God and God is that joy which no one of them truly possesses who seeks anything besides God.

But if I desire anything on my own account and I do not place my God as the goal of that desire, it is obvious that I have become the betrayer of my very self, and the open exhibitor of a hidden fault.

But God wants to be loved in this way, so that no one ought to be mixed with Him in love. Because, if you divide your heart and do not fear to love another being with Him, without a doubt you will see your love deserted by God, Who doesn't deserve to contemplate part of a love. But He accepts either all or nothing, because He has redeemed the whole—since indeed your body and your soul were damned in the sin of Adam your father. Therefore God descended into the womb of the Virgin and, made man, paid the price of your liberation so that not only would He snatch your soul from the power of the demons but that He might also make your body blessed with your soul at the end of the world.

Therefore you have the precept of eternal life; if you wish to enter the lost kingdom recovered again by the blood of Christ, you must observe the commandments of Christ. And indeed, however you desire to ascend into full and perfect joy after your death, you must remind yourself thus in this life— to love God with a full and perfect heart. For the rest, as you do not give yourself now to the love of God, so then you will not have full joy but eternal torment. For when you do not direct yourself with an integral love to your true Creator you are really proved to love a creature of God beyond what is honest and lawful. For the rational soul cannot be without love while it is on its earthly road. Whence its love is its "foot," by which, after this pilgrimage, it is carried to God or to the devil, so that then it may see itself subject to the one it was serving here by its own free will.

Moreover, nothing can be loved except on account of the good which it is—either actual or apparent—and which is within the beloved, or is judged certainly to be within it. Hence it is that those loving the physical appearance, or temporal riches, are deceived through an illusion, as it were. For there is not, in these visible things that are experienced by touch or seen by the eye, the delight that appears or the glory that is imagined or the fame that is chased.

Therefore there is no one who more damnably neglects his soul than he who fixes his eye on a woman for the sake of lust. For when the sight of the eye burns the spirit, soon thought will enter from what is seen, and will generate concupiscence in the heart and will deform the interior nature. Whence suddenly he is stifled by the kindling of this noxious fire and he is blinded lest he see the judgment of the severe judge. Thus also the soul snatched by an unclean and malign love from the consideration of Heavenly things, does not cease to show abroad the signs of its damnation, and unless such a man gives birth to the uncleanness which he has conceived, he despairs inwardly of prosperity. Further, he conceives sorrow in painful concupiscence, whence, deservedly, he brings forth iniquity because to the degree that he melts the more swiftly into muddy delectation, to that same extent he errs about how great is the peril of his soul, which he does not try to discover. And thus the judgments of God are withdrawn from his face. For when he begins to be delighted in carnal desires he does not notice into how great a lake of misery he is falling. Certainly, the judgment of God is that the person who, of his own free will, in contempt for God, is cast down in mortal sin, after this life, with God as his judge, will, unwilling, be condemned. For he will not be able to defend himself in the future from the biting teeth of the nether world who, in this present time, having, when he could, committed mortal sins, did not wish at all to be able to turn himself away from them or even to begin by turning away.

CHAPTER TWENTY-FOUR – *Concerning the filthiness and peril of riotous living; concerning touching; concerning the evil of avarice and concerning improper pleasure as well*

When anyone for the sake of the pure love of God and of virtue and of chastity does not marry, but has enough to do to live in continence and in the embellishment of all the virtues, he acquires for himself, without doubt, a great name among the angels. Because as he did not cease to love God here, thus he will never cease there from His praise.

Moreover, matrimony is good in itself, but when men, for the sake of satisfying their lust, bind themselves under the chain of matrimony, they actually turn a good into an evil, and where they think themselves to progress, there they do not cease to become worse. But the man who loves his wife for the intention that he expects to become rich from it, without a doubt, he is striving to loosen the chain of lust; abounding with delights and riches, he does not boast that he has helped himself with the ordinary medicine for deceitful flesh!

Again, there are perverse men who even burn immoderately for their own wives on account of their beauty, and the more quickly their body is shattered by their passions, the more it is released in satisfying the desires of the flesh. But when they are delighted, they fail, and when they are made fortunate they perish, and when, as it were, they have enough to do to satiate themselves through coveted pleasures, they are miserably pouring out their powers of spirit and body.

For indeed nothing is more perilous, nothing more shameful, nothing more fetid for a man than to pour out his spirit in the love of a woman and to pant after her as for blessed rest. Certainly, after such a deed, that quickly begins to become worthless which, before, he desired with the greatest anxiety as the highest beatitude. Certainly afterwards he recognizes when he considers the brief delight and the lengthy anxiety, that in such a love he turned from the path foolishly and most shamefully. For it is evident that he was linked strongly by the vile chain of unmanageable vanity. But because he did not wish to turn himself to God with his whole heart, he did not recognize his misery before he had experienced it. And therefore he fell into the lake of captivity, because he did not look back to the sun of glory. For if he had perceived a taste of the sweetness of eternal life, carnal beauty (which is false and vain), would never have appeared as so sweet a grace to his spirit.

But, alas, because he does not consider this miserable delectation in the eyes of Almighty God, he does not know himself to be fetid and hateful, in fact, in his conscience, nor does he know how to tear away the illusion. Again, no one is able to give himself to the deceits of the flesh and not wander from the paths of equity. For when the fire of earthly love does not cease to inflame the spirit of a man, it certainly consumes in that spirit every moisture of divine grace and, making it empty and arid, causes its burning ever to swell.

And it also raises up the fire of lust from the fire of avarice so that, in an amazing way, the captive soul, maddened, covets nothing but carnal desires or to multiply riches—placing its end in them, continually lusting to possess them—whence it does not see the while, the torment toward which it hastens. He pays no heed to the words of God and His precepts, and because he hungers for those external things and visible consolations alone, blinded in interior and invisible realities, he goes toward the fire as if with his eyes closed. But in truth, when the unhappy soul has been pulled out from its body, it will know without a doubt in its manifestation, how miserably it has lived while it was in the flesh, where it had judged itself not only not to be noxious, but to be fortunate.

Therefore in everything we do we ought always to take more care about cleanliness of spirit than of body. For it is less evil to touch the flesh of a woman with one's bare hands than it is to pollute one's spirit with evil delectation. But if we touch a woman and nevertheless think in our heart nothing but good, it ought not really be called a sin, nevertheless, even if some temptation of the flesh may arise through this action. For a man does not fall into evil when his spirit remains fixed in God. Indeed, when the heart of the man touching the woman is snatched up into diverse desires or, at another time, is deflected further into an evil sweetness and is not quickly curbed by love of the Creator and the constancy of virtues, know without a doubt that that man supports within himself the fault of uncleanness, although he stands at a long distance not only from a woman but even from a man.

And indeed, if a faithful man is joined to a faithless woman, the next thing is that his spirit will be turned to infidelity. For it is the custom of women that when they have sensed themselves to be loved by men beyond measure, they ensnare their hearts through attracting flatteries, and draw them to those things which their most worthless will shall suggest before they tempt them through plain speech.

For Solomon was wise and existed faithful to God through a certain period of time, but afterward, certainly on account of the love by which he clung to women, he most vilely broke loose from his fidelity and from the precepts of God. Having been established in great wisdom, he was to that extent the worthier to be the more seriously ruined when he allowed himself to be conquered by the foolishness of a woman. Therefore let no one foolishly flatter himself nor, presuming, say of himself, "I am secure! I am not afraid! The caressing world can't deceive me!" when now he hears the most unwise performance of the wisest man.

Certainly spiritual fornication is also avarice by the fact that greed for the love of money opens one's inmost self to the prostitution of demons. When, in truth, before his too great love of money, a man who loved God, His true Spouse, and now deserts Him for the sake of inordinate concupiscence and takes into himself evil petitioners, what is he doing other than committing fornication and idolatry? Therefore, we should try to reveal our hearts as clean in the eyes of Almighty God, insofar as we are able to do so, and to stifle all these most poisonous delights, although they are stirred within us from time to time on account of our fragility, so that, nevertheless, nothing may be seen in our heart in the presence of God except the perfect and the best. For when we become vile in certain things from too great hilarity and when we rejoice in words and in what is seen, although these things and things similar to these can be done in the presence of God by the good soul, nevertheless we are not so ignorant as to conclude they can ever be done to excess in the sight of men.

And therefore moderation must be possessed so that we do not neglect to set a guard for ourselves with caution where we fear that we could be carried into an appearance of evil in anything. But it is good for the servants of Christ to cling to God because they receive the fervor of the fire of the Holy Spirit in the desire of Him, and they sing the delights of eternal love with sweetest harmony of honey-flowing Heaven. Whence the heavens—that is, the saints—have been made honey-flowing. They love Christ so much the more ardently as they realize how much more He has borne for them. For while the spirit of holy men is ingrafted inseparably into the love of eternity, it glories suddenly to have tasted intensely in itself the sweetness of the heavenly life with its melody.

Chapter Twenty-five – *Concerning perfect love; those things that are required for joyous song to result; concerning love and correction*

The excellence of the reward exists in the greatness of the love, so that without a doubt the loving man burns with inextinguishable fire and is replenished within himself by heavenly delight. For whoever loves more fully is placed higher in the kingdom. Moreover, that love is in the heart and where he loves his God more, there he experiences in himself the greater joy.

Therefore, they are mistaken who assert that the man who only rarely or briefly experiences the joy of love loves as greatly as the man who is, as it were, drunk all day long in its sweetness. For certain men love with difficulty, others with facility, but the love of God is the more blessed where it is the easier, it is the easier where it is the more fervent, it is the more fervent where it is the sweeter, and it is the sweeter where it is the more intense.

Love is more intense in men who keep quiet than in those who labor. Therefore, those who stay quiet continuously and love fervently are superior to those who at one time are given to quiet and at another time bend themselves to external ministries.

Indeed, nothing is better than mutual delight, nothing is more pleasant than holy love. For to be loved and to love sweetly is the business of all human life, the delight of the angelic life and of the divine, and the reward of beatitude. If, therefore, you seek to be loved, love, for love repays the lover in kind.

No one ever lost from a good love who did not let go of the end of love. He actually does not know how to rejoice who does not know how to burn with love. And certainly, no one is ever made happier in love than he who is carried outside himself by the vehemence of love, and who, by reason of the magnitude of divine love, catches up within himself the delightful harmony of eternal praise.

But this does not happen to him suddenly, unless, having been turned toward God, he shall have disciplined himself marvelously and ejected from himself every appetite for worldly vanity. For the most part, God pours His ineffable jubilation into His lovers. For the spirit disposed to cleanness received the meditation of eternal love from God; the meditation has been cleansed when it rises in spiritual song. For clarity of heart deserves to possess heavenly harmony and in order that the praise of God may continue steadfast in jubilant song, the soul is enkindled by divine fire and is delighted by ineffable sweetness.

But however much he may perfectly relinquish this world, however much he may continually and insistently pursue reading, prayer and meditation, vigils and fasts, however much he may go after cleanness of spirit and of conscience (so that thus he may, by habit, greatly long for the joy of the saints), however much he desires "to be dissolved and to be with Christ," unless his spirit clings inestimably to Christ and he languishes in sure and determined meditations, loving completely and concentrating without end, and unless, wherever he is or sits or goes he incessantly meditates on this: seeking nothing within himself except that he may love Christ, he actually will not receive the heavenly harmony nor will he resound Jesus and His praises either in mind or in mouth in jubilant song.

Since pride confounds most people—for when they judge themselves to have accomplished something that others did not love, they immediately prefer themselves to those others and undeservedly place behind themselves those who might well be better placed before them. But let them know that that man never knows himself to love who presumes to hold in contempt in his neighbor their common nature. For he does an injury to his own state who does not recognize his own right in another man. Whence he violates the justice of human society who does not honor in his neighbor their common nature. Therefore men wander from the love of God in doing this, nor do they know how to attain to His love, because they do not desire to love their neighbor as they are bound to do.

For either they send the sinner away entirely uncorrected, or, if they begin to correct or accuse him, they bring forth words with such great asperity and rigor that often those to be corrected become worse. For they ought to speak with gentleness so that through sweet words they may be able to draw them on. For immoderate correction drives people to sin the more vilely.

CHAPTER TWENTY-SIX – *Concerning the sighs, the longing, and the humility of the perfect lover; concerning the inequality of worldly love and the love of God; concerning meditation*

The voice of the soul languishing for eternal love and seeking the face of its Creator resounds. "Let Him kiss me," it says, "with the kiss of His mouth" (Cant. 1:1), that is to say, "Let Him delight me by union with His Son." Therefore, indeed, I am languishing for love, because I desire with my whole spirit to discern Him Whom I love in His loveliness.

In the meantime, however, let Him visit me with the sweetness of His love in the labor and struggle of my pilgrimage, and let Him attract my heart to Himself, by transporting it with the heat of higher affections, and (until I shall be able to see my Love clearly), singing, I shall meditate on His most sweet Name held in my spirit.

Truly, even in this world of the present, the man who rejoices to await the desires of his Savior truly flourishes with delights. For there is nothing more joyful than to sing Jesus, nothing more delightful than to listen to Him. For what is heard rejoices the spirit, but what is sung lifts it up to itself. And while I am cut off from those things, I seem to myself, as it were, panting from hunger and thirst, ill and desolate, but when I experience the embraces and kisses of my sweetest One, I abound, as it were, with indescribable delights—my Love Whom true lovers place before all others in love of His immense goodness alone.

Coming, therefore, let Him come into me, pouring in perfect love. Let Him also renew my heart, giving it perseverance. Let Him kindle it and make it fat, removing every impediment to love. Therefore, who shall say that he falls into the stinking uncleanness of the flesh whom Christ deigns to refresh with the heavenly sweetness of heavenly speculation? On account of this is delightfully sung in the following verse, "We shall rejoice in You, remembering Your breasts above wine" (Cant. 1:3), as if this were said: "We seek honor for You, glory for You, we rejoice in Your joys—having relinquished the delights and riches of temporal vanity which make their lovers drunk to such an extent that they do not even know the evils they suffer."

> And though we are not yet permitted to see Your face, nevertheless so ardently do we desire to do so, that if we were living in eternity we would not seek another love. For the longer we live the more ardently we desire You, the greater the joy we experience in Your love, and the more anxiously we pant for You. For by loving You continually, we transcend injurious things and reach prosperity and rejoicing in spiritual things. For that soul, O good Jesus, truly loves You who would more quickly choose to incur a horrible death than consent to a single sin.

Nor does anyone love Christ truly and perfectly who mixes anything into that love besides Him. "For those who love God, all things work together unto good" (Rom. 8:28). For perfect love overcomes suffering. It conquers threats because it does not experience the fear of a creature. It drives out every elation and humbly it yields to everyone.

Whence it is well said, "The upright love You" (Cant. 1:3). The "upright" are the humble—loving truly, neglecting nothing—who are permitted to live in the highest perfection, nevertheless behaving themselves most humble in spirit and in deed. Thus, whoever is a true lover may say within himself, "All excel me in contempt of the world and in hatred of sin, in the desire for the kingdom of heaven, in sweetness, in the fervor of the love of Christ, and in love of neighbor. Some flourish in virtues, others shine with miracles; some are lifted up by the gift of heavenly contemplation, others scrutinize the secrets of sacred Scripture. When I consider the worthy life of so many people next to myself, I succumb as the least among all these, as if I were reduced to nothingness."

Therefore they are the "upright" who bravely flee being bent by earthly things; longing only for the joys of eternity, they break loose from the appetite for all temporal things and flee to the passionate desire for divine love. And they are deservedly said to love God who march along by the straight road and in clear, shining love: there is nothing that they know or seek besides Christ.

Of those who act in the opposite way it is said through the Psalmist, "Let their eyes be shut, lest they see, and their back be always bent" (Ps. 68:24), that is to say, so that they may cling to earthly things and put eternal things after transitory ones. And therefore, the wrath of God is poured out upon them, that is to say, just punishment with the great force of enveloping torments.

For "the upright," having cast aside all simulation, incessantly strain toward the joy of the vision of God in heart, in mouth, and in deed. Nor do they bend themselves to loving any vanity unnecessarily, lest they be confounded in wandering from the paths of justice. Therefore, whoever desires to please Christ should not presume to do anything, either for good or for ill, against the will of Christ.

For it is very horrible to descend to the fire of Gehenna, but it is more detestable to wish to be delighted in a sin for which Christ is able to send one away forever. The soul truly separated from all the vices of the worldly and alienated from the poisonous smoothness of the flesh, given over, on the contrary, to heavenly desires and snatched up by them, rejoicing in marvelous enjoyment because it already experiences in a certain manner the joy of valued love (so that it contemplates the more clearly and is formed the more delectably)— even in this present time, such a soul begs earnestly for the most delightful mouth of its Spouse and for His most sweet kiss, crying, "All earthly things are an aversion to me: I experience the love of delight, I taste the drink of wondrous consolation and I burn assiduously for that sweetness—and may I not fall before a temptation too great, now kept far distant from me! Love makes me bold to call upon Him Whom I love, Who, comforting and filling me full, 'kisses me with the kiss of His mouth.' For I enjoy the more fully the longed-for sweetness, to the degree that I am raised up from earthly thoughts, and where the desires of the flesh are the more completely extinguished, the eternal ones are the more truly kindled. 'Let Him kiss me' by refreshing me with the sweetness of His love, embracing me tightly 'with the kiss of His mouth' that I may not be spilled on the ground and, by pouring in His grace, that I may continually grow in love."

As infants are nourished and sustained by the milk of the breasts, so chosen souls are fed ardently in love by heavenly delights by which they are guided to the vision of eternal brightness.

Certainly the delights of the love of Christ are sweeter than all the delights of the world and all the savors of the flesh; on the contrary, all imagination of carnal pleasures, all abundance of earthly possessions, in comparison with the least sweetness which is poured out by God in the chosen soul, is a misery and an abomination.

> For, however great the difference is between the greatest fullness of secular riches and the greatest in-digence of the poverty of this world, the difference is infinitely greater between the delight of Your love, my Beloved, and the delight of worldly joy which the carnal know, and the worldly work toward, and of which, alone, they boast. For they experience nothing of Your love in which they ought to delight so greatly.

For spiritual gifts direct the devout soul to love ardently, to meditate sweetly, to contemplate excellently, to pray agreeably, to praise worthily, to desire Jesus only, to wash the spirit clean from the filths of sins, to extinguish carnal de-sires, to despise all earthly things, to paint the wounds and cross of Christ on his spirit, and to sigh, panting with inde-fatigable desire for the vision of most glorious brightness. Such are the best perfumes by which the soul, made holy by divine love, is best anointed and beautified.

Chapter Twenty-seven – *Concerning true humility, both in adversities and by the examples of saints; concerning the manner of making progress; concerning meditation on the passion of Christ*

The truly humble do not judge the evil deeds of others, but only their own, and they praise not their own good deeds, but those of others. But reprobates do the contrary, because they rather look for others' sins than for their own, and say their own are little or nothing in comparison to others'. Further, they prefer their own good deeds (if they shall have acquired any) to those of others, whose good deeds they desire to minimize, at all events when they cannot altogether discredit them.

I have suffered indeed to listen to two things. One was when I might know my miserable self (which alone I have despised) to be praised. The second was when I might see my neighbor, whom I have loved in God and for God's sake, reproached or bitten by detractors.

But truly, you who leave the world and try to follow Christ on the road of poverty, desire to recognize yourself, because if you truly renounce the desires and deeds of the world, you bind yourself for the sake of Christ to bear cheerfully the enmities of the world, but to flee from prosperity bravely. For if, ignorant, you do not attend to this, you will depart, deceived, from the love of Christ. Do not wonder, therefore, if you are wearied by diverse anxieties, and if you are afflicted by various temptations, because if you resist constantly, you will be made sweeter and dearer in the presence of God. Remember, because "He has tried them as gold in a furnace" (Wisd. 3:6). For whoever experience inwardly the sweetness of the love of Christ, freely embracing tribulation, do not at all seek earthly comfort exteriorly.

For so great is the sweetness infused in the spirit of the

true lover of Christ that if all the joy of the world were united in one place, he would be delighted rather to run into solitude than to glance at it with his eye a single time. Nor, indeed, is this a wonder, for all earthly consolation seems to him rather desolation than recreation. For the soul which, in customary habit, is visited by the joy of the love of God and whose heart has not withdrawn from His love, is not able to be fed by vainglory, because it would more readily choose to die than a single time wish to offend its Redeemer.

Moreover, so that you may follow after this grace, retain by personal recollection the examples of your repented sins, and try to imitate the life of holy men so that you who are a sinner, nevertheless converted to the service of the Lord, may recover hope, through sinners raised up to the Kingdom and, through the examination of the life of just men, may restrain yourself from all elation. For through the memory of a better thing, the spirit of a holier man is made humble. For whosever life you will discover written or hear read, you will always judge that life as incomparably more worthy than your own. For such lovers of Christ are described, who, for His Name, receive the enmities and asperities of the world, hold prosperities and all vain joys in contempt, are saturated with contempt, shame and scandal, and are tortured in their praises. They live for God alone; dying in life, they are raised up to the fellowship of angels in the fatherland.

For I have fled into solitude because I have not been able to get along with men; indeed, they often block me from joy. And because I have not done as they have done, they have laid both error and indignation upon me, on account of which "I have found tribulation and sorrow, but I have invoked the name of the Lord" (Ps. 114:4).

Therefore, lest we fall into temptation, let us desire to go far away from all earthly desire and continually to keep in mind the crown of eternal glory so that, found keeping watch, we may receive the promised beatitude. In the meantime, moreover, let us make use of such measure that the concupiscence of the flesh may be able to be fundamentally restrained, and that the heart may abandon corporal greed by means of discretion, while the body persists, stable and always strong, in the service of God.

For whoever leaves all things for the love of Jesus, that is to say, he abandons the will of possessing, both persevering and progressing with joy, he shall say, "I have found Him Whom my soul loves" (Cant. 3:4). For Christ is found in his heart when in it there is felt the warmth of eternal love, which desires to be sought without disguise. For Christ descends into the soul in honey-dripping ardor and jubilant song, so that he who has this joy may boldly say, "I have found my Beloved."

But he who, when he prays, sees his spirit lifted up beyond the roof, even beyond the physical heavens (if he does not fail, but always more and more burns to taste eternal things), may await the mercy of Christ full of joy, for he knows that after a few years he will be snatched up to glorious contemplation. Whence, going forward by means of a humble heart into success, let him not grow torpid while he is attaining to the fellowship of eternal quiet.

Moreover, if in prayer the eye of your heart is snatched up to celestial contemplation, this is next, so that your soul, transcending earthly things, may advance in the love of Christ. Indeed, whoever in his praying is not yet lifted up to heavenly things, let him not cease (with discretion), to meditate, to pray and to keep watch while he examines the more sublime things, lest, cast down on the earth, he be trampled by anxieties and pressures.

He says, "Come forth, O daughters of Sion" (that is to say, "O you, reborn souls"), "and see King Solomon in his diadem" (Cant. 3:2), that is to say, comprehend Christ, truly the peacemaker, having suffered for our salvation. Look back on Him and you will see the divine Head crowned with thorns, the face spit upon, the brilliant eyes drooping because of helplessness, the back whipped, the bare breast bloodied, the venerable hands perforated, the most sweet side wounded by a lance, the feet pierced through, wounds penetrating through all the tender flesh, as it is written, "and from the sole of the foot to the top of the head, there is no health in

Him" (Isa. 1:6). Therefore, "Come forth" from your allurements and concupiscences and "see" what Christ has borne for you, so that your crimes may inwardly be cast far away, and your hearts may be educated to the fire of love.

CHAPTER TWENTY-EIGHT – *That the genuine lover despises earthly things and pants for heavenly things; concerning the avoiding of pride and the embracing of humility*

Pay attention, O miserable little man, to how the cruelty of coming damnation sleeps in the delectation of carnal pleasure! Therefore, you ought to resist those people who desire to carry off those things which belong to Christ, that is to say, the virtues.

For before your heart will be able to burn with the love of Christ, it will be free from its appetite for transitory vanity. For the mind loving by the spirit of Christ feeds on the love of eternity alone, and is also delighted in harmonious song. For if the sweetness of eternal love had already continued steadfastly in your soul, it would, without a doubt, destroy the licentiousness of every carnal lewdness, and would allow you, delighting in Christ, to experience nothing besides Christ. For you would neither fall down from Him, nor would you experience sweetly anything other than Him.

Since perfect men, when they have been stripped of their bodies, are immediately made present before the face of God, and are gathered into the seats of blessed rest, they are free to attend to Him, since they see Christ to be God. For those who begin to love Christ truly, afterward do not cease in the great joy of love to resound the loving canticles to the Lord Jesus with honey-flowing ardors.

But nothing earthly delights that man who truly loves Christ, because, beside that magnitude of love, every passing thing becomes worthless. They discern physical things with the eye of the flesh, but with humble hearts the just men contemplate with celestial purity. They are raised up by the flame of heavenly speculation, they feel themselves to be released from the weight of past sin, and they desist from the will of sinning again. Nothing earthly embraces their heart turned entirely into fire, but it is always trying to pierce upward.

Again, those who are ordered toward sanctity, in the beginning of their conversion, through fear of God relinquish the crimes of the world and of vanity, and then they subdue the flesh to strict penitence. Afterward, indeed, having realized the love of Christ for all men and tasting the certain delight of heavenly smoothness, they progress rapidly in devotion of spirit. Whence, ascending step by step, they flower in spiritual virtues, and thus adorned by the grace of God, they arrive, at length, at perfection, which dwells in the heart, in the discourse, and in the deed.

But the man whom the love of Christ has perfectly absorbed acts as if he were dead toward the desiring of these external things. He savors those things that are above, he seeks those things that are above—not those things that are upon the earth. Certainly his spirit, sighing with desire for the heavenly kingdom, increases in love of its Spouse and, rejoicing with infused joy, strips itself of the appetite for earthly things. Replete with the languor of true love, he directs himself with his whole spirit to seeing God in His beauty. Whence, the flame of that love having been kindled, he pants with a single desire for Him, and besides Him, there is nothing that he seeks.

For when the faithful soul ardently desires only the presence of the Spouse, it grows perfectly frigid toward every lust of empty glory. Whence it languishes from love, because it esteems all earthly things as worth nothing, when, sighing thus, it hastens toward eternal joys. For whoever delights himself in the love of Christ and desires incessantly to possess His consolation, not only does not desire human consolation, but also, with great desire, flees it, like smoke offending the eyes.

Indeed, just as air suffused by a ray of the sun and by the splendor of its light is wholly splendor, so the devout spirit, inflamed by the fire of the love of Christ and replete with desires for heavenly joys, seems to be wholly love, for the whole is transformed into another semblance as ineffably delighted as is possible, though its substance nevertheless remains. For when the spirit is enkindled by the fire of the Holy Spirit, it is stripped of all laziness and uncleanness and is made sweet by the torrent of desire for God—always looking up, never falling down, not looking back to earthly things —while it glories in the perfect vision of the Beloved.

Moreover, it is necessary to beware of all pride and elation of heart, because it is this which casts marvelous men into profound misery. For what ought to be more detested, what ought more fully to be punished (indeed, it is a great cause for indignation, and plainly an abomination), than that the most vile worm, the worst sinner, the lowest of all men should appoint himself to lord it over the earth, when for his sake the most high King and Lord of rulers has deigned to humble Himself to such an extent?

But if you consider inwardly the humility of Christ, whatever your state of life has been and however powerful in riches or virtues you have been, you will not find in yourself material for pride, but contempt of your very self and a cause for humility. Therefore, whoever despises sinners, pay attention to yourself, for, by chance, you may make yourself worse than all of them! For the proud, just man displeases God more than a humble sinner.

But when true humility is planted in your spirit, whatever good you do will be done to the praise of the Creator, so that, despising your virtue, you may seek His glory, lest, given over to vanity, you be deprived of the eternal reward.

Ponder, therefore, on Jesus; from the desire of your heart, let your prayer go forth to Him. Let it not annoy you to seek Him incessantly and care to possess nothing besides Him. He is a fortunate rich man who has such a possession! For this possession, relinquish all vain things of the world and He will conquer your enemy and lead you to His kingdom.

The devil, who attacks you, will be overcome; your flesh, which aggravates you, will be subdued; the world, which tries to deceive you, will be disparaged—if your heart does not cease to seek the love of Christ.

But that man is not sitting idle who, although his tongue may be silent, nevertheless in spirit cries out to Christ. Because the body is never quiet in carnal rest while the mind does not decay from desiring the things of heaven, such a man will not be found unemployed if he does not cease to desire eternal things, and he may be always avid for these things.

The meditations of certain lovers of Christ are swift in ascent and uniform in their course. They do not allow themselves to be bent by transitory things or to be transfixed in carnal contaminations. On the contrary, they do not cease to ascend while they are coming to heavenly things. For when the body is wearied in the service of Christ by the supporting of the spirit, often the mind is snatched up to celestial refreshment, and even to divine contemplation.

Moreover, whoever prays devotedly does not have a heart wandering about among earthly things, but lifted up to God in celestial things. But whoever desires diligently to obtain what he prays for, let him attend to what he prays for, Whom he prays to, and to what end he is praying—and let him love Him to Whom he prays, lest, like a reprobate seeking a reward from life, he be frustrated.

Since, indeed, the saints have such profound humility, they judge themselves to know nothing and as if they have done nothing, and they cry out that they are less worthy and more wretched than all other men, even those whom they castigate by censuring them. These saints, following the precept of the Lord, recline in the lowest place; nevertheless, that lowest seat of theirs receives, in the sight of God, not shame but honor, not disgrace or the detriment of their merits, but the reward of praise and of magnificent exaltation to which this humility has best disposed them.

For that humiliation renders praise to Christ, torment to the devil, glory to the people of God. It makes the servant of Christ love more ardently, serve more devotedly and praise more worthily—and it effects a greater fullness in love. But the more fully a man humbles himself, the more he exalts the praise of God.

Moreover, whoever perseveres perfectly in the love of God and love of neighbor and, nevertheless, in his own estimation, judges himself unworthy and inferior to others for the sake of humility, overcomes his enemies, procures the love of the highest Judge, and will be received by the angels into eternal joys when he has passed from this light.

CHAPTER TWENTY-NINE – *Instruction of the unsophisticated and of beginners desiring to love; concerning the avoidance of women*

The soul, the faithful spouse of Jesus Christ, casts out pride, for it loves humility profoundly. It abominates foolish glory for, desiring only the joy of eternity, it follows Christ. It hates carnal fulfillment and smoothness because, tasting the sweetness of eternal honey, it burns to experience always the love of its most dearly beloved. It does not possess an evil wrath, because, for the love of Christ, it renders itself prepared to endure all things for the love of Christ.

But it does not know how to envy others because, ruddy with true love, it rejoices with the progress and salvation of all men. Certainly, no one is envious unless he is, in reality, lesser and judges himself to be greater; whence, he prepares calumnies against others, lest they should seem to be equals to him. Or, if the other is said among people to be greater than he, or more beautiful, or more powerful, immediately, touched with the sorrow of jealousy, he is saddened.

But the soul which has been kindled even a little bit by the fire of heavenly speculation cannot seek that vainglory of transitory praise. From this situation it is plainly obvious, therefore, that men envy and bite at one another because they have nothing from the love of God Who is present in all the chosen ones. Where, therefore, there are others who love God, they desire for their comrades the same progress they desire for themselves.

Therefore, if you desire to excel in the love of God, let all earthly praise be abominable to you, and extend your spirit bravely to embrace, for the sake of Christ and in pursuing eternal things, the disdain and irritations of men. Choose more quickly to experience the torment of fire in punishment with the damned than to share in their faults with them.

But whoever loves Christ ardently and lives secure in His love, singing with luxurious joy, will find it more delightful to himself to fall into eternal fire than to sin mortally a single time.

Again, such are the saints because they live in purity; they despise all earthly things and, from fervor and from spiritual joy, they sing by making melody, who previously spoke. They burn with the love of Christ, they desire heavenly sights, and they direct themselves always to good works, so far as in them lies. They abound with the delights of eternal life and nevertheless they appear most vile to themselves; among others they see themselves as the farthest away and the lowest.

Therefore, try, you who hitherto have been uninstructed and a neophyte, to resist your spiritual enemies bravely. Do not let depraved thought rest in your heart; on the contrary, practice prudence against the snares of the devils. When an unclean imagining or thought contrary to your intention approaches your mind, do not desire to succumb, but fight manfully; cry out incessantly to Christ while you don the armor of God.

And if you desire to imitate those who hold the world in contempt, do not think about what you are giving up, but consider what you are holding in contempt. Consider with what affection you are presenting your vows before the face of God. Consider with how intense a desire of love you are offering your prayers, with what ardor God ought to be seen, and with what ardor you are languishing to be joined to Him.

If you hate every sin perfectly, if you seek nothing of transitory things, if you refuse to allow your soul to be comforted by earthly solaces, if you savor the things of heaven, if you desire continually to contemplate heavenly things and, most of all, the Son of God, if you speak moderately and wisely (because he whose spirit is melted by the honey of divine love and by the sweetness of the song of Jesus speaks only when he must do so)—here, in these things, and well exercised in this way, at some time you will reach perfection.

Certainly, God approves such contempt of the world. For

the soul that is delightful through the luster of its conscience and beautiful through the charity of eternal love can be called the dawn of Christ because, purged from vices, it flowers with virtues and rejoices with the delight of the song of jubilee like the harmony of the birds. Therefore, we should fix our whole intention to obey God, to serve God, to love God and in every good work that we do we should endeavor to come to God.

For what is it worth to desire earthly things or to strive after carnal love when we shall have from them nothing lasting except the wrath of the Judge?—that is to say, eternal punishment. Love certainly stirs up temptations of the flesh; lest one seek perfect cleanness, it blinds one, it hides one's committed sins, it hurries one incautiously to the commission of new crimes, it inflames one toward all depraved delights, it disturbs all quiet, it impedes one lest he love Christ ardently, and it disorders all virtues previously acquired.

Accordingly, let whoever freely desires to love Christ not take a backward look with the eyes of his spirit toward the love of a woman. Women, if they should love men, go mad because they do not know how to keep measure in their loving. Moreover, when they are loved they sting most bitterly. They have one eye of snares, the other of true grief. Love distracts their senses, perverts their reason, transforms the entire wisdom of their mind into foolishness, separates their heart from God and subjugates the soul as captive to the demons.

And the man who regards a woman with carnal love (though not with a will filled full of lust) does not keep himself immune either from illicit actions nor from unclean thoughts, but frequently experiences himself as fetid in his faults and intensely delighted in the committing of greater ones.

But the physical beauty of women deceives many men, whose concupiscence sometimes even subverts the hearts of just men so that what had begun in the spirit is ended in the flesh. Beware, therefore, lest in this way you have discourse, in the beginning of a good conversion, with the beauty of a woman because thence, seized by the illness of poisonous delectation, you may be dragged, knowingly deceived and rashly conquered by the enemies, toward preferring and fulfilling the uncleanness of spirit.

So flee women, with discretion, so that your thoughts may always be far distant from them, for although the woman may be good, nevertheless, with the devil attacking and suggesting, and her beauty also enticing you, your will might delight in these things beyond measure, because of the weakness of the flesh. But if you muse incessantly on the love of Christ and keep Him everywhere in your attention with fear, I judge that you will never be deceived through the false flatteries of a woman. On the contrary, however greatly you see yourself enticed and tempted by empty flatteries, if these flatteries are like so much sawdust and fable—which they are— you will hold them in contempt and to that extent you will certainly be everywhere the stronger in the joy of the love of the Lord.

Wonderfully indeed does Christ work in those He loves; He snatches them up to Himself by a tender and special love. But they do not desire the voluptuousness or the beauty of the flesh, they consign all temporal things to oblivion, they do not love the success of the world, and they do not dread other enemies of His.

Such men love intensely to be solitaries, so that they may run without impediment in the joy which they experience in divine love. To them it seems not hard, but most sweet, to suffer for the sake of Christ. For let the man who desires to venerate worthily the victory of a martyr perform his devotion by the imitation of that martyr's spirit and virtue. Let him hold to the cause of martyrdom though he does not undergo its suffering; let him serve patience, in which he will reach the full victory.

Moreover, the soul, leaving the foolishness of wicked love behind, goes forth firmly on the road to life, in which the pledge of the sweetness of eternal life is tasted greedily. Experiencing this consolation, this soul asks its Beloved to give it this customary consolation continually, so that it may conquer every transitory delectation, and to refresh it invisibly and pour into it the grace of perseverance, lest, fatigued, it fall in diverse errors.

But if any young man should begin to do well, let him always ponder how to persevere, that he may not become torpid nor ever desist from his good intention. But let him always progress in spirit, so that he may ascend from the lesser to the greater. Since he has left behind the darkness of error and has despised and ejected the poisoned sweetness of a seductive life, taking possession of the narrow road, he embraces the delight of sublime devotion. Whence he climbs by means of gifts poured into him by the Holy Spirit, as if on a ladder to the heights of divine contemplation. Here, refreshed and delighted by the ardor of eternal love, he abounds with heavenly delights, so far as it is permitted to mortals.

Then the beloved soul, filled by various disturbances and afflicted by the fire of temptations, is not able to experience the sweetness of love just as it is in itself. Nevertheless, having experienced the joy of love, and clinging to its Beloved by means of a stable course, however much it may miss that wondrous sweetness, it loves Christ with so great a desire that it will persevere for His love alone.

But how praiseworthy is His most gracious aid! In it the truest lover has experienced that it consoles the mourners, sweetens the desolate, calms the disturbed and destroys disturbances by dissipating them. The soul separated from the vices of the world and alienated from carnal desires is purged from its sins. Whence it knows as present to itself a certain delight of future joy, by which it is confirmed in hope and is made certain concerning the kingdom about to be obtained. And in this life it gives Christ from burning love and the ornaments of spiritual gifts, with the flowers of virtues a cup of delectable wine, which Christ, pleased, accepts; He, for the sake of love "drinks from the torrent on the road" (Ps. 109:7).

CHAPTER THIRTY – *Concerning the hidden judgment of God on backsliders who ought not be judged by us; a strong attack on the acquisitive*

But certain people are accustomed to inquire how it can come about that most who had led the harshest life and seemed to have abandoned the joys of this world utterly, afterward do not fear to fall back to their vomit, and ought not finish by a good end. Let us avoid in silence judging them with temerity, if we wish not to make mistakes. It is not our place in the present time to know the hidden judgments of God.

Moreover, all things, however He works them out, will be made manifest after this life. All the ways of the Lord are agreeable judgments. That is to say, they are true and just. He neither damns this man apart from wondrous justice, nor chooses that man for life without great mercy, which is also just. Just so, we ought to consider that "the abyss, like a garment, is His clothing" (Ps. 103:6).

On this account we ought to fear while we are on the road, and never ought to be incautiously presumptuous, for man does not know which he may be worthy of—hatred or love—nor by what end he may be about to withdraw from this light! Good men ought to fear lest they fall into evil, while evil men are able to hope that they may rise again from their malice.

Further, if men should endure in their greeds and wicked deeds, in vain do they judge themselves secure in the area of mercy, when, indeed, their iniquity has not been forgiven. For sin is never forgiven unless it has previously been abandoned, nor then, certainly, unless satisfaction is promised and the sinner sets himself to fulfill the promise as quickly as he can.

Moreover, there are powerful and rich men of the world

who burn insatiably in acquiring the possessions of another, and from their riches and goods stir up their earthly magnitude and worldly power. They buy for a small price what, according to its transitory substance was of great value, or accept, in royal offices or appointed by great men, very many treasures, without merit or repayment, so that they may be made powerful by delights and pleasures and honors.

Let these men listen not to me but to blessed Job. He says, "They lead their days in good things, and in an instant they descend to hell" (Job 21:13). Behold, they lose everything in a single instant that they have desired to acquire through their whole life. With these things tarried the wisdom of this world (which is called foolishness before God) and they recognized the prudence of the flesh, which is an enemy to God.

Afterward the powerful will powerfully suffer torments for, knowing God and glorifying not God but themselves in their musings, they have vanished; calling themselves wise, they have been made foolish. And those who have experienced the glory and delights of this world have reached to the depths of stinking hell.

Certainly, among all who are allured by the vices of the world, as I judge the matter, concerning none should so small a hope of salvation be held in any way, than of those whom the common folk of the world name "the grabbers." For although they pour out all their strength and youth in obtaining other people's possessions through lawful means and through unlawful means, afterward, in their old age, they rest as if securely, holding on to what they have possessed illicitly. But because their conscience is timid, their wickedness gives testimony for their condemnation. For they are simply ceasing from unjust exactions, they are not terrified to use other people's goods as they were their own property. Perhaps if they were to give back other people's goods totally, few things might remain for themselves, but because they are proud, they would blush to beg—or, rather, they couldn't endure to fall from their pristine honor. For the same reason, they say they are not strong enough to dig (Luke 16:3). And thus, deceived by demons, they choose to avoid worldly misery so that they may suffer eternal and infernal misery without end.

And then, while such men rule in the world and oppress lesser men by the power of their tyranny, for others, assuredly, the fact of their never having been exalted onto such a summit in this exile ought not be feared, but rather should be rejoiced over. For, lest His beloved souls should become like the "grabbers," they are restrained by God, as the Psalmist testifies when he says, "Do not be afraid when a man is made rich, and when the glory of his house is multiplied" (Ps. 48:17). For when the rich man shall perish, he will not take up all his things, nor will his glory descend with him; on the contrary, not a drop of water reaches to the tongue of the rich man burning in Hell. For, dying, he loses all his glory, and only his sin (for which he will be crucified in eternity), will descend with him to the dark land.

CHAPTER THIRTY-ONE — *Why contemplatives do not completely pay attention to external songs; concerning the error of finding fault with them; concerning the method of progressing in contemplation*

Since, moreover, in the church men and women singers, dedicated to praising God and stirring up the people to devotion, are ordained in their ranks, indeed certain men have come to me asking why I do not choose to act as the others do, although they often see me attending the solemnities of the Mass. For they have judged me to have erred in this, asserting that all ought to sing physically in the presence of the Creator and to sound the music of the external voice. On this account I have been silent, because they were entirely ignorant of the way in which I have sent forth melody and have brought forth sweet harmonies for the Mediator.

Moreover, they have judged that no one has received spiritual songs because they themselves are unable to understand by what process such things may come to pass. And if indeed it is madness to judge this—that another (if he is perfectly bound to God) may not particularly receive from his Beloved any special gift which is not given to the many, because they themselves have found nothing of such a gift in themselves—accordingly, I have indeed taken thought to lay out in a certain manner some kind of a response, and not to be altogether undone by the disapprovers. For what concerns those people about the lives of others whose customs, they are not ignorant, excel their own lives in many ways? And by how much the more are they superior in those things which cannot be seen!

But isn't God allowed to do as He pleases? But are their eyes wicked because He is good? And do they not wish to confine the will of God to the measure of their own? All men belong to God, don't they? So He lifts up those He chooses to life, He leaves those He chooses to leave, He gives what pleases Him to whom He chooses, and when He chooses, in order to show forth the magnificence of His goodness, doesn't He?

Therefore I judge that these people complain and backbite because they wish that others, superior to them, might come down and conform themselves to these lesser persons in all things. For they judge themselves to be superior, when in merit they are inferior.

Here, therefore, my soul has discovered the boldness to reveal to some extent my music, which rises up from the fire of love. In it I rejoice in the presence of Jesus and sound breaths of the most delightful harmony. Further, they even stand more extraordinarily opposed to me for this reason, that I have taken care to flee the audible songs which are to be made use of in the customs of the church, and also the instrumental melodies which can be heard by those standing around. (As far as this matter is concerned, I am among these things when necessity demands my hearing Mass, which I was not able to hear elsewhere, or because a solemn feast day has forced it, on account of the envious bites of the people.) For I long to be sitting so that I might attend to Christ alone, and so that He might give me the spiritual song in which I might offer Him praises and prayers in worship.

Those arguing do not believe me, and therefore have been trying to reduce me to their shape, but I cannot abandon the grace of Christ—and for foolish men who have not recognized in any way what I have experienced interiorly! I have endured their talking and I have done what had to be done according to the state into which the Lord transported me. Accordingly, I shall make this public, returning thanks to the glory of Christ, in order that they may not rave longer this way at other people of this kind, nor presume next, with temerity, to judge those sitting still. For what I have done by this undertaking is not from simulation nor by imaginary things, as certain men have interpreted concerning me. Many men have been misled by these people, suspecting themselves to have entered upon what they have never received.

But in truth, an invisible joy has come into me, and in reality I have been thoroughly warmed within myself by the fire of love, which has assuredly lifted up my heart from these lesser things so that, rejoicing in Jesus, I might fly a long way from external harmony into the interior harmony.

And so that I might detest contamination and I might avoid the vanities of words, I have struggled also not to take in foods unnecessarily, nor indiscreetly to restrain myself—however much I may be said to have given myself over to the homes of the wealthy, that I may eat well and revel in delicacies! But, God acting, I have kept my soul ordered otherwise, so that I might savor heavenly things more than the deliciousness of foods. And consequently I have not ceased, assuredly, to love solitude. I have chosen to dwell reserved, apart from men. Except for having gathered the necessities of the flesh, I have received my comfort continuously from Him Whom I have loved.

For without a doubt, it ought not be affirmed that anyone, in the beginning of his conversion, should climb to the heights of the contemplative life, or fully experience its sweetness, when it is well known that contemplation is acquired after much time and with great labor. It is not given all at once to anyone who wants it at random, although it is possessed with great joy. For it is not in human power to receive it, nor in truth can labor of any kind, however much extended, merit it. But it is given from the goodness of God to the truly loving, who, assuredly, have desired to love Christ beyond the estimation of men.

Whence many, after penitence, have fallen from innocence, again falling to pieces in sloth, on the contrary, and into the abominations of the Egyptians. For they have not been burning up in love, and have experienced the delightfulness of contemplation so superficially (and have experienced it so rarely), that they have been strong enough to stand when they were tempted.

Or, really, influenced by tedium and wearied by manna they desire the fleshpots, that is to say, they desire to dwell among secular feasts and consolations. Indeed, an appetite for the love of God makes the desire for the kingdom of heaven strong in contempt of the world and, with the reading of or meditation on sacred books joined to it, in the hatred of sin. For, usefully disciplined in these things, the devout and educated soul has fortifications against the darts of the enemy in readiness. Moreover, it is a confusion to the devil when we bring the word of God forward for every temptation.

Enduring in upright fashion and bearing the burden and heat of the day in patience, and never letting themselves be induced into the delight of deceptive sweetness, after many tears and assiduous prayers, they will be enkindled by eternal love and will experience the heat in themselves, enduring without end, because the fire blazes up in their meditation.

Therefore the chosen one, for the sake of love absolutely desiring Christ alone, and transforming himself into his Beloved, has no earthly substance nor desires to have any, but following Christ through poverty freely chosen, lives content on the alms of others when his conscience is clear. Formed by the savor of heavenly delight, he will pour out his whole heart in love of the Creator and will labor at kindling heavenly desires by daily increase, since, indeed, everyone turning away from this world, if he genuinely desires to be enkindled by the fire of the Holy Spirit, does not grow cold in leaning upon prayer and meditation.

For from these things and from the tears accompanying them, when Christ grants His favor, the spirit will be marvelously set ablaze to love. Having been burnt, it will be delighted, and having been delighted, it will be raised up into the contemplative life. Moreover, the soul goes forth into this excellence while it flies away through excess and is snatched up beyond itself, and to its mental eye an opened heaven displays secrets to be contemplated.

First, indeed, he must be disciplined assiduously through not a few years in praying and meditating, scarcely gathering the necessities of the body. Thus, burning in pursuing these things, he shall live, and having cast out all pretense, he shall not grow torpid in seeking for divine love and experiencing it by day and by night.

And thus from hence the Omnipotent Lover, animating His beloved to love, raises him up on high beyond earth-born things and the tumults of the vices and of vain musings, so that never shall "dead flies destroy the smoothness of the ointment" (Eccles. 10:1), for they vanish fully by means of death.

And thereafter, at length, love will become sweet to him, he will be made drunk with divine and most delicate sweetness, and he will taste the supremely wonderful honey, so that he may experience in himself nothing except the comfort of the savor poured into him from heaven, and the sign of the highest sanctity.

Further, having been anointed, he will try to guard this true sweetness—since the man who experiences in his senses and in reality his heart burning with the ardor of eternal love will certainly not separate his spirit from the light-giving mystery flowing with honey, since indeed those who were judged not unequal to him possess so great a love only through imagination. Because of this, those who exist not in truth but in shadows do not fear unworthily to usurp for themselves the first place, when they have been called to the wedding feast. Without a doubt, they will descend with shame in the just multitude, and will take the lowest seat. For of these men it is said, "A thousand fall at your side, ten thousand at your right side" (Ps. 90:7).

But O, that they might know themselves and pry into their own consciences! Then they would never become presumptuous and, comparing themselves to the merits of others, they would not insult their betters, since the lover of the Godhead whose interior heart is penetrated at its foundation by the love of invisible beauty, who has the whole innermost portion of his soul made glad, rejoices with the most agreeable fervor, because he has yielded himself to continual devotion. Uninterruptedly, when Christ wishes it (not through his own merit), he will receive within himself the song sent into him from the heavens, and his meditation will be changed into melody, and his spirit will linger in marvelous harmony.

For it is angelic delightfulness that he receives in his soul and that very song, although he will not resonate praises to God with those very words.

This harmony is similar in quality to that of the angels, although not so great nor so clear (on account of the corruptible flesh which burdens the loving man here on earth). The man who experiences this has also experienced angelic song, although it may not be of the same beauty on the pilgrimage as it is in the fatherland.

For the music belongs to the song, not to the verse which is sung. That praise is angelic food. In it some pilgrims likewise delight, rejoicing in Jesus, but by means of the most ardent love, when they have already received within themselves discernment of the eternal praise which is sung over and over by the angels to God. Hence the psalmist sang, "Man has eaten the bread of angels" (Ps. 77:25).

From thence, therefore, his nature is renewed and he is transported into divine glory, and the most blessed beauty, so that he may be both sweetly and divinely sonorous, because thereafter he may also experience within himself the delights of eternal love when he sings unweariedly with the greatest delightfulness.

In any case, on account of this gift, things fall out for the lover in this way. I have never found this in the writings of other doctors, nor have I heard it expressed—namely, that that song will burst forth even up to the mouth and he will sing his prayers with spiritual harmony and heavenly smoothness, and the song will become much impeded by his tongue.

For in the face of the abundance of interior joy and the singular sonority being breathed forth, he makes a delay, and what before occupied no more than the space of a single hour now often will fill almost half a day. If indeed he will sit solitary when he receives this gift, mixing himself as little as possible with others for psalmody, he will particularly not sing with other men.

I'm not saying that all men should do this, but let him to whom the gift is given do what he pleases, because he is being led by the Holy Spirit and his life is not led according to the words of men. Further, his heart will remain in clarity and fire, and he will be lifted up into marvelous melody. He does not regard the person of man, and therefore he is judged by many to be foolish or rustic. For he will praise God in jubilant melody. Indeed, he utters praise to God from his inmost heart and his voice reaches even to the heights with the sweetest song, which the Divine Majesty is delighted to listen to.

He has a beautiful face and the King desires his beauty. Accordingly, he holds within himself uncreated Wisdom. For Wisdom is drawn out from hidden things, and its delights are to be with the lovers of eternity, for it is not found smoothly in the land of the living. Moreover, it remains in him of whom I have spoken before, because he is entirely melted in the love of Christ and all his innards cry out to God.

His cry is singing love, for it raises a great voice even to the ears of God. It is the desire for the good, and the affection for virtue. His cry is beyond the world because his spirit desires nothing besides Christ. His inner man has been ignited with the fire of love, so that his heart, shining and burning, does nothing externally that cannot give expression to the good. He praises God in jubilation, but in silence—not for the ears of men, but in the sight of God, and with ineffable smoothness he utters songs, that is, praises.

CHAPTER THIRTY-THREE — *That spiritual song has no sympathy with that which is external; the motive and error of those who say the opposite; concerning how infused and inspired knowledge differs from that which is acquired*

But let the man lifted up in sanctity in this gift know that he is experiencing the song of which I am speaking, if he does not have the strength to sustain the clamor of Psalmsinging, unless his interior song is reduced to meditation and he has fallen to the recitation of exterior things. Moreover, that certain among the singers or psalmodizers are distracted in their devotion is not from perfection but from instability of spirit, because the words of others interrupt and confuse their prayers, a thing that certainly does not befall the perfected man.

Indeed, stabilized men are such that they are not able to be distracted by any clamor or tumult, or by any other thing whatsoever, from prayer or meditation, but through such things they are separated only from their song. For that sweet spiritual song is indeed exceedingly special, because it has been given to the most special people. It does not harmonize with external songs, which are repeated in the churches or in other places. Moreover, it is greatly in discord with all things that are formed by the human and the external voice to be heard by bodily ears, but among the angelic choirs it has acceptable harmony and is commended with admiration by those who have recognized it.

See and understand, men, and do not choose to be deceived! For I have pointed out to you, for the honor of Almighty God and our convenience, why I fled the singers in the churches and by what reason I have not loved to mix myself with them, and why I have taken to not listening to people playing on organs. Indeed, these things produced an impediment by the pleasantness of their sound, and forced them most brilliant songs to fail. Therefore, it is no wonder if I have fled from what might confound me; I would have been blameworthy in this if I had not desisted from that which I knew drove me from my most delightful song. In any case, I would have erred if I had acted in any other way, but I have not been unacquainted with Him from Whom I have received the gift. On this account, I have conformed myself utterly, so that I might perform His Will, lest He withdraw what He had lavished out of kindness on an ungrateful man.

I delighted, in any case, to sit in solitude, so that, settled outside the tumults, I might sing more meltingly and might experience, by the burning fervors of my inmost heart, the most delightful jubilation, because I might accept that joy without ambiguity about its rewards—Whom I have loved inestimably above all things.

Certainly my heart has not been made bestial in physical concupiscence, nor have I received from creatures the consoling song which I have rejoiced singing in Jesus. Love, indeed, was led forth to this place so that I might not stand still in a condition by which the unworthy are weighed down, but that I might be raised up above every height of visible things, both enkindled and illumined by heavenly fire for praising God, Whose praise here is not beautiful in a sordid mouth.

On this account, to him to whom is thus opened the window impenetrable to all men loving something other, beyond the One, it is no wonder if his nature is transformed into a nobility of inexplicable dignity, made free and light-giving. All who do not now know how to love and experience delight in Christ will be ignorant of that noble liberty in eternity.

Nor ought I, without a doubt, to have ceased from a most cleansed devotion on account of the detractors who have put their malevolent teeth into my innocence, and I ought to have conquered completely all impiety and to love those who have stirred up evil to a greater extent for me. And after that, grace for the lover might be increased, while he does not attend to words thrust out into the wind, but he will really extend himself in heart to his Beloved and indefatigably pursue what has been set forth.

And thus the affection for vanity vanishes here, and true love breaks forth in the spirit, so that the soul of the loving man, not growing cold, instead persists in comforting warmth and the heart might never be shaken from its continual thinking of the most dearly Beloved. Indeed, in this constancy, the excellence of love falls down upon the lover so that, lifted up into the fiery heavens, he is there ineffably set on fire for loving, and burns more fully within himself than anyone will be able to express. He embraces the ladder of the graces, and from them he receives wisdom and subtlety, so that he may know how to speak among the most brilliant men and so that he may boldly bring forth what he has deduced ought to be said, however ignorant and foolish he may previously have been judged to be—and may even have been.

But taught by acquired, not infused, wisdom, and inflated by involved argumentations, they have scorn within themselves for this man, saying, "Where did he study? From what doctor has he learned by listening?" They do not judge that the lovers of eternity are instructed by the interior Doctor, so that they may speak more eloquently than those taught by men, who have studied for the sake of vain honors all the time.

Moreover, if in former times the Holy Spirit inspired many men, why indeed will He not now raise up lovers to gaze on the glory of the Lord, when approved modern men are not unequal to those of prior times? Moreover, I do not draw this approbation from men, who often make mistakes in their approvals, choosing men such that God despises them, and despising those men whom He chooses.

But such men are entirely approved whom eternal love sets on fire in their inmost being, and whom the grace of the Holy Spirit inspires to every good. They are men who, marked by the flower of every virtue, rejoice continually in the love of God and trample under the feet of their affections all things which belong to the vain joy of the world and the false honors of a proud and execrable life. Without a doubt, these men are rejected by men, but in the sight of God and of the holy angels, they are commended as magnificent. Their hearts stand unshaken to bear all adversities, nor do they allow themselves to be moved around by the wind of variety. And at length they are carried away to Christ with sublime sanctity, when they whom men, choosing, will accept, are cast down into damnation and are dragged into torment without an end, to be crucified with demons.

Chapter Thirty-four – *Concerning the super-excellence of the melodious song of joy and that it cannot be spoken of nor written about; concerning the love of those who sing; concerning the pride of those possessing acquired knowledge*

In fact, not without reason is the lover of the Almighty snatched up to contemplate the highest things by the intellect, and for the singing of most loving songs breaking forth in the soul. He burns ardently and visibly with the fire of love, and he is enlarged into sweet-flowing devotion, living in the hymns which most beautifully breathe forth the honey of the Mediator.

Leaving off song, he is introduced by Him into every pleasantness and, a fountain of internal fervor bubbling up into delight, he is sustained within His embraces. The beloved, made drunk in the most intense ardors, is provided, by means of singular solace, with the vigor of a most agreeable passage. Indeed, glittering, he shines whiter than snow, and glows redder than the rose, for he is set ablaze by divine fire and he is adorned by his purity of conscience, walking in white robes.

Therefore he has been raised up to this condition from among others in secret, for in his spirit a melody remains and the honey-dripping fullness of ardor lingers so that not only might he offer rich holocausts within himself, and render praises to Christ in spiritual music, but also that he might stir up others to loving, so that they might hasten to give themselves up devoutly and perfectly in God. Thus it is fitting, even in this exile, for the man loving Him and clinging to Him in his whole heart, to rejoice. For that delight which he has tasted by loving Jesus overcomes every sense.

Nor am I adequate to recount even a little way the least point of this joy—for who can express ineffable fervor? Who can lay bare infinite sweetness? On the contrary, if I wished to speak this ineffable joy as it might appear to me, it would be as if I were to try to empty the overflowing sea drop by drop, and to force it entirely into a small hole in the earth by dripping it in! Certainly, I, who scarcely taste a drop of that excellence, cannot unlock for you in any way the immensity of that eternal sweetness, nor can you, made obtuse by your senses and made distracted by carnal musings, do so. On the contrary, if you had natural wisdom and were bound to divine services, you would be able to seize it. If, notwithstanding, you were to try to savor heavenly things absolutely, and you were to desire to be enkindled by divine delight, without a doubt the delight of that very sweetness would flow into you abundantly and, by filling it again, would drip wonderful rejoicing into the penetrable places of your spirit. For the fuller you will be with this love, so much the more capable of that joy you may judge yourselves to be. Certainly they will place themselves the nearer to God eternally who in time ardently and delightfully have loved Him.

But those who are empty of divine love, are filled with earthly crimes and thus cling to empty fables; they seek pleasures in the exterior good things, which are seen, and are forgetful of interior good things, whose height is hidden from mortal eyes; while they pursue transitory comforts with their whole intention, they vanish from glorious perpetuity in its elevation.

Accordingly, it is evident that cupidity will live in exile in the future, but love will reign. The opposite is done in the present time by many people, on the contrary, so that cupidity is often introduced into the royal hall by many people, while love is jailed (like one consenting to ruin), cast out from the kingdom into exile.

But nevertheless, love has discovered a small habitation in the hearts of chosen men. It withdraws from the proud; it rests in the humble. Many miserable people are deceived who imagine they love God when they do not love Him. They think they can let themselves be occupied by external affairs and can truly enjoy fully the love of Christ Jesus with sweetness. And they judge that they can run back and forth through the world and be contemplatives, a thing that those who love God fervently and have gone forward into the contemplative life judge to be impossible. But these "inspired" people, not imbued with celestial wisdom but inflated by acquired knowledge, judge badly concerning themselves, and do not know how to hold on to God with love here in this life.

Hence I cry out and say with my affection gazing upward, "O God, make me safe, for Your holy one is failing" (Ps. 11:2). The singing of hymns fails and the voices of the singers grow silent. The ardor of the holy lovers does not appear. A man, whoever he may be, declines into his evil way; the tribulation that he conceives in his heart he does not hesitate to bring forth into effect. Their days are consumed in vanity and their years with haste. Alas, the fire of concupiscence devours the young man just as it does the virgin, eats up the suckling child with the old man.

> But for me, O good Jesus, it is good to cling to You, for my soul shall not come into their counsel, but, sitting, I shall rejoice for You alone, Who grow sweet when You are praised, so that it may not be hard but flowing with sweetness to praise You continually, not bitter but sweet beyond all corporal and worldly delights to overflow with praise. Indeed it is delectable and desirable to devote oneself to Your praises, for everything that exists, created by such great Love, certainly gives forth fragrance with wonderful savor.

And thus the lover, burning with desire in those bodiless embraces, and panting to look upon his Beloved with his intellectual eyes (having been purged of all spurious and vanishing thoughts which do not tend toward the One), undoubtedly has this cry to his Creator stirred up and breaking forth from the inmost marrow of affectionate love, as if he were crying out from a long distance away. He raises his interior voice, which is not found except in the most ardent lover (as ardent as is possible in this life).

Here I fail through the lack of wisdom and the dullness of

natural talent, for I do not suffice to describe this cry nor even express how great it may be or how like a pleasure it is to meditate on it, to experience it and to utter it, even in the small measure I can! But I cannot describe it to you, nor will I be able to, for I do not know how to overcome my own senses—unless I would choose to say more loudly, "That cry is that song!"

Therefore, who shall sing for me the songs of my singing, and the joys of my affections with the ardors of love, and the burning of my loving youth, so that at least from my friend's songs of love I might trace out my substance and the measure of melodies in which I might be judged excellent. Oh, that he might become known to me, if by chance I might find myself exempt from unhappiness, and—what I do not presume to preach on my own authority, for I have not yet found what I greatly desire—oh, that I might rest with sweetness in the comforts of my friend!

Since indeed if I should judge that cry to be that song utterly hidden from external ears (which, and truly, I dare announce it to be), oh, that I might discover the author of that song, the man who might sing my glory for me—if not in speech, nevertheless in writing—and that he might draw forth by singing and linking notes those melodies which I, bound up in the most noble Name, have not blushed to utter in the presence of my Beloved!

And indeed this man, to me, would be lovely above gold and I would not exchange all the precious things that can be possessed in this exile for him. For the loveliness of virtue dwells with him and he examines the hidden secrets of love more perfectly. And then I would love him as my heart, nor would there be anything which I would intend to hide from him, for the song which I desire to understand he would express for me, and he would unfold the rejoicing song of delight for me more clearly. Truly in this unfolding, I would rejoice more fully or certainly I would emulate him more fully, since the fire of love would be shown to me and the sonorous jubilation would shine forth the more visibly. Also my clamorous thought would not be turned aside without a praiser, nor would I labor if I were in uncertainties.

But now the overwhelming apathies of exile weigh me down, and their aggravating molestations scarcely allow me to subsist, and when I will burn inwardly with uncreated heat, I skulk outside the door without light, like a dark and unhappy man.

Therefore, my God, to Whom I offer devotion without simulation, will You not remember me in misery? For I am wretched. I stand in need of mercies. You will lift up the lassitude, which binds me, into light, so that I may possess what I desire, won't you? And You will also transform the labor by which I pay back what I have owed into a mansion of delight, so that melody may persist where sadness was lingering and I may see in the beauty of His loveliness the Beloved Whom I desire, and may praise Him eternally, held in His grasp, for I languish for Him.

CHAPTER THIRTY-FIVE – *Meditation of one who languishes for love and his desolation in regard to a comrade; how he arrived at the fire of love in an orderly way*

O Jesus, when I burn in You with jubilation and the burning glow of love continually pours itself out so that, O most Loving One, I would embrace You fully, I am separated from that for which I pant most delightfully. In addition, anxieties occur and a vast solitude shuts off the way, and does not allow the swellings of lovers to be built into oneness here. But oh, that You might show me a comrade on the pilgrimage, so that my lassitude might be gladdened by his exhortation! And the chain of an indestructible sigh, if it is not broken quickly by Your most delightful vision, will squeeze in so many ways that it will draw Your lover to leave the confinements of flesh and by the intensity of his love to be thrust out in the presence of Your Majesty.

But in the meantime, exulting in Your hymns, may I be carried away sweetly with the companion whom You have given me, and may we be gathered together in words of sincerity without controversies. Truly feasting in the pleasantness of love, we might, by turns, reveal the most loving songs until, led forth from this external penitentiary, we might be introduced into the interior dwelling-place, at the same time receiving a seat among the heaven-dwellers who loved Christ in the same manner and measure.

Alas! What shall I do? How long do I suffer delay? Where shall I flee, that I may enjoy happily that toward which I hasten? I am poor and hungry, confined and afflicted, wounded and pale on account of the absence of my Beloved, for the approaches of love crucify me and hope that is deferred afflicts my soul. Hence the cry rises from my soul and melodious meditation hastens to the banquet among the chorus of banqueters desiring to be lifted up even to the hearing of the Highest, where, when it shall have arrived, it makes known its business and says,

> O my Love! O my Honey! O my Harp! O my psalter and canticle all the day! When will You heal my grief? O root of my heart, when will You come to me so that You may raise up with You my spirit, looking upward for You? For You see that I am wounded vitally by Your super-brilliant beauty, and my lassitude does not release me. On the contrary, it rises greater and greater in its growth and present penalties press me and fight me, so that I hasten to You from Whom alone I hope for my comfort and the remedy about to be seen.

In the meantime, who will sing for me the end of my trouble and a termination in tranquillity? On the other hand, who will announce for me the fullness of my joy and the consummation of my song, that from these things I may indeed receive comfort and I may rejoice with delight for the reason that I do not know how near that perfection, and the end of my unhappiness, may be? Whence I might bring forth the excellent cry and my voice might soften the hardness of my Beloved, so that if He whips, He may strike a single time and, punishing little by little, He may not forever laugh about the sufferings of the innocent!

From this I shall be able to be called happy, and to possess interiorly the most pleasant drink without any uncleanness and, my anxieties everywhere eliminated, to dwell in the perfection of sanctity and sound the praises of heavenly joy with the celestial symphony, since indeed I do so even among these disruptions. The ardor of love, sweetly sounding, has existed within my secret places and the honeyed memory of Jesus in my marrow. They bemused my mind as if with music, so that, delighted, enlarged in jubilant song which I received from the Heavens, I might not experience the poisoned sweetness of unworthy delight, a delight which those who flourish in beauty of the flesh possess, and that no turbulent earthly element might hold me.

O most beautiful One, and preeminently lovable in Your beauty, remember that on account of You I have not feared transitory power, and be mindful how I have cast from me every love which allures the incautious to all those things which prevent them from loving You, God, in order that I might cling to You, and that I might flee from fleeting beauties, which lead men captive and send mere women into malice. Nor has it pleased me to play juvenile jokes which, through their impurity, subject ingenuous souls to the servitude of folly.

Then I have not ceased to show You a heart touched by desire, but You have held it that it might not flow down into the diverse desolations of concupiscences, and You have sent into it the memory of Your name, and You have opened the window of contemplation to its eye. At length I, devout, have run to You in song, but first my heart has grown hot with the fire of love, and I have broken forth within myself in most loving songs. If You have not removed these things from Your sight, the greatness of Your compassion, by which You do not allow Your lovers to be consumed beyond measure in cold places, might remind You that You might mitigate (as I judge them) my miseries and might not turn away my lassitude from Your face. But my lassitude persists in my soul, until You will have given what I have desired with such great ardor. By love of You, my flesh has withered away and become worthless among the beautiful men of this life.

My soul languishes from the influences of this love in order that it may see You Whom it has desired ardently, and that it may stand by in these seats of celestial secrets, and that it may rest quiet with the society which it has desired, and that it might be raised up to that place where, among the hymn-singing angels, it might enjoy You perfectly without end.

For behold my innermost parts have boiled up and the heat of love has consumed the clogging of my heart which I have hated, and it has destroyed the disastrous joy of unclean friendship and the thoughts which were inept, and it has even uprooted abominations for examining. And thus, without simulation, I have risen in an orderly manner to loving (I, who before have slept in the diverse deviations of my errors, involved in obscurities), and there I have delectably experienced the delight of most agreeable devotion, where I grieve myself the more greatly to have failed.

Listen, I beseech you, my friends, that no one may seduce you. These things, and encouragements of this kind in the sight of the Creator, are emitted from the fire of love, and no other stranger, who is disturbed here in this life by the temptation of vain and useless thoughts, dares to draw forth such things from the immense delight. Nor does anyone dare to do so who does not continually hold his spirit directed toward Christ, without contradiction or being pressed by another kind of great affection round about a creature, so that the motion of his heart does not totally cross over into God because he finds himself linked to an earthly affection.

On the other hand, he is excelling in love whose heart has repeatedly sung songs of this kind of love, and hidden in interior feasts, he has not looked back upon external insanities. Further, wonderfully delighted in eternal desires, gazing upward, he raises himself into Heaven whence, burning with the sweetest delight, he is made drunk with a most pleasant drink of a heavenly exhalation and whence, placed before (rather, transformed by) the ardors of future felicity, so that he may evade all temptations, he is established in the height of the contemplative life and then, continuing his song, he glories in praise of Christ.

CHAPTER THIRTY-SIX – *Concerning the different gifts of the chosen; how holy men make progress toward love by praying, meditating, loving, enduring adversities, and hating vices; that love comes forth from God and that recollection of Him is necessary for the lover; that the lover neither falls in carnal temptations like others who are imperfect, nor is he damaged by the lit tinder God allows him to endure*

Moreover, the chosen ones who superabound in love and direct themselves to loving rather than to anything other with their whole spirit, have marvelously manifested to us the secret of lovers. They have received superfervidly and supernaturally the fire of love and, with inestimable affection, they burned for their Beloved Jesus.

For the beloved of God are disposed to various gifts. Some have been chosen for doing, some for teaching and some for loving. Notwithstanding, all the saints desire the same thing, and run toward that same life, but by distinct paths, for each one of them, predestined, climbs step by step to the kingdom by that path of virtue in which he is most fully exercised, although if that same virtue in which he excels should cling more ardently to the delightfulness of divine love, it would certainly be more powerfully assessed in the greatest quiet. Indeed, he really arrives at God, and receives as a reward that mansion and seat of eternal glory which Christ has ordained for His most perfect lovers to have forever.

Therefore, lovers who were recommending glorious songs of love used to say that the man who is chosen principally for loving diligently cares for and strives after that especially, so that his heart may never draw back from his Beloved, and so that for him the memory of Jesus may be like music at a feast, and in his mouth it may be made sweet beyond honey and the honeycomb. But the longer he has exercised himself in spiritual studies, the more delightful they will appear to him. Then he will draw his spirit away from inane things and depraved musings, and dispose it toward desire for the Creator. He collects it totally into Christ and in that fountain of delight he fixes it, and so that he may love Him alone, and in Him alone may be delighted, he prays incessantly. Then already do sweet affections come into his soul, and marvelous meditations, inclined to God alone.

Having ruminated on these things and with his intention stretched forth in this spirit, they affect him ineffably and, with great delectation and pleasure of spirit, they lead him to the contemplation of heavenly things. And they purge him from the appetite for worldly comfort, so that the lover of God may seek nothing in the world except that he may be able to live in solitude and there abandon himself to his single-hearted desires for the Creator.

But afterward, strongly and well exercised by praying and meditating, giving himself over to the most intense quiet, killing every impiety and uncleanness, taking on the arduous journey with discretion, he eagerly goes forward in the strength of eternal love and ascends above his affections, entering into what is opened to his mental eye, in speculation on celestial mysteries.

There also, a love that his soul has not previously known begins to burn, and (while in this love he is occupied in useful things), to boil up—now more intensely, now more mildly —as much as the corruptibility of the flesh, by aggravating and often pressing it down with various vexations permits, so that even the soul itself, anointed with heavenly delight and breathing out in heavenly blandishments, may animate itself so much in going forward in desire that it may even weary the soul to remain in mortal flesh. Nevertheless, it freely sustains the adversities that touch it, for it rests agreeably in the joy of eternal love, nor can all those things that happen take away that jubilation which, delighted, it has received in Jesus. On the contrary, the ineffectual machinations of the devil fly away, and the deceptive vanity of earthly honor rushes away into contempt, and carnal softness is neither sought nor loved.

Those things are really armed against the chosen ones of God so that, united, they may rush in unexpectedly to the subversion of those who hold conversation in heavenly things. But they do not make progress, but they are cast down headlong, for the holy lover of God, in the Name of Christ, unshaken, and as if without repugnance, may glory, saying, "You, moreover, are my guardian" (Ps. 3:4),

> so that the malicious attacks of hostile beings opposed to me render me unquiet

"my glory"

> for I glory in You, not in my virtue which, although it cannot be except from You, deservedly ought to be brought back to You in its entirety and nothing be given to me

"and exalting my head"

> that is, that same highest part of my soul by which the inferior parts are ruled, You protecting them. Raising my soul to the joy and contemplation of heavenly things, You do not permit it to be cast down by the vile delights of the world and involved in these inferior things. In any case, it is "the head," for You have made it fat in the oil of spiritual gladness so that it might be made stout by love.

"and it might be a chalice for me" (Ps. 22:5)

> that is, a cup of interior sweetness

"making drunk"

> my soul with love of the Creator, and calmed, I lie turned away at the foundation of my being from the love of temporal things and thus, as if with delight, aware of nothing of earthly joy or annoyance, I shall be led forth into an eternity brilliant with light.

Moreover, in this excellent smoothness of love, the conscience shines white, for purity persists there, and the heart glows delectably. And the spirit burns, made glorious by rewards, nor does it deign to regard the pleasures of this exile. On the contrary, it embraces more willingly the bitter things

of the world than it follows its sweet things, for, enjoying unfailing delights, it does not cease to cling to the love of Jesus
so ardently that you can overturn the order of the world as
quickly and as easily as you can call this spirit back from the
love of its Savior. For it hates all things that are contrary to
divine love, and it burns indefatigably to fulfill those things
which it sees and knows are pleasing to God.

For this man will not send away by whatever means any
pains or miseries standing in his way, but will hasten to do
the will of the Lord the more ardently on their account; for
this reason, he might look forward to suffer something of
difficulty. But he meditates or desires no other thing except
that he may truly love Christ and do His good pleasure in all
things, and incessantly.

And indeed, he receives this ardent will from his Beloved
in His goodness. And then, his spirit is enriched by devotion
from God Who chooses it, so that it might be such that he
might remain a perfected lover of Christ, so that it might be
made a vessel of election which has been filled full with the
most noble liquid of the sweetness of celestial life—and so
that the Name of Him Who has been chosen out from thou-
sands might continue in an indelible and perpetual memory,
and that he might preserve It within himself by continual
meditating.

Thence, through divine assistance, he shall cast from him
all impediments to love; he shall also continually be delighted
in God, for the darts of the enemy shall not prevail against a
lover of this kind. But he will receive from his Beloved security in conscience with the inestimable clarity of inner
sweetness, and he will pant to send forth his spirit hour by
hour, for, living in the intimate cry, he cheerfully expires
daily in the ardor of love, so that no vileness of spiritual corruptibility may remain.

When continual meditation on God has cast out every iniquity that the malignity of the enemies suggests, the fire of
love, lingering in the spirit in a real way, purges all the contagions of sins which are accomplished by inborn concupiscences. Nevertheless, established in the highest sublimity,

thus secure, it is brought about that he may be absolutely on guard against negligence, and that he may expel it from himself as a plague-bearing enemy. He may not lose solicitude and fear while he lives here, for where a man is better and more acceptable to God, there he burns more fully in love, and is further stirred up by these goads of love to a more earnest and stronger doing of those things which correspond to their state of life.

And through this he is always solicitous that the memory of his most sweet Beloved may not fall away for a moment from his spirit, so that not only in habit but also in act he may possess and meditate on Him, Whose precept it is, as he well knows, to love Him with his whole heart. And he fears intensely lest he be drawn to offend Him, even in those things that are smallest.

Not only does he extend himself and press forward with his whole desire to the fulfillment of that which is commanded—that Christ be loved with the whole spirit—but he is also seized by great delectation, so that he may never be made oblivious to his most dearly Beloved, nor, likewise, wish to be separated from His love, sinking himself down to temporal delectation, even though he might be able to do without punishment whatever he had the power to do. For he has experienced that spiritual caresses are sweeter than physical loves. On this account, it would be a wonder if he should fall down into such great absurdities, so that, having spurned spiritual gifts, he were to prepare himself to be subject to these fictions and this fantasy-like felicity, or, cemented in carnal beauty, he might desire to use those things which every holy lover of God hates. Without a doubt, concupiscence of the flesh has shamefully deceived certain people, and beauty, exposed in things seen, has sometimes attracted even the wise and the devout to illicit embraces, for they were not perfectly grounded in love, nor did they cling utterly to eternal love. Pushed into temptations on account of this, while they seemed to ascend, before they were able to arrive at the heights they tumbled further down.

But without a doubt, the true lover of eternity holds himself tranquil among temptations, and he earns a crown for himself in this fight in which others, unstable, are completely destroyed. Nor do those beloved of Christ cease to cut away all obstacles, and they pour out their hearts totally in the presence of the Creator. And in no way like those who have not fixed their feet in love: cast down, from the ladder of effort, they have become feeble. Rather, unchangeably preparing for eternal joys, they continue stably in their beginning, nourished and educated in the sweetness of celestial savor, so that they may shine for those who are outside, by the example of their sanctity, and that they may burn sweetly within themselves with the fire of love.

Certainly, however much they mortify the errors of carnal affections through their appetite for cleanness, no one in this life may be able to extinguish to the full inborn concupiscence, or to be so perfected that he may be strong enough to live in flesh and not sin. And in this regard, he will not be perfectly healed here, but in that fatherland where glory much strengthens the intellect in discerning God and perpetual peace attacks anxieties and vexations on every occasion and it expels them, so that there may be no anxiety of corruption, since indeed eternal blessedness consummates its triumph.

In the meantime, however, this spirit must keep watch and sigh in the persevering love of fire and desire to avoid the delectations of visible vanity. For he may endure in this condition even to death, but in death the kindling-wood of sin perishes, and the lassitude of nature, so that the chosen one, whoever he may be, handling himself skillfully in loving and strengthened with heavenly grace, armed by chastity against this same kindling-wood, may fight glorious battles and vanquish all who mark out lovers in a hostile way.

Hence, when battling in a healthy way, he conquers and is not overcome. He is raised up into admirable pleasure to which all his interior qualities give applause. For he perceives the mystery of love being breathed into him, and he ascends higher in warmth flowing with honey, and contemplates with jubilation the honey-flowing praises pouring out for the lover by means of the hastening to destruction (or, rather, to nothingness) of the carnal affections in their motions. Many add to this, asserting that there sounds in their heart a sweet something and a song by which they are seized, knowing, and are soothed, but they have not explained (so that I have been able to recognize it), how meditation is transmuted into song, how the melody lingers in the spirit, and by what jubilation it sings its prayers.

CHAPTER THIRTY-SEVEN – *That the true lover loves a single Beloved; concerning the two forms of rapture—by being taken outside the body and by the raising of the mind into God; concerning the excellence of the second*

The ardor of the spirit languishing from the beauty of God shows pure love, for it requires nothing outside of his Beloved, and it extinguishes internally all other affections. For thus freely the spirit in that which it loves is smoothly carried, and the very joining of the wills of the lovers is stably confirmed when it does not run to meet what would impede the lover from his resolution, nor force him to go back again to any other thinking, so that, loving with the highest felicity, it adds to his desire, and swiftly, every relationship having been removed, he runs into the embraces of his love.

Among these delights which he tastes, moreover, he experiences in love so sweet the secret sent into him from Heaven, which no one here knows unless he receives it, and bears within himself the potion which intoxicates lovers rejoicing in Jesus, and makes them happy so that they do not cease to hasten toward their sitting in heavenly seats and enjoying the glory of the Creator without end. Sighing toward this, pressing on to heavenly sights and inflamed to the marrow, all their inmost parts rejoice to be illuminated by splendor flowing with delight, for they feel themselves made glad in the most pleasant love, and melted in the joy of songs in a marvelous way.

Whence their meditations are honey-sweet in their ministry, for even by studying and meditating on Scripture and even in writing or dictating, they think of their Beloved and they do not withdraw from using their accustomed instrument of praise. Indeed, what a wonder it will be judged, when one spirit may be filled with two things at once, or at any rate intended at the same time. That is, he may offer his praises and loves to Jesus by singing, rejoicing in spirit, and at the same time, with this, he understands the things that are in books, and neither offends the other.

But this grace has not been granted to everyone indiscriminately, but to the holy soul, to the soul inspired in a most holy way, for whom the excellence of love shines, and in whom loving hymns commonly break forth, Christ inspiring them, and he resounds ineffable in jubilant singing as if already his hymn-singing in the sight of his Creator had been effected.

This soul, knowing well the mystery of love and rising eagerly with an intense cry to his Beloved, exists most acute and perspicacious in intellect, subtle in senses, not scattered by the single things of this world but entirely collected in one God and fixed in Him, so that in purity of conscience and shining cleanliness of spirit, he might serve Him Whom he is dedicated to love, and show himself too. Where indeed the love of the lover is purer, there God is more present and nearer to him. And because he rejoices more purely in God, he experiences more fruitfully from the goodness and beneficent sweetness of God how purely He is accustomed to pour Himself into lovers, and with what incomparable rejoicing He flows into the hearts of the pious.

Further, that love is pure when there is not now mixed in with it affection for another thing, and he does not have an inclination toward the enjoyment of another delectable beauty of a bodily creature. But on the contrary, with the knife-edge of the spirit cleansed, he is entirely stabilized in a single desire for eternity, and with liberty of spirit he continually looks up into the heavens. How is he to be seized by the beauty of another thing toward which he cannot direct himself, and which he is not able to love?

But nevertheless, it is clear that the word "rapt" can be understood in two ways. In one sense, indeed, it indicates that one is so carried off outside the senses of the flesh that during the time he is "rapt" he does not experience anything in the flesh, nor can anything be done by the flesh. Nevertheless, he is not dead but living, for this soul makes his body live. And whenever holy men and the chosen are "rapt" in this way, it is for their use and their instruction, like Paul who was "rapt" to the third heaven. And it is in this manner that even sinners are "rapt" when they are carried away in vision at any time, so that they may see either the joy of good men or the punishments of the reprobate, for their correction and that of others, as we read in many sources.

In another way a man is said to be "rapt" by the elevation of his spirit to God through contemplation, and this is the manner in all perfected lovers of God and only in those who love God. And this condition is as rightly called "rapt" as the other, for it is done as by a certain violence, and as if contrary to nature. On the contrary, it is truly supernatural that from a vile sinner is made a son of God who, filled with spiritual joy, is carried into God. This kind of "raptness" is greatly desirable and worthy of love. For Christ has always had divine contemplation, but never the absence of control of the body.

The one way is to be "rapt" by love while in the senses of the flesh; the other way is to be "rapt" from the senses to another vision, either terrifying or soothing. I judge it better to be "rapt" of the love in which a man may most greatly merit. For to see the heavenly things given as our reward does not belong to merit.

And thus they are called "rapt" who are wholly and perfectly bound to the desires of their Savior and who powerfully ascend to the summit of contemplation. They are also illumined by Uncreated Wisdom, and deserve to experience the fervor of Uncreated Light by Whose beauty they have been "rapt." Moreover, these things befall the devout soul when all its meditations are ordered to divine love and all the wanderings of its spirit pass over into stability. Now it does not fluctuate nor hesitate, but with all its affection drawn down into One and settled there, it desires Christ with intense ardor, extended and directed toward Him, as if there were no one beyond the two of them—that is, Christ and that loving soul.

Whence the soul is glued to Him with an indissoluble chain of love, and, flying through excess of spirit, outside the enclosure of the body, it drinks of the supremely wonderful small cup from the heavens, to which it would never have attained except that it was "rapt" by the grace of God from its feeble affections, established in the sublimity of the spirit in which, without a doubt, it received the health-giving gifts of grace.

When, therefore, the soul considers eagerly and with an unshakeable and free heart, only these divine and heavenly things, it sees its spirit "rapt" and carried away even beyond everything corporal and visible into the heavens (it is near at hand, without a doubt), so that it receives and experiences the fervor of love within itself in a real way. And then the soul melts in the song of honey by its sweetness. For he who is chosen for it gains this from that "rapture."

On account of this, "rapture" of that kind is great and marvelous, for it excels (as I judge it) all the actions of life, for it is judged to be a certain taste of eternal delight. And it exceeds, if I am not mistaken, all other gifts that are conferred by God on the saints in their pilgrimage for their merit. For in this they merit a higher place in the fatherland, for through it they have loved God on their road more ardently and more quietly.

The most intense quiet is implored as much as possible for seeking and retaining this "rapture," for in too much motion of the body, or by inconstancy and wandering of spirit, it will never be either received or held. Therefore, where anyone chosen is raised up to this state, he lives in great joy; filled with virtue, he dies in secure delight and after this life he stands among the angelic chorus, more excellent and nearer to God.

But in the meantime, he has sweetness, burning fervor, and song (which have been discussed at length above). By these he serves God, and loving God, clings inseparably to Him. But because the body which is corrupted aggravates the soul, and the earthly habitation greatly depresses the meditating of the senses, he does not always rejoice with the same facility, nor cry out continually and in all things with a song of equal clarity. For sometimes he feels more of burning fervor and sweetness and he sings with difficulty. But when he is "rapt" to singing with great sweetness and facility, nevertheless, although his fervor may be felt to draw farther away, often he even flys away into song with the greatest pleasure, and goes forth—and he may even recognize that that fervor and sweetness are truly present within him.

Nevertheless, fervor is never without sweetness (however much it may sometimes be without song); it even impedes the song of the body and the din of those making a tumult forces it to turn back into thought.

However, these two are present more clearly in solitude, for there the Beloved speaks to the heart much like a shy lover who does not embrace his friend in the presence of everyone nor kiss her amiably, but greets her in an ordinary way, as he would an outsider. The devout soul, separated from outside business as much in spirit as in body, and desiring to enjoy only the delights of Christ, burning for Him also, is soon present in sweet-sounding jubilation and, enjoying it marvelously, he pours forth melodies to Him Whose sign he receives, because he will not now willingly bear external sound any further. And this is spiritual music, which remains unknown to all who are occupied with the business of the world—licit or illicit. Nor is there anyone who knows it unless he has desired to have time for God alone.

CHAPTER THIRTY-EIGHT – *The desire of the lover for God is unfolded; the love of the world is made plain by many detestable examples; that mindfulness of God does not linger in the lovers of the world*

But I am binding Your love, sweet Jesus, within me with an indissoluble knot, seeking the Treasure Whom I desire. And continually I come upon lassitude, because I do not cease to thirst in You. Hence, like the wind, my grief will vanish, for my reward is the melody which no one among men sees. My inner nature is turned into very sweet song and on account of love I languish for death.

The light-filled excellencies of the rewards delight, and the advances of love torment with joy when they approach what they would sustain and, in the sustaining, refresh. But those things that show to the languishing lover his Beloved fail. They wound me that I may languish, and they no longer fully heal my lassitude. On the contrary, they rather increase, for languor is augmented with the increase of love. "Thus my life fails in grief, and my years in sighs" (Ps. 30:11), for I am separated from my Beloved and the desire of death is deferred and the healing of miseries delays. And with cries I rise up and say, "Woe is me that my exile has been prolonged!" (Ps. 119:5).

Love is that which torments, love is that which delights. It torments because it does not quickly give what is much loved. It delights because it refreshes with hope and pours in inestimable consolation in these ardors. And indeed it vigorously increases languor when, through the joy of love, the song of songs is present within the soul and the fire, abounding, supplies an increase for the sweet love—and nothing is so pleasing as to imagine in what way death is life.

For the flower in which this thought is happily cherished

cannot be finished. On the contrary—what may seem a marvel—the glory that continually grows greater in the lover makes death and the melody into one thing at the same time. For when I shall have come to death, the fullness of my beatitude, which the Almighty Whom I love is about to lavish on me, begins. My seat is actually prepared in the place where love does not know how to grow cold or to slip down into torpor. His love, of course, enkindles my heart, for I can feel His fire, whence the strength of my soul does not know servitude when I have been wholly confirmed thus in the comfort of love. I fail before love, and I expend all my time in holy sighs, and in this there will be no shame for me in the sight of the angels of God toward whose fellowship I pant ardently. By firm hope I expect to be consummated with them, and now praise, rejoicing, will more powerfully release the languishing man and the sweet-sounding beatific vision will show him plainly what he has loved.

But woe indeed to those whose days, consumed in vanity, have failed and whose years have perished with rushing around without the fruit of love. They languish with unclean love and for the sake of the beauty of putrid flesh, which is nothing but a garment of decay and corruption. Without sweetness they are led to death.

Indeed, the fire of cupidity and wrath falls upon them and they have not seen the sun of eternal light. These men go away into destruction; walking after vanity, they are made as empty as those things they have loved. Just so, when they shall be judged they shall see a Christ hard and unbearable to their eyes, for in this life they have not known Him soft in their hearts. But those who know Him within themselves here will see Him pleasant there without a doubt.

For the way we exist for Him now, so will He appear to us then. To lovers, indeed, He will be lovable and desirable, but to those who do not love Him, He will appear hateful and cruel. Nor is this a change on His part, but on ours. For He is the same immutably, but every creature will see Him in such a way as he has deserved to see Him. For like an object, He shows Himself of His own free will to each person as He chooses. Whence at the same instant, He shall appear pleased to the just and angry to the unjust.

Indeed, the love of a rational soul moves within it so that whether a man be good or evil, he is judged according to that love. Nor is there anything so efficacious for meriting the joy of eternity as the love of Christ, nor does anything more lead into extreme damnation than love of the world. Therefore, let eternal love inflame our spirits and let wicked and hateful love of carnal affections be expelled far away. Let the sweetness of the heavenly life inebriate us so that it may not please us to love the bitter sweetness of the present life, for "the poison of the dragons" (Deut. 32:33), that is, the worst malignity or the bitterness of deceit, is the "wine of the impious" (for drinking that, they are thus made drunk, because they do not pay attention to what the future may be for them) and "the poison of asps" (that is, a killing wickedness is a death-bearing drink to them). In addition, the condition is incurable, for their malice is incorrigible.

For the world has lying charms of miseries, riches of vanities, wounding flatteries, plague-bearing delights, false felicity, insane pleasure, frantic, hateful delight, a shadowed noon in the beginning, in the end eternal night. And the world has unsalted salt, savorless savor, deformed beauty, horrible friendship, soothing mornings, stinging evenings, honey that makes bitter, fruit that kills. And the world has the fetid rose, the joy of lamentation, the melody of dejection, the celebration of contempt, truly the nectar of death, the adornment of abomination, the seducing leader, the oppressing prince. And the world has the jewel bewailed, the mocking praise, the livid lily, the clangorous song, the putrid beauty, discordant concord, tread-upon snow, desolate solace, and a kingdom without resources. And the world has a nightingale bellowing louder than a cow, the blackbird voice ignorant of melody, the sheep wearing a wolf's pelt, and the dove raging more than a wild beast.

Therefore let us flee bodily and unclean love whose tail has a sting although its face soothes, whose flower is steeped in gall and who bears the breast of a viper, however much it may conceal it, whose savor cuts off the soul from God, and whose bath boils with the fire of Hell. Its gold is turned into ash, and its treasure will send forth sulphurous fire. This is the love cutting off clemency, madness full of charm, which does not allow the soul bound to itself to be joined to the assemblages of the saints or to be delighted with divine love.

For truly, to those who have their affection inclined toward the love of a creature of this world, it is ponderous and seems unbearable to meditate about God, although the memory of Him may be most pleasant and may make the thoughts marvelously sweet. For if they shall have begun to meditate about God, suddenly it slips from their spirit and they go back to their original thoughts in which they have voluntarily rested for a long time. Certainly they are joined by their evil custom, nor with such infirm and impure spirits can they savor the bread of angels—without great and lengthy exercise of spiritual meditations and the casting away of corporal imaginings.

For they have the palate of their heart defiled by the fever of injurious love, on account of which they are not able to experience the sweetness of celestial glory. Indeed, if, in some way, a thought of good should come into their spirits, when it does it does not linger there. The traces of divine inspiration suddenly expelled through the root of evils, they go from bad to worse and run there the more damnably, where they have not acquiesced in that good by which they are touched.

Thus, the chosen who have been inflamed at their foundation by divine love and cling inseparably to Christ, if at any time evil or unclean thoughts should strike their souls and exert strength to enter, soon, looking up to heaven, they cast them out and extinguish them with the fervor of their intention. They stir themselves up to You by that good custom, so that they take up into themselves nothing earthly nor anything of poisoned sweetness in which they may be delighted. For he whom perfect love burns does not experience sin or unclean pleasure. On the contrary, he exults in his God the more powerfully, and neither anguish nor uncleanness makes him sad.

CHAPTER THIRTY-NINE — *Concerning the many forms of friendship of good and evil men and whether friendship can be dissolved; concerning the rarity of friendship; concerning friendships of men and women; concerning true friendship and how the chosen delight in it in this life; concerning the lack of wisdom of those certain people who abstain too much or have been too much deprived; concerning carnal friendship; concerning the splendid dress of men and women*

Friendship is the joining of wills, agreeing to these things and dissenting from these things. This friendship can exist between good persons and between bad persons, but with differing affections.

The greatest friendship ought to exist between God and the soul that holds its will conformed to the divine will in all things, so that what God wills the soul itself wills, and what God does not will the soul itself does not will. Thus indeed the friendship between them will be full.

But in human affections, where there is true friendship, it would not be fitting that distance of bodies create a separation of souls. Rather, the indissoluble bond of cemented friendship more strongly relieves the desolation of physical distance, and the friend judges himself as living with his friend when he sees the constancy of indissoluble wills. This, indeed, is true friendship, when the friend holds himself toward his friend as toward himself, when the friend is another self, and he loves him for his own sake, not for the useful thing that he hopes he will receive from him.

But, it may be asked, if one of the friends should err, should the friendship be dissolved by the other? For certain men have claimed that there can be no perfect friendship except between those who are alike according to virtue. But how is that friendship perfect which can be dissolved by erring, even a single time? Now it is not perfect, and thus, little by little, it can come down to nothingness—which is contrary to the reason for true friendship, by which one is loved for his own sake, not for the sake of his usefulness or delight. Since indeed it is not necessary among friends for the one to be changed on account of the change of the other, friendship, when it is a virtue, is impossible to be laid aside in anyone without his change.

Therefore it is not necessary that friendship be laid aside on account of the error of one. On the contrary, if it were true friendship, it would be the more solicitous to call back the erring one, although it might be suitable that friendship be called love where it wishes and procures good for the friend as far as the very self, and can be disrupted by no error while they both live.

For friendships are easily dissolved when there are not discovered in the friend those things on account of which he is loved, that is, when the friendships are not useful and delectable (for which things friends are now loved). And such friendship is a fiction, because it is not able to endure unless it retains its delectability and usefulness.

But that, by reason of which there is a true friendship, is not dissolved in the friends while they are alive. Therefore, neither is true friendship dissolved while they are alive. But though one person errs, the other can still live; therefore the friendship can still endure if it is forever true, even though one party goes astray. For each loves the other for his own sake, that is, according as they are good. ("Good" must be understood not as goodness of behavior, but as goodness of nature.) For nature forces a man to seek for himself a faithful friend, and when he intends to protect faith and gratitude he does nothing in vain. Therefore, that friendship which is natural may not be dissolved while nature exists unless (in an injury of its nature), nature, beloved, should resist—which nature is in no way able to do unless it has been oppressed by corrupt customs. Therefore the friendship kindled by anything that is not itself the thing that is loved fails, and is extinguished, while the very thing that incited love is not possessed—so that if habits or wealth or beauty should make friendship continue, by the habits' straying, the wealth's failing, the beauty's annihilation, the friendship likewise vanishes, and of him who had such a friendship is it said: there is nothing more unhappy than to have been happy.

But the friendship that nature stirs in friends is cast down by no poverty, is erased by no error, is ended by no deformity while the nature that is the cause of that friendship exists.

Such friendship is purely natural, and therefore neither meritorious nor demeritorious (unless it works something contrary to the law of God), and further, it has great delight connected with it, in which there is also neither merit nor demerit. For true friendship cannot exist without the mutual delight of the friends, their desirable conversation and the speaking of consolation. This friendship, if it has been shaped by the grace of God and is made whole in God, brings everything back to God and tends to Him, is then called a holy friendship and is greatly meritorious.

But if on account of this friendship anything contrary to the divine Will is done by the friends, it is a perverse friendship, fetid and most unmeritorious.

Moreover, I do not know by what misfortune it now occurs that with difficulty and rarely is a faithful friend to be found. All seek those things that are theirs. No one has a friend of whom he says, "He is to me another self." For they sink down to their own uses and delights and they do not blush even to perpetrate fraud on their very friends; whence it is plain that they are friends not truly but feignedly, for they do not love men but direct themselves either to the good things of men or to their adulations and their favors.

Further, although friendship between men and women may be perilous (for delectable beauty easily allures the fragile soul and temptation seen gives rise to concupiscence of the flesh and often leads to pollution of the spirit and of the body, and thus the familiarity of women to men commonly proves detrimental to virtue), nevertheless, such friendship is not illicit but, on the contrary, meritorious if it is undertaken with a good spirit and is loved for the sake of God and not for carnal delight.

For if women see themselves despised by men, they might complain about God, Who has created them such that men hold them in contempt, and they might perhaps despair of their salvation, even judge themselves desolate if they do not receive counsel or aid from men. Certainly, reason works less vigorously in them, whence they are easily led astray and quickly overcome. On account of this they have very great need for the counsel of good men. But they are badly managed by bad men, for they are much more prone to the delight of the flesh than to the clarity of sanctity.

There is a certain natural love of a man for a woman and of a woman for a man which no one lacks, not even a holy man, following the nature instituted by God from the beginning. Through this love existing together and in harmony with one another, they rejoice companionably by natural instinct. Indeed, this love further keeps their delights as in mutual conversations and in honorable touches and in a pleasing sharing of life. Nevertheless, through this love a man merits nothing unless it has been shaped by Love, nor does he lose merit unless it has been blackened by a fault. For if evil motions should surge up, from which they should think of desire and tend toward it, without a doubt they belong to death for that deed, for they sin against God.

Therefore they are shamefully mistaken who say that all our deeds, whether interior or exterior, are meritorious or unmeritorious, for they strive to destroy natural delights and actions, or at least they contend that these things are not within us, and thus they do not fear to introduce confusion to a noble nature.

But that friendship or familiarity of men and women is illicit and prohibited by which, having been filled full with the pleasures of carnal affections, they come together in vile concupiscence and, putting eternal things behind them for temporal comforts, they seek to flourish by corporal loves. These people fail seriously besides, and they most of all who have received Holy Orders. These come to mere women like sinners, saying that they are dying for love of them, and almost consumed with immense desire and the conflict of their thoughts—and thus these men lead these light and unstable women on to a misery of life, present and future. But these men will not remain unpunished, for they carry with them their damnation, of which, through the Psalmist, it is said, "An open sepulcher is their mouth, by their tongues they acted deceitfully; judge them, O God!" (Ps. 5:11).

For God wishes women neither to be absolutely despised by men nor to be seduced through their empty flatteries, but to be instructed faithfully and lovingly in all sanctity and virtuousness for the salvation of their soul and body. But now there is rarely found a man who does so. Nay, rather (which is to be mourned), they desire to mold them either for rewards or to acquire their own peculiarity. Whence it frequently happens that if they instruct in one thing, they destroy and confound in another, and lest they offend, they either do not wish or do not dare to forbid those things which it pleases women to use—however bad these are.

But this is true friendship—the consolidation of loving people, the consolation of spirits, the relief of anxiety, the expulsion of worldly sorrow, the reformation of sinners, the augmentation of sanctity, the diminution of wickedness, the multiplication of the merits of good men—when a friend is drawn in turn by his friend from evil through healthful counsel, and is enkindled to do good, when he considers in his friend the grace which he desires to have within himself.

Therefore, holy friendship ought not to be spurned. It has the medicine for every misery. For it is from God that, among the calamities of this exile we may be restored by the counsel and helps of our friends, while we are coming to Him where we shall all be disciples of God and, in eternal seats blessedly gathered together in Him Whom we have loved and in Whom and for Whom we have friends, we shall glory without end.

From that friendship I can except no one, however holy, who needs it—unless by chance there be someone such that to him not men but angels should minister. But there are some who rejoice in divine love and are so inebriated by His sweetness that they can say, "My soul refuses to be comforted by the things of earth" (Ps. 76:3)—that is, by the consolation by which lovers of the world comfort one another. Nevertheless it is fitting that they be delighted, according to nature and according to grace, in these things that are necessary to the body and in men.

For who eats or sleeps or accepts relief from heat or cold without delight? Who has a friend and is not delighted in his presence by his conversation, his sharing of life, and his partaking of good? No one, certainly, unless he is insensate and lacking in reason, for in these things and in others of this kind, human life is comforted, even that which is holiest and rejoices the more fully in God.

Therefore the sentence "My spirit refuses to be consoled by the things of earth" (Ps. 76:3) is not to be understood of such things, but of fetid and unclean things, and of the illicit consolations of the things of the world. For after this is said, "For You have delighted me, O Lord, in the things You have made, and in the works of Your hands I shall exult" (Ps. 91:5). Who refuses to accept that consolation, who confesses himself to exult in the works of God? "But the unwise man does not recognize these things, and the foolish man does not understand them" (Ps. 91:7).

But certain men who have the zeal of God, but not according to knowledge, who when they desire to cast away superfluities are even led incautiously to cut off from necessities, judge it not possible to please God unless they afflict themselves immoderately through too much abstinence and bareness. And although pallor of face may be the beauty of the solitary, it is not nevertheless their service rightly ordered, for although they are commanded to castigate their body and to reduce it to the servitude of the spirit, nevertheless these things are maintained not to kill, but to serve for the honor of God, until He Who has joined them together shall separate the soul from the body. Therefore such men as are harsh to men and bitter in themselves also do not recognize the protection of friendship, for they have not held to its way.

Love of blood-kin, indeed, if it is immoderate, is called carnal affection and ought to be disturbed, for it impedes one from the love of God. But if it is moderate it is called natural and does not disturb one from divine service, for nature, as far as it is of this kind, does not work against the Maker of nature.

Finally, the women of our time are justly reprehensible who, in so great and such marvelous vanity, have invented new ornaments, as much for the head as for the body, and have led forth these invented things because they inflict horror and astonishment on the beholders! For not only is it contrary to the command of the Apostle that they proceed, in gold and in the twisting of hair, as servants of pomp and lasciviousness, but even contrary to human honesty and divinely instituted nature, they place on their heads horns for themselves, wide and horrendous in magnitude, made from hair not rooted in them! Of these women certain ones, studying either to veil their shame or to augment their beauty, color their faces with the rouge of an impure deceit, and whiten them. Further, both men and women use up garments cut out by the new fashion, not considering what may be becoming to nature, but what the new vanity of rumor, suggested by the devil, may introduce.

Moreover, if any very rare man should wish to correct them concerning such things, he would be laughed at and they would rather reflect upon an inane fable than upon emendation. Therefore they go away and they fall. They are captured and they are ensnared. These ladies, and the women who are called free-born, may wish to be decorated for time and to be deformed in eternity, for after glory has been finished, they will experience infernal punishment. In this life they loved, not Christ, but the most vile vanity of the world, crowning themselves with roses beforehand, that they might wither—but now, let us pass on to other things.

CHAPTER FORTY – *That at all times and in every act there ought to be intermingled the love of God, which does not fail either in prosperity or in adversity; concerning its excellence and a comparison of it; concerning tears converted into melody.*

The love of God takes up to itself with marvelous rejoicing the soul of the man whom it perfectly penetrates and sets it truly ablaze by the fire of the Holy Spirit, and does not permit it to stray for a moment from the memory of so great a love. It ties the spirit of the lover so that it does not fly away toward vain things and continually tends in to the Beloved.

We are able, certainly, if we are true lovers of our Lord Jesus Christ, to meditate on Him while we go on, and to hold on to the song of His love while we sit in the assembly, and we shall be able to keep the memory of Him at the table, even in the very tastes of food and drink. But we ought to praise God for every little morsel of food or every small cup of drink, and among the intervals of the acceptance of nourishment and of small morsels, we ought to resound these praises with honeyed sweetness and spiritual cry and desire. We ought to pant toward Him in the midst of feasts.

And if we should be engaged in manual labor, what prevents us from raising our heart to heavenly things and from retaining the thought of eternal love without ceasing? And thus at every time of our life we should be burning with fervor, not torpid; nor will anything remove our heart from this love, except for sleep.

Oh, how great the joy and gladness that flows into the lover! Oh, what blessed and truly desirable sweetness fills his soul! For love is life, lasting without an end, where it is fixed and made solid in Christ, when neither prosperities nor adversities will be strong enough to change that love following its loving affection rooted in heavenly things, as the wisest men have recorded. Then, without a doubt, it turns night into day, shadows into light, annoyance into melody, punishment into pleasure, and labor into the sweetest rest.

For this love is not imaginary or simulated, but true and perfected, directed inseparably toward Christ, resounding melody to the Beloved with harmony. And if you have loved in that manner (as I have shown), you will stand glorious with the best and the most honorable in the kingdom of God for that life-giving vision Itself.

But in the meantime, you shall valiantly overcome all attacks of demons, all insurgent motions of the flesh and of concupiscences for worldly things in the ardor of love and the strength of prayer. You shall also conquer the delight in apparent loveliness, so that you shall not wish for the sake of anything that can be valued to be dishonored a single time. With this, certainly, you will abound with internal feasts and you will experience the delights of eternal love, so that you will recognize the sign in certitude, and as if in knowledge, that you are a lover of the Eternal King. Nevertheless, this does not happen to anyone unless either God has given it to him or he has truly experienced, lingering within himself in this life, a great part of his future reward.

But what do I say about these things to those others who, although they are chosen, nevertheless have not had that potion? I wonder now and then about myself, because I have spoken concerning the excellence of the lovers of God, as if anyone who wanted to would be strong enough to ascend to that reality, when it is not done by flying nor by running but by Christ's loving and elevating and accepting.

Actually the smallness of my natural capacity does not know how to open up that which, like a stutterer, I have tried in every way to show. Nevertheless, I was compelled to say something concerning the ineffable, so that those listening or reading might desire to imitate, discovering that every love of a worldly thing, however beautiful and pleasing, when compared to divine love is a sorrow and a misery.

On account of this, look to your intelligence and know how greatly the Lord has done wonders for His lover and has lifted him up on high, nor allowed him to be cast down into unworthy, vain love, but has guarded him within Himself most pleasantly, to love stably.

Indeed, love is continuing thought with inborn desire for the beautiful, the good, and the lovable, for if a thing that I love is beautiful and not good, I prove that I love it unworthily, but if it is good it ought to be loved.

But love of a creature, although it may be good and beautiful, has been forbidden to me, so that I may offer and reserve all my love for the fountain of goodness and beauty—so that He may be my Love Who is my God and my Jesus. For He alone has beauty and goodness from Himself. No other things whatever are beautiful and good except from Him, and the nearer they approach to Him the more beautiful and the better they are. Therefore He is most fittingly loved Who contains all those things in Himself that ought to be sought by a lover. Since He withdraws nothing from his share, He is the rather able to be loved most ardently.

For if I loved anything else my conscience would bite me, because I would not be loving rightly. I fear lest that which I am loving would not thus love me back, and if I were not to be afraid about that, nevertheless I would be struck here by death, which separates those loving badly and devastates all their vanity.

Besides, often adverse things occur that disturb the serenity and delight of lovers, but he who loves God truly and with his whole heart exists so much the more purely in conscience as he knows himself the more burning in divine love. Whence he experiences his most loving Beloved, from Whose sweetness death cannot separate him. On the contrary, he finds his Beloved perfectly then, when he passes from this world and is most truly joined to Him, so that then he may never be placed at a distance from Him, but may run eagerly into His most delightful embraces and may glory without end, seeing plainly Him Whom he has loved, Him Whom he has desired.

And thus I compare this love to inextinguishable fire, which no force of hostile power can cast down, and the softness of no flatterer can conquer. This love purges us from our sins and in immense ardor burns up all obstacles which would impede us from loving, and in the most fervid flames of divine love it renders us more shining than gold and more light-filled than the sun. That love brings us spiritual medicine—nor, I judge, is there anything among all those things that can be listed by the clerics that thus sustains and calms us, and purges us from every stain of iniquity, as burning love of the Godhead and continual meditation on the Creator.

Tears customarily wash us clean from sins and sorrow of heart removes damnation, but ardent love exceeds all these inconceivably, and makes the soul most excellently resplendent, whence, and for all that we can do, it acquires the heart of the Eternal King and deserves to contemplate Him in singing joy.

I am not saying that tears are useless, nor am I saying that sorrow of heart is unsuitable, or that it ought not be loved in this exile. But I admire anyone in such great rapture of love from jubilant song that he cannot weep in his devotion, either in praying or in meditating. On the contrary, I proclaim and declare that song to be more truly prayer, and the meditation of so great a lover, converted into song and melting in a melody of heavenly sweetness, so that an angelic, rather than a human, song resounds. In this rapture, marked out with honey-flowing fervor, he is raised up, not to mourning but to rejoicing, so that as if tears had been withdrawn, he rejoices continually in the very fountain of truth and eternal joy.

And although our doctors assert that perfected men ought to weep, and where they are the more perfect, there they are in tears the more abundant, as much on account of the miseries of life as for love of the fatherland. Indeed, for me a marvelous languor flows out in divine love, and the compunction of physical tears has ceased for the greatness of inner sweetness. Moreover, the man who does not burn with eternal love must, of necessity, be purged with tears, but for the man who languishes with love of eternity, love is sufficient as a torture for him! For there is no wound more serious, nor more sweet, than that of love. Certainly, although such a man may implore it, he is not permitted to weep. Most greatly, in secret devotion, raised by the Holy Spirit to that place, then his spirit rises upward and with the sweetness of angelic delight he sings to God his praises and loving meditations.

For if the seat of love is on high, for it moves quickly even into the Heavens, it seems to me that even on earth he is subtle and artificial who makes men, once lovely, dark and pallid, forces them to pine away that they may be virile, to fail that they may be strong. Whence it approaches more closely to the quiet of eternal glory that a man mix himself bravely with those singing for the Creator. For where a man loves the more ardently, there he sings the more smoothly and feels the more sweetly because he has desired the more strongly. For although the road may seem harsh and long to non-lovers, nevertheless, love joins God and man, and, by brief labor, fashions those who endure it.

CHAPTER FORTY-ONE – *That perfect love joins one to God, renders him inseparable from God and causes mindfulness of God, but the love of the world falls into nothingness; concerning the nature of true love—stable and perpetual, sweet, smooth and useful; concerning false love—full of poison, shameful and putrid*

That act of love is perfect, that is if we separate our spirits from the love of creature in our marrow and join them truly and inseparably to God alone; and the more perfect we have been in this work, the better we are.

That act is above all others, for everything that we do ought to be referred to that end, so that we may be perfectly one with our God. But many things draw one back from that union, for instance, the delectable beauty of the world, the vanity of men and women, riches and honors, and the praise and favor of the people. Therefore, we must exercise ourselves to fulfill this act by putting behind us and obliterating all the things that could impede us.

For the love toward which we are climbing in this work is more burningly fervent that ignited charcoal and produces its effect in us absolutely, for it will make our souls burningly ardent and resplendent. This is the love that cannot be deceived by a creature, and it cannot be defrauded of its eternal reward in heaven.

Moreover, who is able to sustain the flame of this love for a long time (if one could persist in the same way always), but he is often tempted, lest it consume nature through the body, which is decaying and annoys the soul? (For the corruptible flesh itself does not allow the spirit to be borne continually into God.) Indeed, the fervor of actual devotion is interrupted through sleep and immoderate exercise of the body, or labor. Ardor is not, nevertheless, extinguished, but it is not experienced as it was at first. Certainly, it returns to us when we return to God and it causes us to convalesce from our infirmity of spirit and gives us ease. Further, it snatches the body away from many kinds of disorders while it guards us in sobriety and temperance. It also may raise our souls to celestial desires, so that we may not be delighted by the lower things of earth.

This is the love that carries off Christ into our hearts, and makes our spirits flow with honey, so that we may break out in melody from interior hymn-singing and rejoice in breathing them forth. Nor, I judge, is there any pleasure like this one, for it makes a man drunk with sincere delight and delights him with holy sweetness. Indeed, the soul that is raised up by sacred fires is purged, nor does there remain in it anything rusty or hidden. But all is penetrated by sweet-sounding pleasure, so that the interior nature seems transformed into a divine glory of love. Thus indeed eternal love rejoices and pours in copious delight, so that its friends do not know how to bend down to another affection for a creature of this world, so that they may freely melt in praise and love of Christ Jesus.

Therefore, learn to love your Author if you wish to live when you have departed from this place. Do this so that you may love God in your life, if you wish to live after your death. Yield your spirit to Him Who can guard it from eternal and temporal griefs. Whence, let not your heart be separated from Him, although you have been placed in adversity and misery, for thus you will be strong enough to possess Him with joy and to love Him without end. For in this you show yourself a true lover, if you do not allow the memory of God to stray from you, whether prosperous things come to you or adversities occur.

O good Jesus, Who have given me life, also lead me, sighing for it, into Your love. Take to Yourself my whole intention, so that You may be my whole desire, that my heart may not love anything outside of You! Sorrow and harshness will fall far from me, and what I desire will also come if my soul may hear and receive the canticle of Your praise. Let Your love remain in us always and without ceasing; from it we are able to experience Him; on account of it, make my meditation stable in Your power, so that nowhere may it disappear in vain and useless phantasms, nor at any time be deceived by errors. But let it not bend down toward earthly felicity or loving or praising. To the extent that my spirit has been cleansed by You, may it thus burn in Your love, so that by no event, sudden or foreseen, may it grow cold.

For if I have loved any creature of this work, that might of my own free will please me in all things, and if I have placed in it my joy and the end of my comfort and desire, when it comes to me, I shall be able to fear a burning and bitter separation, for all the felicity which I have in love of this kind is nothing but weeping and anxiety in the end, when now it is near because pain will torment the soul most bitterly.

And thus every pleasure which men gaze toward in this exile is comparable to hay, which now flowers and grows green, but at once vanishes, as if it had not been. Thus without a doubt does the joy of this world appear to those who consider it properly, and to those following after the comforts of captives for themselves, it never remains fixed in the same state, but always passes away until it is led back into nothingness.

Nevertheless, all men exist in labor and disturbances, nor is there anyone who will be able to avoid them. But this is the nature of faithful and unfeigned love, that it persists in perpetual stability and it is not changed by whatever new thing may befall it. On this account, the life that will be able to discover that love and really recognize it in the spirit is transformed from sorrow into ineffable joy and converted into the mystery of melody. For he will love the melody and, by rejoicing in Jesus, he will be made like a small bird, singing even to his death. But perhaps in death he will not be cut off from the solace of singing love, if indeed he may taste death and not rather, living, fly over to his Beloved. Then, after death, he will be marvelously raised up in praise of the Creator and will abound inestimably with delights in singing and

he will rise up quickly into the seraphic cry, so that in praising, he may shine and serve continually without end. There
the embraces of love will be present and the delight of lovers
will be bound in the heart; the joining of dear ones will stand
stable in eternity. The honey-flowing mouth will offer delicate kisses and their love for one another will never cease.

For me, the presence of my Beloved generates an immense
joy and security, nor am I mindful of any disturbance with
Him. All opponents vanish, no other affections and concupiscences match it; on the contrary, they are checked and they
disperse, and only He Whom alone my spirit has ardently desired, refreshes me and envelops me.

Moreover, you will have loved Christ with your whole will
and for your hatred you will have every sordidness of iniquity.
You will have given over your heart to Him Who redeemed
it, so that He may be your possessor through grace, not the
devil through sin.

In whatever way your soul has sought Christ truly and
fearlessly, and has not wished to stop seeking until it shall
find Him, in this way shall you be led to eternal glory and
you shall serve before your God on a blessed seat. Therefore,
I advise you to love as I have explained; take your place with
the angels. See to it that you do not sell this glory and honor
for the sake of the vile vanity of carnal pleasure. Take care
diligently, lest the love of a creature separate you from the
love of the Creator. Do not hate a misery on earth, indeed,
unless it can cast away your pure love and disturb you, for
perfect "love is stronger than death" and true "jealousy is as
hard as Hell" (Cant. 8:6).

Love, indeed, is a light load, not burdening but relieving
the man who carries it. It makes young men rejoice with old
men; victors rejoice in it, having seized the booty of the demons; battlers against the flesh and the world are protected
in it. Love is spiritual wine, making drunk the spirits of the
chosen and making them advanced and virile, so that they
may forget the poisonous delight of the world and not care to
recognize it, but on the contrary that they may disdain it
energetically.

On this account and concerning sacred love, no one loving can lose, but he must necessarily profit much. For if it is held faithfully in the heart, love will remain in the soul of the lover without punishment in whatever way lovers have spoken about it, for love profits, pain destroys—profiting by truth and destroying utterly those things that are opposed to it. Therefore, the heart loving perfectly does not experience pain nor disturbance, nor is it sad nor turbulent, and this is so since perfect love and dejected mourning do not make compacts.

Then again, what is done freely is not done by punishment, but the lover works voluntarily and freely. Therefore he does not have misery in his work, but he is happy, coerced in nothing, groaning is nothing, but always showing himself joyful and blithe.

Therefore love is the sweetest and the most useful thing a rational creature ever receives, for love is the most acceptable and delightful thing to God. It not only links and joins the creature to God by the embraces of wisdom and delight, but also constrains flesh and blood, lest the man flow forth into deceptive sweetness and deviate into the diverse concupiscences of errors. In this love the heart heals, and our life grows strong and persists. Certainly, I have never found a better or more pleasing mansion, for love joins me and my Beloved, and from two makes one.

However, carnal love shall prosper and perish just as does the flower of the field in the summer, and it will not be, exulting and existing, any more fully than if it had lasted only for a single day. Certainly it subsists thus for a little while, but then it will decline into a sorrow and thus, without a doubt, it will be made bitter in foolish lovers. Their pride and their play in false beauty will be cast down into putridness and shame, for they have already been cast down into the torment which will be with them in eternity. This will not pass away, as their false felicity and the joy that they have had in the splendor of their beauty have disappeared in vain, and everything in which they have been delighted will swiftly pass away.

But God gives beauty to men and women not so that they may burn for one another, despising their Creator (as now frequently befalls all men) but so that, recognizing the benefits of the Lord their God, they may glorify Him with all their heart and love Him incessantly, and that they may continually sigh for that permanent beauty, compared to which all earthly beauty and glory is nothing. For if a pleasing form appears in the servants of the world, what will be the beauty in the sons of God, established in Heaven? Just so, may we love ardently, because if we have loved in sweet-sounding delight, we may sing to Christ with melody, Whose love conquers all things, and therefore we may live in love and also die in it.

I do not know a sweeter pleasure than in my heart to sing to You, Jesus, Whom I love, the song of Your praise. I am ignorant of better and more abundant happiness than to experience in my spirit the delightful warmth of Your love.

Of all things I judge it to be the best to fix Jesus in the heart and in no way to desire anything else. For He has the first good of loving who has a lover's tears with sweet lassitude and the desire for eternal things. But that same Christ, in a manner of speaking, languished for our love, when, in order that He might acquire us, He hastened with so much ardor to the cross. But it is truly said, "for love goes before in a dance and leads a chorus": what brought Christ so low was nothing but love.

Come, my Savior, to console my soul! Make me stable in love, so that I may never stop loving! Destroy sorrow when I must die, for there is no sinner such that he will not be able to rejoice if he is perfectly turned toward You. Be mindful of Your mercy, O sweetest Jesus, so that my life, shining, may be filled with virtues. So that I may conquer my enemy, grant me strong deliverance! In this manner, I beseech You that I may not be lost with the son of perdition. For from this holy love my spirit has been enkindled; I have been placed in the languor of seeing Your majesty, just as, made the bearer of poverty, I despise the dignity of earth and do not care about any honor. For my friendship is glory. When I had begun to love, Your love sustained my heart and allowed me to desire nothing besides love. Then You, O God, made my soul burn with sweet light from which, through You and in You, I shall be able to die and not experience sadness.

And thus love is delectable in the loving heart. It devours unhappy disturbance in the fire of fervent love. Hence it has been given sweetness, chiefly by mediating music and caressing the soul, for there You, my God and my Consoler, have prepared Your temple. Certainly the glory for which I sigh exceedingly is delicious, nor can any man live more greedy in such a desire. Whence my loving soul, adorning itself as a bride, in the King of high sovereignty speaks thus, "Let Love hold my heart in His unbreakable embraces" and places itself in such bondage and entwines itself in such a great inclination with marvelous teaching that it is pleased to think about dying more fully than about living.

For as a flower that cannot die, so is the friend burning with love, and his joy joins death and melody fitly together. For in the beginning of my conversion and of my singular purpose, I thought that I wished to be made like the little bird that languished beyond love for his Beloved, but by languishing also rejoiced, by reaching in himself what he loves, and in rejoicing sings, and by singing languishes, but in sweetness and ardor.

For the nightingale is carried away the whole night to indulge in singing and melody, so that it may please Him to Whom it is joined. How much the more should I sing to Christ, my Jesus, with the greatest sweetness, Who is the Spouse of my soul, through the whole present life (which is "night" in respect to future shining light), so that I may languish, and by languishing that I may fail before love! But in failing I may grow well and be nourished in love, so that I may rejoice, and in rejoicing that I may sing the delights of love with pleasantness. As if from a pipe there sounds singing and burning devotion, and it emits burning songs to the Most High interiorly, but also offerings from the mouth in pledge of divine praise, to the extent that the eager soul exists to love and never fails by sadness or torpor from the desire which it has received.

Certainly integrity of intention, promptness of will, actual fervor of desire, and conversion to God through the continuation of meditation, which are in holy souls, do not allow them to sin mortally—or if through fragility or ignorance they should sin, at once they are stirred up by these stimuli toward true penitence, nor will they linger in sins for a long time, even if they have adhered to delectable things. But the venial sins that they commit are inwardly consumed in the fire of love—unless, by chance, some people are pressed down by such negligence because they did not wholly judge that to be sin in which they fell and their love did not suffice to erase all the punishment owed, or unless the tribulation by which sin is inwardly purged is not borne.

But in the ascent of love, the heart of the loving man burns. More burning than fire is this marvelous heat which both rejoices the spirit most sweetly and chills and shades it from the fire of the vices.

O good Jesus, give back to me the heavenly musical instrument of the angels, so that in it I shall be snatched up to sing Your praises continually. What You have given to me, ignorant of it and not recognizing it, now give to me again as one experienced and begging for it! Soothe me, burning in the delight of love, so that at my death I may be found ablaze, and with a singing joy descend into my soul! Show me smooth caresses in Your good pleasure, so that my excesses may be punished and purged in this manner here, where in Your mercy You have known me, consequently, clinging to You—not in the way You in Your wrath handle those flourishing for this world, to whom You grant prosperities temporally and reserve for them eternal torments! Certainly the lovers of the world are able to know the words or the songs of our singing, but not the canticle of our songs, for they read the words but they are not able to learn, in addition, the note and tone, and the smoothness of our odes. O good Jesus, bind my heart in the thought of Your Name and I am not strong enough not to sing it already! Therefore, have mercy on me by perfecting what You have prepared. Your true lover, excited in the joyful song of melodious meditation is so seized that it is impossible that there be such sweetness from the devil, such fervor from anything created, such song from human ingenuity—in which things, if I should persevere, I shall be saved.

Moreover, it is fitting that he who wishes to avoid sin most perfectly should wish to commit no slightest sins. For he who knowingly and willingly falls into the smallest sins, often, incautious, will run into greater ones. Certainly it belongs to love to wish to incur great misery more quickly than to sin even a single time. Indeed, it is not at all necessary to that man (on the contrary, it would be ridiculous) to seek here delights and riches, fortitude and beauty, who is, in the judgment of the eternal King, established as an eternal soldier with perfect decency of his members and loveliness of color, where there will be neither superfluity nor diminution, and he shall minister in the heavenly hall of the most high Emperor for ever and ever. Amen.

In preparing this translation of Richard Rolle's *De incendium amoris* (*The Fire of Love*) and *De emendatio vitae* (*The Mending of Life*), I have used five manuscripts, two of which have been published as printed texts.

For *De incendium amoris* there are two versions in the forty-two extant Latin manuscripts,[1] a long and a short. The long has been conclusively identified by Margaret Deanesly as Rolle's original text,[2] while she sees the short as an abridgment[3] made by one of Rolle's admirers[4] who was probably a conventual religious and not a solitary[5]—possibly by one of the nuns of Hampole.[6] Deanesly believes the audience intended for the short text was more interested in Rolle's teaching on the mystical experience than in his personal life.[7]

The short form—more like the usual medieval treatise on the subject, as Miss Deanesly notes[8]—appears in nineteen manuscripts, the long in sixteen, and fragments of either text appear in the remaining seven.

One of these manuscripts contains both the long and the short forms of the *Incendium.* The manuscript (Cambridge University, Emmanuel College MS 35, folios 16–19, 25–59, 63–99), described in detail by both Miss Allen[9] and Miss Deanesly,[10] contains a number of spiritual treatises by Rolle and other writers. This manuscript belonged at one point to John Newton (d. 1414), the treasurer of York Cathedral from 1393 until his death.[11]

Newton, having obtained an autograph of Rolle's *Incendium* (now probably not in existence),[12] compared it to the version he had in his manuscript. He found that Rolle's manuscript contained thirty-nine passages[13] his own did not, and made use of margins and inserted pages to copy in the missing material; in addition, he corrected even single words where Rolle's text differed from his manuscript.[14] Thus Newton expanded what we have come to call the "short" text into the so-called "long" text,[15] adding to it a table of contents, which provided in a single list the descriptive titles (probably not Rolle's) for each of the book's forty-two chapters.[16]

Newton ended his reconstructed copy of the *Incendium* with the declaration, "*Hic correctus per librum quem sanctum Ricardus de H. propria manu scripsit*" ("This has been corrected by means of the book which the holy Richard of Hampole wrote with his own hand").[17] In the absence of the Rolle autograph, Miss Deanesly argues, "The note renders Newton's notes authoritative for the text,"[18] a conclusion with which Miss Allen concurs.[19]

For these reasons I have chosen Cambridge University, Emmanuel College MS 35 as the basis for my translation of the *Incendium*, using Miss Deanesly's extremely accurate printed version of the manuscript (1915) with its excellent introduction and scholarly notes, together with the microfilm of the manuscript itself, for my work.

A choice of the best Latin manuscript to serve as the basis for a translation of *De emendatio vitae* is less clear. While there are ninety manuscripts extant which contain the *Emendatio*,[20] none of these is immediately traceable to a Rolle autograph, and they differ distinctly, though not substantially, from one another, thanks to "medieval editorial activity."[21] Attempts are being made,[22] with the aid of a computer, to establish the *stemmata* among the ninety, as a preliminary to the establishment of an authoritative text for the work, but the project is still in progress.

Given this situation, I have chosen two manuscripts for my source of translation on the basis of antiquity, legibility, and geography. They belong, according to Dr. Amassian's analysis, to two distinct branches of the same major division of the manuscripts.[23]

The first, British Museum MS Additional 34763, folios 19–44[v], formerly known as Phillipps MS 11928, is the earliest dated manuscript containing a work of Richard

Rolle.[24] The date, 1384, places the copy within forty years of Rolle's death (1349).

The second, Cambridge University MS Mm., v., 37, folios 94[v]–124[v], is also called the Book of Christopher Braystones. It was made, beautifully, about 1400.[25] The book was once owned by Christopher Braystones, a Benedictine monk of St. Mary's, York, later chaplain to Thomas Spofforth, Bishop of Hereford. Braystones obtained from Spofforth and several other bishops, including the archbishop of York, "an indulgence of forty days to the devout reader of a chapter of the *Incendium*."[26] The indulgence is recorded on the flyleaf of this manuscript, perhaps in Braystones' own hand,[27] and Braystones himself, according to a note just below the indulgence, written in a different fifteenth-century hand, gave the manuscript to the Carthusian monastery at Beauvale, Nottinghamshire, which he entered after serving as Spofforth's chaplain.[28]

Thus, though there is no provable connection between Newton and Braystones,[29] this manuscript, like Newton's, has close associations with the northern counties and with York, its Cathedral and its hierarchy—Rolle's own place and diocese.

Finally, in addition to Latin manuscripts, I have consulted the two manuscripts and one printed text of the earliest English translation of the *Incendium* and *Emendatio*, in order to determine what the contemporary understanding of Rolle's texts was.

The translation is that of Richard Misyn, who completed the *Emendatio* in 1434 and the *Incendium* (long text) in 1435, according to the texts' colophons.

Of Misyn himself we know only what these colophons tell us—that he was a Bachelor of Theology, was a Carmelite, and served as Prior of the Friary at Lincoln.[30] In addition to its being the closest in time to Rolle, Misyn's translation is of interest because the chapter titles he provides for the *Incendium* have been translated almost literally from those supplied by John Newton[31] in the text discussed above. These titles appear in only three manuscripts of the long text—Newton's own and the two copies made from it.[32] Thus, the earliest English translation of the *Incendium* is linked directly to the Latin manuscript having the closest connection with the vanished Rolle autograph.

Preparing his text of Misyn's translation for publication by the Early English Text Society (which printed the volume in 1896 as No. 106 in its Original Series), the Reverend Ralph Harvey discovered that the manuscript on which he based his edition, Oxford, Corpus Christi College MS 236, folios 1ʳ–56ᵛ, was neither Misyn's autograph nor a "consistent dialectical text"[33] as had been assumed previously. The dates appearing in the colophons seemed quite plainly to belong to the translations themselves, rather than to this manuscript. Harvey eliminated the possibility of a binder's error (the 1435 *Incendium* appears before the 1434 *Emendatio*, and the colophon of the former shares a sheet of vellum with the beginning of the latter)[34] and deduced a copyist. A study of grammar, spelling variants, and errors typical of a scribe rather than an author confirmed him in this opinion.[35] Nevertheless, he considered it the best text available, and used it.

In addition to, and as a corrective for, this manuscript and Harvey's printed edition of it, I have used the other fifteenth-century manuscript of the complete Misyn translation, British Museum Additional MS 37790, folios 1–95. In this manuscript, the *Emendatio* appears first, folios 1–18ʳ, followed by the *Incendium*, folios 18ᵛ–95. In her study of the Rolle manuscripts, Miss Allen concludes that it is probably not Misyn's autograph, despite the chronological arrangement, since the Revelations of Juliana of Norwich, which follow the Rolle/ Misyn text (folios 97–115), "refer to her as 'yet alive, 1413,' and it is obvious that the same scribe could not have written both 1413 and 1434–35 as an actual record of the date when he was writing."[36]

A. *Prologue to* Incendium amoris

In reverence for our Lord Jesus Christ and wishing to satisfy your desire and request, Sister Margaret, I, the simplest of educated men and the least profitable in my living, have undertaken to translate this work from Latin into English for you, and for others who do not understand the intricacies of Latin. I want it to increase your spiritual comfort and to edify many souls.

And since it is true that God's pleasure and the spiritual life of man entirely consists in perfect love, this holy man, Richard Hampole, has named his book *Incendium amoris*, that is to say, *The Fire of Love*. I do not intend to alter this book either in meaning or in substance, but I mean to write faithfully, according to my understanding, a clear version of the text.

Therefore, all you who shall read this book, if your discretion should find anything in it worthy of thanks, give praise for it to God and to this holy man [Richard Rolle], but if you should find anything said amiss, attribute it to my lack of skill. Nevertheless, I object to any reform of it with the intention to write or to say anything against the Faith or against the judgment of Holy Church, as God is witness.

Furthermore, sister, have in mind the mortality of this life, and always keep some holy reading in your hand. For if you preserve holiness, you will not love fleshly sins—and holiness consists, as I said before, in perfect love.

But what is perfect love? Certainly you have perfect love when you love your God for Himself (as you ought), when you love your friend in God, and when you love your enemy for the sake of God. For God is not truly loved without love of your neighbor, nor is your neighbor truly loved without love of God.

Perfect love, therefore, consists in love of God and love of your neighbor, and love of God consists in the keeping of His Commandments. Therefore keep His Commandments and in your prayers (or your contemplation, when you enter upon it) plainly forsake all worldly thoughts, and forget the burden of all outward things. Pay attention to God alone, and take heed only of Him. If you find any doubts, submit them to serious counsel, lest you err, especially in such things as touch on the twelve articles of your Faith, such as the Holy Trinity, and other different things as are written skillfully in this holy book following, for our instruction.

B. Colophon: Misyn Incendium amoris

Thus ends the book De incendium amoris of Richard Hampole, hermit, translated into English at the request of the Lady Margarete Heslyngton, recluse, by Brother Richard Misyn, Bachelor of Sacred Theology, then Prior of Lincoln of the Order of Carmelites. In the year of our Lord 1435, on the feast of the Translation of Saint Martin, Bishop, that is July 4, written and corrected by the said Brother Richard Misyn.

C. Colophon: Misyn Emendatio vitae

Thus ends the twelve chapters of Richard Hampole, translated into English by Brother Richard Misyn for the information of Christian souls. In the year of our Lord 1434.

These texts are translated from Harvey's edition of the Misyn translation prepared for the Early English Text Society, cited below. Text A: Harvey, pp. 1–2. Text B: Harvey, p. 104. Text C: Harvey, p. 131.

Appendix III – *Scriptural Quotation*

Like many another medieval writer, Richard Rolle, though for the most part he uses the Vulgate, sometimes quotes Scripture by ear. For instance, in Chapter Three of the *Emendatio*, he renders Matthew 19:28 as "*Vos qui reliquistis omnia et secuti estis me sedebitis super sedes duodecim iudicantes duodecim tribus Israel*," where the Vulgate reads, "*Jesus autem dixit illis, amen dico vobis quod vos qui secuti estis me in regeneratione cum sederit Filius hominis in sede maiestatis suae. Sedebitis et vos super sedes duodecim iudicantes duodecim tribus Israhel.*"

Since, again like many of his contemporaries, he does not provide citations with his quotations, it is sometimes difficult to ascertain his source. (In this case, Rolle's words diverge less from Matthew's text than from any other of the Evangelists' versions!)

In quoting the Psalms, Rolle almost invariably uses the *Psalms emended according to the Septuagint*—that is, the *Gallican Psalter*.

When Rolle's use of Scripture has been simply allusive or illustrative, as is usual in the *Incendium*, I have translated the passage without providing either the Latin or the source. When he explicates the Scriptural passage, or uses its words as a framework for his own meditation or exhortation his usual practice in the *Emendatio*, I have provided both Latin and source.

Except where the use of the Scriptural passage in Rolle's text requires a more literal rendering, I have used the Jerusalem Bible for the English translations of Scripture. However, in the case of the Psalms, I have followed the Psalm numbering of the Vulgate rather than that of the Jerusalem Bible, even where I have used the Jerusalem Bible translation.

NOTES

Introduction

I. THE AUTHOR

1. Margaret Deanesly, *The Incendium Amoris of Richard Rolle of Hampole*, University of Manchester Publications, No. XCVII; Historical Series, No. XXVI (New York: Longmans, Green and Company, 1915), p. 37.

2. Reginald Maxwell Woolley, ed., *The Officium and Miracula of Richard Rolle of Hampole* (London: Society for Promoting Christian Knowledge; New York: The Macmillan Company, 1919), p. 5.

3. Frances M. M. Comper, *The Life of Richard Rolle Together with an Edition of His English Lyrics* (London: J. M. Dent and Sons, Ltd., 1929), p. 3.

4. T. W. Coleman, *English Mystics of the Fourteenth Century* (London: The Epworth Press, 1938; reprinted Westport, Connecticut: Greenwood Press, 1971), p. 66; Comper, p. 3.

5. Hope Emily Allen, *Writings Ascribed to Richard Rolle, Hermit of Hampole, and Materials for His Biography*, The Modern Language Association of America Monograph Series, III (New York: D. C. Heath and Company, 1927), p. 430. This work will be called *Writings* in future notes.

6. Comper, pp. 3–4.

7. Comper, pp. 311–14; Woolley, pp. 82–93.

8. Coleman, p. 66.

9. Hope Emily Allen, *English Writings of Richard Rolle, Hermit of Hampole* (Oxford, at the Clarendon Press, 1931),

p. xii. This work will be called *English Writings* in future notes.

10. Coleman, p. 66.
11. Deanesly, p. 37.
12. Comper, p. 301.
13. Comper, pp. 5–6.
14. Allen, *Writings*, pp. 433–35.
15. Allen, *Writings*, p. 444.
16. Comper, p. 301.
17. Comper, p. 301.
18. Allen, *Writings*, p. 496.
19. M. L'Abbe Feret, *La Faculté de Théologie de Paris et ses Docteurs les plus célèbres*, III, 247–50, and Dom Maurice Noetinger, "The Biography of Richard Rolle," *Month* (January 1926), quoted and discussed at length in Allen, *Writings*, pp. 490–93.
20. Allen, *Writings*, pp. 493–97.
21. Allen, *Writings*, p. 494.
22. G. C. Heseltine, *Selected Works of Richard Rolle, Hermit* (New York: Longmans, Green and Company, 1930), p. x.
23. Allen, *Writings*, p. 496.
24. Coleman, p. 68.
25. Allen, *Writings*, p. 495.
26. Noetinger, quoted by Allen, *Writings*, p. 490.
27. Allen, *English Writings*, pp. xx–xxi.
28. Allen, *English Writings*, p. xxi; Dom David Knowles, *The English Mystical Tradition* (New York: Harper and Brothers, 1961), pp. 52–53, 55.
29. For example, Allen, *Writings*, pp. 492–93, 497–98.
30. In an article by E. J. Arnould, appearing in *Bulletin of the John Rylands Library*, XXI, i (April 1937), reprinted in his edition of the *Melos Amoris* as Appendix II, 210–38; this is the opinion of Knowles, p. 51, note 7.
31. Knowles, p. 55.
32. Allen, *Writings*, p. 495.
33. Allen, *Writings*, p. 448.
34. Comper, p. 301.
35. Clifton Wolters, trans., *The Fire of Love by Richard Rolle* (Baltimore, Maryland: Penguin Books, 1972), p. 12; Allen, *Writings*, p. 448.

36. Allen, *Writings*, p. 448.

37. Comper, pp. 301–2.

38. Wolters, p. 14.

39. Deanesly, p. 40.

40. Wolters, p. 18.

41. Wolters, p. 19.

42. Wolters, p. 15.

43. Objections, when they were raised, concerned not Rolle's right to be a hermit, but the alleged irregularities of his leading of that life, particularly in his moving from place to place. See Deanesly, pp. 39–40.

44. Comper, p. 302.

45. Comper, p. 302.

46. Comper, p. 302.

47. Comper, p. 302.

48. Comper, p. 303.

49. Comper, p. 303.

50. Wolters, p. 14.

51. Allen, *Writings*, pp. 449–58.

52. Comper, p. 303.

53. Allen, *Writings*, p. 459.

54. Comper, p. 303.

55. Allen, *Writings*, p. 460.

56. Allen, *Writings*, pp. 460–62.

57. Comper, p. 304.

58. Allen, *Writings*, pp. 460, 462.

59. Comper, pp. 304–5.

60. Allen, *Writings*, pp. 462–63, 472.

61. Comper, p. 305.

62. Allen, *Writings*, pp. 467–70.

63. Comper, p. 306.

64. Deanesly, p. 39.

65. Comper, pp. 306–7.

66. E. J. Arnould, "Richard Rolle of Hampole," Chapter 11 in *Pre-Reformation English Spirituality*, ed. James Walsh, S.J. (New York: Fordham University Press, c. 1965), p. 140.

67. Wolters, p. 15.

68. Dom Gerard Sitwell, *Spiritual Writers of the Middle Ages*, Twentieth Century Encyclopedia of Catholicism, Vol. 71, Section IV: The Means of Redemption, Vol. 40, ed.

Henri Daniel-Rops (New York: Hawthorn Books, 1961), p. 89.

69. Wolters, p. 15.
70. Sitwell, p. 90.
71. Allen, *Writings*, p. 480.
72. Allen, *Writings*, p. 488.
73. Allen, *Writings*, pp. 470, 471–88.
74. Knowles, pp. 51–52; Allen, *Writings*, pp. 481–82.
75. Comper, p. 308.
76. Allen, *Writings*, p. 502.
77. Allen, *Writings*, p. 502.
78. Allen, *Writings*, p. 507.
79. Allen, *Writings*, p. 506.
80. Comper, p. 308.
81. Allen, *Writings*, pp. 507–8.
82. Comper, p. 308.
83. Comper, p. 308.
84. Allen, *Writings*, p. 506.
85. Comper, p. 3.
86. Allen, *Writings*, p. 517.
87. Comper, p. 3.
88. Coleman, p. 66.
89. Allen, *English Writings*, p. lvii; Coleman, p. 66.
90. Deanesly, p. vi.
91. See the *Melos Amoris* and the *Judica Me*, for the clearest examples.
92. Allen, *Writings*, p. 508.
93. Allen, *Writings*, p. 518.
94. Wolters, pp. 15–16.

II. THE WORKS

1. Allen, *Writings*, p. 201.
2. Allen, *Writings*, p. 209.
3. Allen, *Writings*, pp. 228–29.

Appendix I

1. Hope Emily Allen, *Writings Ascribed to Richard Rolle, Hermit of Hampole, and Materials for His Biography*, The

Modern Language Association of America Monograph Series, III (New York: D. C. Heath and Company, 1927), pp. 209–23.

2. Margaret Deanesly, ed., *The Incendium Amoris of Richard Rolle of Hampole,* University of Manchester Publications No. XCVII, Historical Series No. XXVI (Manchester, England, at the University Press; London: Longmans, Green and Company, 1915), p. viii.

3. Deanesly, p. 84.

4. Deanesly, p. 89.

5. Deanesly, p. 88.

6. Deanesly, p. 89.

7. Deanesly, p. 84.

8. Deanesly, p. 88.

9. Allen, pp. 215–16.

10. Deanesly, pp. 12–15.

11. Allen, p. 215; Deanesly, p. xix.

12. Deanesly, p. 14.

13. Deanesly, p. 83.

14. Deanesly, p. 14.

15. Deanesly, p. 63; Allen, p. 215.

16. Deanesly, p. 232, note 3; p. 63, note 4.

17. All translations are mine, unless otherwise noted.

18. Deanesly, p. 14.

19. Allen, p. 215.

20. Allen, pp. 230–45.

21. Margaret Amassian, "Richard Rolle's *Emendatio Vitae* (Latin and English)," a paper in the series Medieval Spiritual Treatises: Resources and Methods for Editing, presented at the Twelfth Annual Conference on Medieval Studies, sponsored by the Medieval Institute, Western Michigan University, May 1977.

22. Amassian (Fordham University), and others.

23. Amassian, fig. 5.

24. Allen, pp. 236–37.

25. Allen, p. 234.

26. Deanesly, pp. 51–52.

27. Deanesly, p. 52.

28. Deanesly, p. 52.

29. Deanesly, pp. 76–78.

30. Rev. Ralph Harvey, M.A., ed., *The Fire of Love and*

The Mending of Life, or The Rule of Living of Richard Rolle, Hermit of Hampole, Translated by Richard Misyn, Early English Text Society, Original Series No. 106 (London: 1896), pp. xiii–xiv.

31. Deanesly, pp. 7, 14.
32. Deanesly, p. 7.
33. Harvey, pp. ix–xi.
34. Harvey, p. x.
35. Harvey, pp. x–xiii.
36. Allen, pp. 223–24.

BIBLIOGRAPHY

Allen, Hope Emily. *English Writings of Richard Rolle, Hermit of Hampole.* Oxford, at the Clarendon Press, 1931.

Allen, Hope Emily. *Writings Ascribed to Richard Rolle, Hermit of Hampole, and Materials for His Biography.* The Modern Language Association of America, Monograph Series III. New York: D.C. Heath and Company, 1927.

Amassian, Margaret. "Richard Rolle's *Emendatio Vitae* (Latin and English)." A paper in the series Medieval Spiritual Treatises: Resources and Methods for Editing, presented at the Twelfth Annual Conference on Medieval Studies, sponsored by the Medieval Institute, Western Michigan University, May 1977.

Arnould, E. J., ed. *Melos Amoris.* Oxford: Basil Blackwell, 1957.

Arnould, E. J. "Richard Rolle of Hampole." Chapter 11, pp. 132–44, in Pre-Reformation English Spirituality, ed. James Walsh, S.J. New York: Fordham University Press, c. 1965.

Biblia Sacra iuxta Vulgatem Versionem. Adiuvantibus Bonifatio Fischer, O.S.B., Iohanne Gribomont, O.S.B., H.F.D. Sparks, and W. Thiele. *Recensuit et brevi apparatu instruxit* Robertus Weber, O.S.B. Stuttgart, Germany: Würtembergische Bibelanstalt, 1969.

Coleman, T. W. *English Mystics of the Fourteenth Century.* London: The Epworth Press, 1938; reprinted Westport, Connecticut: Greenwood Press, 1971.

Comper, Frances M. M. *The Life of Richard Rolle Together with an Edition of His English Lyrics.* London: J. M. Dent and Sons, Ltd., 1929.

Deanesly, Margaret. *The Incendium Amoris of Richard Rolle of Hampole.* University of Manchester Publications, No. XCVII; Historical Series, No. XXVI. New York: Longmans, Green and Company, 1915.

Feret, M. L'Abbé. *La Faculté de Théologie de Paris et ses Docteurs les plus célèbres.* III, 247–50.

Heseltine, G. C. *Selected Works of Richard Rolle, Hermit.* New York: Longmans, Green and Company, 1930.

The Jerusalem Bible, ed. Alexander Jones, *et al.* New York: Doubleday and Company, Inc., 1966.

Knowles, Dom David. *The English Mystical Tradition.* New York: Harper and Brothers, 1961.

Misyn, Richard, trans. *The Fire of Love and The Mending of Life, or The Rule of Living of Richard Rolle, Hermit of Hampole,* ed. Ralph Harvey. London: Early English Text Society, OS 106, 1896; unaltered reprint produced by Kraus Reprint Company, 1979.

Noetinger, Dom Maurice. "The Biography of Richard Rolle." *Month* (January 1926).

Petry, Ray C. *Late Medieval Mysticism.* The Library of Christian Classics, Vol. XIII. London: SCM Press, Ltd., 1957.

Sitwell, Dom Gerard. *Spiritual Writers of the Middle Ages.* Twentieth Century Encyclopedia of Catholicism, Vol. 71, Section IV: The Means of Redemption, vol. 40, ed. Henri Daniel-Rops. New York: Hawthorn Books, 1961.

Wolters, Clifton, trans. *The Fire of Love by Richard Rolle.* Baltimore, Md.: Penguin Books, 1972.

Woolley, Reginald Maxwell, ed. *The Officium and Miracula of Richard Rolle of Hampole.* London: Society for Promoting Christian Knowledge; New York: The Macmillan Company, 1919.

Specializing in Old and Middle English, M. L. del Mastro holds a Ph.D. in English Literature from Fordham University and teaches English, by choice, at Polytechnic Preparatory Country Day School, Brooklyn, New York. Dr. del Mastro has also prepared translations of *The Rule of St. Benedict* (in collaboration with Anthony C. Meisel, Ph.D.), (Doubleday Image, 1975), *The Revelations of Divine Love* of Juliana of Norwich (Doubleday Image, 1977), and Walter Hilton's *The Stairway of Perfection* (Doubleday Image, 1979).